Gail Hamilton

Sermons to the clergy

Gail Hamilton

Sermons to the clergy

ISBN/EAN: 9783337087678

Printed in Europe, USA, Canada, Australia, Japan

Cover: Foto ©ninafisch / pixelio.de

More available books at **www.hansebooks.com**

SERMONS TO THE CLERGY.

BY

GAIL HAMILTON,

Author of "Country Living and Country Thinking," "Gala Days," "A New Atmosphere," "Woman's Worth and Worthlessness," &c.

And Moses said unto the Lord, O my Lord, I am not eloquent, but I am slow of speech and of a slow tongue.

Behold, they will not believe me, nor hearken unto my voice: for they will say, The Lord hath not appeared unto thee.

And the Lord said unto him, Who hath made man's mouth? Have not I the Lord?

Now, therefore, go, and I will be with thy mouth, and teach thee what thou shalt say.

BOSTON:
WILLIAM F. GILL AND COMPANY,
309 WASHINGTON STREET,
OPPOSITE OLD SOUTH CHURCH.
1876.

CONTENTS.

	PAGE
THE IMPERIOUSNESS OF TRUTH	9
ADAM	33
THE "BLUE BLOOD" OF CANAAN	63
OUR CHARITIES	87
RELIGIOUS BEGGARY	169
HEAVENLY HEATHENISM	207
PRAYER	227
TEA-PARTY SALVATION	245
THE LAND OF BROKEN PROMISE	259
MISSIONARY MUSINGS	291
THE LAWS OF ANGER	331
THE SIGHING OF THE PRISONER	347
FAIR PLAY	375

THE IMPERIOUSNESS OF TRUTH.

SERMONS TO THE CLERGY.

THE IMPERIOUSNESS OF TRUTH.

THERE is, and there can be, no conflict between scientific truth and religious truth. Scientific men so far as they are honest, and religious men so far as they are honest, are in pursuit of one and the same object. All controversy, all apparent contradiction, springs from the ignorance of the persons who are engaged in it. From a few facts that come within its ken, the Church constructs a system of theology; and from its few facts the world constructs a system of science. Both, by reason of the limited knowledge of the constructors, must be very defective; and from these defects it follows that the two systems clash, inevitably clash. But between the divine plan of theology and the divine framework of science is no clashing. They are not simply harmonious: they are one. Science is but a knowledge of the divine method. What else is theology? Both have God for the basis and background. Even if the votaries of science refuse to speak the divine name, they are equally in search of the divine Being. God is not less God, because you call him an original Principle.

What, then, are we striving for, — to defend our own, or to discover the divine system? Who believes that he has found all truth? Who believes that he has discovered enough to make it worth while to expend his breath in defending it, except so far as attack and defence are the handmaids of discovery? Certainly no theory is indispensable, except the theory which comprehends all things; and that we shall never compass in this world. No fact is fatal, so it be a fact. As a fact it must have its appropriate niche in the temple of Nature, "whose builder and maker is God."

Yet a clerical discussion of certain scientific theories closes with this statement: —

"Such, in a word, is the question which the thinking portion of the religious world are now considering. Shall we refuse to admit the possibility that these views can be true, under the idea that they exclude the existence of creative power? or shall we gladly receive them, if we find them sustained by the evidence, on the ground that they vastly magnify the extent and grandeur of its action?"

If this be true, the religious world is surely stultifying itself with a remarkable and appalling unanimity. If this be true, the religious world has not yet learned the A, B, C, of discovery in any truth whatever. Such truth as it holds, it holds by imposition or by accident, not by original acquirement; for its method is all wrong. It speaks as if truth were a matter of choice and of consequences. By its own confession, it does not ask, "Is this true?" but "Will it do for us to admit that it is true?" It is not concerned to know what the facts are, but whether it can stand the consequences of admitting those facts. The argument is not, "The Darwinian theory is the correct theory, and must therefore be accepted;" but, "In spite of all ecclesiastical fear, the Darwinian theory is not only not opposed to church-teachings, but really upholds them. Therefore we need not be afraid to receive it."

In scientific investigation, consequences are not to be considered. Falsehood is always dangerous: truth is always harmless. Where it seems to be injurious, it is more often the preceding and surrounding falsehood, than even the injudicious application of the truth, which works woe. This very Darwinian theory is a case in proof. No one knows whether it be true or false, or whether our theory of the Creator be true or false; but, granting both to be true, the one is, as the writer quoted says, absolutely harmless to the other. It was supposed to be subversive of the divine Being only by those who did not comprehend the theory. But whether harmful or harmless is not the question. The only question is, What is truth? It is irrelevant, it is mere charlantanism, to ask on what ground we shall receive views: if we find them sustained by the evidence, that is ground enough. The sole point is, are they sustained by the evidence? If they are, we must receive them, whether we like it or no, whether they subvert, or confirm, our theories. There is no choice in the matter. God is not the God of this world by sufferance, but by sovereignty. He borrows no leave to be, from *savant* or saint. He cannot be volatilized out of his universe by chemical agency, nor kept in it by any labored harmony of the Gospels, or geology of Genesis. If he is here at all, he is here by his own will and act, and here to stay.

One might say that the Darwinian theory had as few facts to stand on, and had to go as far to get them, as any theory ever framed by man; but that is not to the purpose.

Not entirely alike, yet not wholly dissimilar, is another paragraph from a religious review: —

" The reduction of the biblical doctrine of the Devil to a mythical personification of evil, and of the account of the fall to a poetic representation, admits a principle of interpretation fatal alike to the historical and the moral weight of the Scriptures."

Here both the statement, and the principle which underlies it, may be questioned. It is by no means certain that an allegorical interpretation of the fall of man is fatal to the historical or moral weight of the Scriptures; and, if it be, what of it? The issue is not, What becomes of the Bible if the Devil was a myth? but, Was the Devil a myth? It is not to be asserted that a story written in a certainly remote and a probably indefinite past, in a country and among a people wholly different from our own, is to be understood precisely as we should understand a story of America to-day. Nor is it to be denied that large portions of the Bible are poetical and literary, not scientific or metaphysical. Even its history is not the history of Hume and Gibbon. Language itself has changed significance in changing skies, and often puts us at loggerheads. The Devil, we all agree, got into the Bible by a myth; and it is surely not unreasonable that he should go out the same way. The first account of the creation says nothing about the fall of man. The second says nothing about the Devil. The only *Deus ex machina* is a serpent. That serpent cannot be turned into the Devil, except on the principle of poetic interpretation and mythical personification. So we are not called upon to admit the principle. The principle is already there. "'Nobody asked you, sir,' she said."

This principle is more nearly vital than fatal to the

historical and moral weight of the Scriptures. I do not care particularly about the Devil. A bad man is a bad man, whether he is tempted of the Devil, or whether he is drawn away of his own lust, and enticed. It is rather satisfactory, on the whole, to have some one to lay the blame on besides ourselves. At any rate, Satan is under precisely the same laws as ourselves, and to be combated exactly as if he were a vile inclination or a bad habit. But on what principle do we in ninety-nine cases proffer an allegory as the true interpretation, and in the hundredth case not only deny the allegory, but decree that an allegorical theory would destroy the Bible? How can it be lawful to poetize a snake, and not only unlawful, but revolutionary, to poetize the tree he coiled on, according to the old pictures? We do not hesitate to accredit our Roman Catholic brethren with the woman sitting upon the scarlet beast of the Revelation. Why may we not use equal freedom towards the woman parleying with the serpent of Genesis? The seven heads and ten horns of the beast are not more suggestive of poetry than the tree of the knowledge of good and evil that springs in the garden. Who is it that says to poetry and parable, "Thus far shalt thou go, and no farther"? What sovereign commentator has announced, "Every story of the Bible thou mayst freely allegorize; but the story of the Devil and the story of the Garden of

Eden thou shalt **not allegorize**; for, in the day that thou touchest that, thou shalt surely die, and the Bible with thee"?

When our creed declares that we hold all Scripture to be given by inspiration of God, every one yields ready assent: when it goes on immediately — as if the **one** thing were involved in the other — to constitute the Bible our complete rule of faith and practice, the only rule to direct us how we may glorify God and enjoy him, we do not always have our thoughts sufficiently about us to consider whether the **second** proposition is really implied in the first, or whether it is actually true, or what it definitely means.

I suppose creeds are not framed for keeping people **out of** the Church, but, rather, to keep out heresy, to keep out **dangerous** theological falsehood. The benefit arising from church organization is **so** great, or must be assumed to be so great, that we surely ought to aim at bringing into the church-fold all who can be brought in with truth and honor. It will be agreed by every one, that we ought not to impose needless restraints, that we ought not to demand belief in statements of questionable purport and of doubtful authority.

What does it amount to when we say that the Scriptures are our only sufficient rule of faith and practice? They are not like a rule of arithmetic. They are not like a statute of law. These are, for the greater part, exact, and to be definitely applied. The only way in which the Scriptures furnish a rule is in supplying principles, in softening and purifying the heart, in tranquillizing the temper, in developing the conscience, and putting us in the right frame of mind to make a rule for ourselves. They furnish a rule, just as the quarry furnishes to the sculptor his angel: he must dig it out. When the Scriptures do give a rule, the first thing we do is to show how often it ought to be broken. The sacred writer makes a statement, and we at once turn to and prove beyond a doubt that he does not mean what he says. "Owe no man any thing but to love one another," says Paul; but who refrains from borrowing money on that account? "Whosoever shall smite thee on thy right cheek, turn to him the other also," says Christ; but, if a man smite us, we prosecute him at the North, and knock him down at the South. "Swear not at all," said the same divine person; and we not only swear, but hold that an oath is a peculiarly sacred and solemn thing. I do not say that we are contumacious or rebellious in doing thus; but, so long as we are in fact chiefly a law unto ourselves, why do we pretend in our creeds to take the Scripture as our only rule of faith and practice?

We have a great theoretical dread of rationalism: nevertheless we do constantly bring our own reason to bear upon the precepts of the Bible. The most conscientious, the most devout, the most orthodox, does not make the Bible his only rule of faith and practice. He puts the Bible and his own common sense together; and the two furnish him a rule. Why is it worse to say that we consider our own reason as authoritative as the Bible, than it is always to interpret and construe the Bible by our own reason? When the Bible contradicts our judgment, we do not obey the Bible, and fling our judgment to the winds: we follow our judgment, and say that the passage is obscure; that it means something different from what it appears to mean. We explain it all away. We think we can get more truth out of witnesses, with oaths than without oaths: so when Christ said, "Swear not at all," we say that he only meant, swear not except in certain circumstances. When the Almighty says, "I loved Jacob, and I hated Esau," it conflicts with our ideas of what God ought to do; and our most scrupulous commentators do not scruple to say that God did not really hate Esau, but only loved him less than he did Jacob. When God said unto the man, "In the day that thou eatest thereof, thou shalt surely die," we affirm that he only meant that man should on that day become liable to death. What is this but making our human judgment paramount to Scripture?

This is precisely what the Bible authorizes us to

do. I find no scriptural warrant for making the Bible our only rule of faith and practice; but I find abundant warrant for making the Bible an authoritative referencebook for faith and practice; and the human reason the proper and prescribed investigator. It may be, as is asserted, that the Westminster Confessions and Catechism, and the Thirty-nine Articles, and the Dordrecht Formulas, are unsurpassed as specimens of logical precision; and, if what we wanted were perfect logical systems and statements, we might go farther, and fare worse. But what we want is not a perfect logical circle above our heads, but concrete divine truth in our hearts. Now, with all respect to the creed-makers, it seems to me that the Scriptures give a better account of themselves than any man has given of them. For displaying the origin and object of Scripture, its precise relation to human life, its precise place in the divine economy, and its best showing in our creeds, I do not think Nice, Athanasius, Prelate, Pope, or Puritan has ever surpassed Paul.

"All Scripture is given by inspiration of God, and is profitable for doctrine, for reproof, for correction, for instruction in righteousness."

There we have no iron-clad "rule," at once rigid and fragile, unbending, and therefore constantly breaking. It is a precise statement of the case, as broad and elastic as the truth itself, needing no explanation and no supplement. It makes the Bible not a rule, but a repertory of wisdom, goodness, truth, and love, of divine principles, out of which we are to frame our own rules on our own responsibility.

Even this great responsibility is not overwhelming. The human reason which is to work on the Bible, — that mere human reason which some flout at, and which many seem to look upon as an insidious foe, — that very reason has been much encouraged by these Sacred Scriptures. "There is a spirit in man; and the inspiration of the Almighty giveth them understanding," says Elihu in the Book of Job. Only twice in the Bible is the word "inspiration" used. In both places, it is the inspiration of God. In one passage, inspiration gives us the Bible: in the other, it gives us understanding. If it is said that Elihu, the son of Barachel the Buzite, is not as good authority as Paul, I can only say that the statement is one that can hardly be proved or disproved. It is certain that though Elihu waited, as was proper, being a young man, till the three friends had ceased to answer Job, yet, when he did speak, he was as vigorous and pointed and decisive as any of them. And though we are told that the anger of the Lord was kindled against the other three, and they were forced to humiliate themselves before Job, not a word of rebuke was passed upon Elihu. Does not this silence give assent?

But we are not dependent upon Elihu's testimony. The Lord himself " answered Job out of the whirlwind, and said, Who hath put wisdom in the inward parts? or who hath given understanding to the heart?" implying more strongly than a mere assertion could that God himself gave understanding. Solomon tells us expressly, that out of the mouth of the Lord cometh knowledge and understanding; that, to the man that is good in his sight, he giveth wisdom and knowledge and joy. "If any of you lack wisdom," says James, "let him ask of God that giveth to all men liberally, and it shall be given him." On what authority do we throw distrust and suspicion on the human reason, when God himself has so often and so kindly urged us to use it in studying his Word and himself? Why do we shorten his arm by asserting that the Bible is all we have to go by, when he has promised to shine directly into our own minds, and to let us know, if only we will follow on *to* know?

It is feared and asserted that a reference to human reason would open the door to all sorts of heresy; that leaving out certain forms from our creeds would be bringing in certain other forms whose root is evil, and whose fruit is death. We must raise barriers against an " ever-restless, ever-developing, never-finished, progressive theology." It will not do to confine ourselves to Bible statements, because Bible words do not mean to people now-a-days the same that they meant to people when they were uttered. They have lost something of their significance, of their solemnity. Words which meant then only one thing now mean whatever you choose. Explanation and interpretation have so perverted the sacred texts, that the Bible can no longer be trusted among the people unsupported, but must be bulwarked with gloss and comment, by — by whom? One is just as far off as another from Bible times. Arians and Arminians, the dark ages and the renaissance, heresy and schism, brood with equal gloom over us all. If the language of the Bible has been perverted to almost any meaning that a pretentious rationalizing may put upon it, how shall we know which of those meanings to incorporate into our creed as the true one? If the sacred writers confined themselves to simple statements, because their hearers were too near the facts to make any mistake, and if we are so far off that we are liable to great mistakes unless we have additional elaboration, formulated statements, inferences and systems lifted into the realm of fundamental truth, in whom rests the authority to make these additions, and to formulate scriptural simplicity, and to say, once for all: This is what Christ meant, this is the real gist of Paul's words? Have we an apostle among us? The prophets, do they live forever? Where is that fountain of interpretation of which, if a man drink, he shall mistake no more? Who has had this supplementary inspiration, which not only illuminates the Scriptures to his own edification, but authorizes him to impose his interpretation as the condition of union with Christ's visible Church on earth?

No one will deny the claims of truth. Sharp and positive convictions are better than an indifferentism naming itself with the name of liberality. Let the Presbyterians govern themselves by a synod, and the Congregationalists guide themselves by a council, and the Universalists stay in a church that believes God is too good to damn them, and the Unitarians in a church that believes they are too good to be damned. We need advocate no levelling of necessary barriers, no sentimental union of feebleness and fustian; but if there are advantages in belonging to the Church, if the communion of saints, if the sacrament of the Lord's Supper, be a sacred and solemn privilege, we have no right to exclude from its participation those whom the Bible does not exclude. Ye take too much upon you, ye sons of Levi, when ye graff the wild olive-branches of your own conclusions into the good olive-tree of God's gospel, and call it all alike the vineyard of the Lord.

Few of us who have read the story of Samson have not marvelled at the means which Samson took to avenge himself on his father-in-law. We can very well believe that he carried off the gates of Gaza to the hill of Hebron; for we have seen, in the picture, exactly how he did it. It is easy to understand that a thousand men should be slain by the jawbone of an ass; for such slaughter is not wholly unknown to modern society. Any remarkable feat of strength may with impunity be ascribed to Samson; but the capture of the three hundred foxes argues, besides superhuman strength, an " infernal activity." And when we observe that these foxes were not only caught, as might be possible in a trap and in time, but were caught all at once, and were tied every one tail to tail, and that a burning firebrand was secured firmly in the midst between every two tails,—so firmly that a good many of the foxes must have run a considerable distance before the brand dropped off, if it dropped off at all,— it must be admitted that very large draughts are made on the childlike faith. For what motive had Samson? To catch three hundred foxes, and tie firebrands to their tails in order to set your neighbors' cornfields on fire, savors of the Western mode of preventing mosquito-bites; viz., to catch your mosquito, give him chloroform, and extract his teeth. It would seem easier to burn up every cornfield in Massachusetts with flint and steel than to catch a hundred foxes, not to mention fastening a firebrand between their tails. Was Samson afraid to go into the cornfields? But did he not have to forage after the foxes quite as extensively? Would not the same cunning, agility, and strength which could capture, collect, accoutre, and despatch three hundred foxes, have enabled him to slip into as many cornfields, and set fire to them all?

It is amusing to see how nimble our commentators become in the chase of those three hundred foxes. The foxes turn into jackals at the first clip. The captor is furnished with a pair of mittens little less than miraculous. He is allowed as many assistants as the case may require. The foxes, become jackals, are sent over the country in swarms. Samson is granted an indefinite extension of time. The Greek term "jackal," we are told, means *nimble;* and the Persian jackal is a *glowing coal.* The red fox has a tail like a burning torch; and the Greek word "fox" means "a bright, burning tail." Ovid, in his Festival of the Cerealia, and the Feast of Vulpinaria, and the tradition of the glow-worm carrying fire, all point back to the fire-foxes of the Philistines. What with fable, etymology, and natural history, we become bewildered, and, in the confusion of law and legend, find ourselves quite ready to welcome that learned Hebraist who rises to explain that some little quirk of a letter, some little dubious twist in the tail of a comma, has made those foxes out of a shock of corn, and sent them clattering across our common sense through all these hundreds of years. It was not foxes that Samson caught. He simply gathered shocks, sheaves, bundles of corn, and such combustible matter, fastened them together, and set the fire leaping across the field, to the destruction of both shocks and standing corn, vineyards and olives. It was what any shrewd Danish "fire-bug" might have done, — to our nineteenth-century sense, a perfectly natural way of setting the farms on fire. We are willing those three hundred foxes should rest in peace; and for us, before we fash ourselves with strange stories, we will look to our P's and Q's.

In the laws given to the Israelites, after they had left the land of Egypt, we find the stern sentence, "Thou shalt not suffer a witch to live;" in obedience to which mandate, thousands of men and women — the offscouring of the earth, and saints of whom the world was not worthy — have suffered death at the hands of men. Massachusetts has, I believe, the honor of having first reared the standard of rebellion and revolt against the devil of persecution, of torture, and of death; and that devil she cast out. But, before he went, he so tore and bruised her, that the world remembers only how the evil spirit foamed, and raged, and remembers not that the foaming and raging were because she withstood him to the face, and crushed him down, and cast him out. So her good is evil spoken of. But Giles Corey bore the *peine forte et dure;* and the venerable white hairs of that saintliest of women, Rebecca Nourse, floated from the gallows-tree; and the Rev. Mr. Burroughs was torn from wife and babies in the wilderness, and doomed to the felon's death,—because, far back in the twilight of time, a *Thus saith the Lord* had rung out through the smoke of Sinai, and reverberated over the plains and the desert: "Thou shalt not suffer a witch to live." Now comes up a wise man of the East, and joins hand with sundry wise men of the West, and all jointly and severally declare that the true rendering and reading is, "Thou shalt not suffer a witch to get her living." The Most High did not command his people to do to death these wizards and witches; but he forbade them to allow the trade of necromancy to be carried on in their community.

The dead cannot rise from their graves to receive or to give atonement; and, long before this, I trust that the Rev. Mr. Parrish has found dust enough on the golden streets to bestrew his garments of repentance for the children whom he led astray, and the men and women he hunted down. Long before this, I trust, have the torture, the ignominy, and the shame which wrought the death, and shrouded the grave, of Rebecca Nourse, been lost in the light and glory of heaven. But, for all the living, there is hope that the lesson of our fathers' mistake may not be lost.

It is of very little consequence in itself whether

sheaves, or foxes, set fire to the Philistine vineyards. It is not of the first importance, whether, in one particular passage, a witch was commanded to be slain, or to be forbidden the practice of her arts; for there are other passages of similar purport. It concerned Abram chiefly, whether the Moreh to which he passed were a burning, perhaps arid, plain, or a sheltering and restful oak. There is authority for both. The point is, that, on certain words of Holy Writ, men of learning and piety differ so widely as to change the whole meaning of statement and command, — differ, in at least one instance, by all the distance that stretches between life and death. How unwise is it, then, how unscientific, how impious, to pin our faith upon a word! How absurd to make the gates of heaven swing or shut to any open sesame which one, or close sesame which another, may think himself to have found in the Bible! How derogatory is it to the divine Being to suppose that he would make salvation turn upon any one or two, or a dozen, interpretations in a book, when a dozen other interpretations are admitted to be so doubtful that the world cannot agree upon their truth! If, when the Bible speaks of so simple a thing as a fox, I am expected to believe it means a jackal, and am not a heretic if I think it means a shock of corn, why shall I bar from heaven, and from the table of our Lord on earth, my brother who cannot understand that "baptism" in the Bible means "immersion," or my brother who cannot comprehend what the word "trinity" means, which is not in the Bible at all? If some scriptural words are vital, and other words are not vital, then we need a supplementary revelation to tell us which are the vital words. From the simple fact that the revealed word of God is dotted with statements, which, whether from lapse of time, or change of language and manners, are to us practically incomprehensible, I rather infer that intellectual comprehension of theological truth is not essential to salvation, but that, "in every nation, he that feareth God, and worketh righteousness, is accepted with him."

I do not suppose we have departed any farther from the faith once delivered to the saints than the divine Being knew we should depart. When he inspired the sacred writers, he knew just as well what the perversions of a pretentious rationalism would do with the words as our modern theologians know what it has done with them. And if he still let the words stand as symbols of faith, and tests of piety, cannot we afford to let them stand? Perhaps the ark of God is not so unsteady as it seems. Perhaps it will not topple over, even if we leave it to its own divine strength. It has been brought forward as one great proof of the divine origin of the Bible, that it was not confined to one age and one people, but was adapted to all ages and all peoples. What becomes of this miraculous adaptation, if it must be supplemented and interpreted and appendixed, and generally pieced out and filled in, before it can safely be trusted as a lamp unto our feet and a light unto our path? Christ himself says, "Whosoever believeth in me shall never die." But we have discovered that men may say they believe, and yet say nothing; may call Christ the Son of God, and yet mean nothing. Therefore we are not contented that they should confess Christ before men. We will not even let them simply confess Christ before men. We build up a wall of logical precision, and verbal exactness, and metaphysical distinction, and say that any man that entereth by the door into the sheepfold, and climbeth not up this way, " the same is a thief and a robber." Would it not be better, like Christ, to put a generous construction on men's motives, to believe that he who is not positively against Christ is on his part; that, if a man cares enough about Christ to believe in him in any sort of way, he will not lightly speak evil of him; that, if he calls him the Son of God, he certainly means nothing bad? He may be yet far off from the full assurance of faith. He may see the Lord only through a glass very darkly; but why is he to be treated as a hypocrite, a pretender, and a foe, to be barred out with formula and exegesis, to be unmasked and exposed, as it were, and not rather welcomed in, though "not to doubtful disputations"? Is not a man more likely to be built up in the faith inside than outside the Church? How, then, can the salvation of the world be furthered by multiplying tests beyond those which God himself laid down? If Christ could trust the general honesty of human nature in confessing him, why cannot we?

And why is an "ever-restless, ever-developing, never-finished, progressive theology" a thing to be guarded against? Has any man, or any school of theologians, ever found out the Almighty unto perfection? A very high authority, long ago, declared, that, "touching the Almighty, we cannot find him out." If he be indeed infinite, must not the science that treats of him, unless it is a dead science, be "ever-restless, ever-developing, never-finished, and progressive"? It will make a thousand mistakes; but the greatest mistake which theology can make is to fold its hands, cease to develop, cease to progress, and say, "It is finished." All the ages and all the worlds may strive, by searching, to find out God; and though the search is most blissful in process, and most blessed in results, always behind it remains the Almighty, forever found by the sincere seeker, yet forever and forever to be sought.

ADAM.

ADAM.

ADAM'S fall is a very discouraging circumstance.

All the machinery of life aims to bring man into a state of moral excellence. Churches, schools, newspapers, are to make him good and wise. The great obstacle is, that he has in himself so much bad blood, and is surrounded by circumstance so untoward. A child seems to be made up of the traits of many generations. He gets brightness from his mother, deception from his father, a furious temper from one, self-restraint from another, indolence from a third, and a thousand little strains of strength and weakness which once variegated the lives of ancestors whom living eye has never seen, and who sleep in forgotten graves. One propensity we try to curb, one tendency to develop. We do not expect to accomplish great things with the generation now on the stage; but, if we can only get this rising race started fair, we have great expectations of the race that shall come from them. Weak and wicked parents make weak and wicked children. Given one generation of upright, noble, healthy men and women, and the world is fairly started on its career of reform.

But, when you have secured your noble men and women, you are, at the farthest, only where we started six thousand years ago. Churches and schools, family training and piety, have produced, let us say, the upright generation; but it is no better than was Adam. Adam was upright and noble. He inherited no bad blood, no weak trait. No stern father, no indulgent mother, helped to spoil him. No society flattered and fooled him. He was a perfect and holy man. God was his teacher and intimate friend. All his powers were balanced, all his faculties in harmony, all his wants natural, all his tastes innocent. Yet, at the first touch of temptation, down he went, and all the generations with him.

And it was no great temptation, either. If it were proper, and to the purpose, one could find it in his heart to be thoroughly angry with Adam for bringing us into our estate of sin and misery on such slight provocation. Adam's descendants, all degenerate as they are, resist a thousand stronger temptations every day. There are many sins into which it is hardly surprising that a man should fall. When the appetite for wine has once taken firm hold of him, the wonder is, that he should ever dispossess himself of it. It is not incomprehensible that men and women will sacrifice wealth, ambition, even honor, to love; for love is a passion so absorbing, so overpowering, that judgment and reason may be held captive in its thrall. It is inconceivable that a man should commit fraud to gratify a love of display and self-indulgence; but it is not inconceivable that he should commit forgery to conceal fraud, and commit suicide to escape the penalty of forgery. But Adam had nothing that was worthy the name of temptation; and he had every thing else. There was his wife made on purpose for him, and made out of his own flesh and blood; so that he could not find fault with her. There was no other woman existing to be compared with her to her disadvantage, or to make it possible for him to think he might have done better. No overweening appetite tempted him, for he had perfect liberty and perfect likings, except in one direction; and there is nothing to indicate that he ever so much as looked in that direction of his own accord. He had not a single want or wish ungratified; and all his gratification was moderate, reasonable, and wholesome, — as salutary in effect as it was pure in enjoyment. He was called upon to crucify no natural propensity, to exercise no form of self-denial. The forbidden tree was pleasant to the eyes, and good for food; but so was every tree in the garden. There was no reason why he should wish to eat of this tree, except that the Lord God had told him not to. And this Lord God was no tyrant, no mere far-off unseen monarch even, but a familiar friend in whom he trusted, who had given him all things richly to enjoy, who had brought all the creatures of the earth to him to acknowledge fealty, and talked with him as a man talketh with his friend. Now, I believe, that, all fallen and sinful as we are, there are thousands of men and women on the earth to-day who would stand such a test, and call it nothing. They would do, even for an earthly friend, for friendship's sake, what Adam would not do for the sake of the Lord God. Every boy who gives up smoking to please his father and mother resists a temptation infinitely stronger than that which beset Adam. For, let it be always remembered, Adam was not hankering after the forbidden fruit. There is nothing to show that he had even so much as thought of it, or was any thing but indifferent to it, when up came a beast of the field, and suggested to Adam and Eve that they should try it. That was all. One would say a thousand beasts of the field might have beset them, a thousand serpents hissed out suggestions, in vain. What was a serpent in comparison with the Lord God? Adam knew perfectly well that the beasts of the field were inferior to himself; for he had been set to have dominion over them. He could not, of course, comprehend the Almighty; but he knew enough to know that he was Sovereign, sovereignly good and wise, and to be revered, obeyed, and adored. Yet upon the first suggestion of an irresponsible, unhelping, slanderous serpent, they disregarded his wishes, — I will not say disobeyed his commands, — apparently without the smallest compunction, misgiving, or remorse, as simply, coolly, and heartlessly as if they had been used to disobedience ever since they were created. Veterans in faithlessness could hardly have done worse.

Now, if these things are done in a green tree, what shall be done in a dry? If Adam, pure, perfect, holy, with no acquired weakness from habit, with no treachery of inherited traits, with no temptation from ungratified wants, and no promptings of pride, could thus wantonly fall into the first silly sin that he *could* stumble upon, how shall the present generation, all borne down with the weight of accumulated crime, enervated by centuries of weakness and vice, beset by temptations that Adam never knew or dreamed of, — how shall such a generation even think of maintaining itself upright? How can we be expected to stand where Adam fell? And suppose we do stand, suppose we do secure an upright generation, what guaranty have we that it will not, upon the second temptation, lapse into vice, repeat the ruin of Adam, and so give us all our work to do over again? What hinders the world's progress from being at best but a perpetual moral see-saw — now up, next down? And what encouragement have we to help a man to his feet, when his first act after he gains them is to fall flat upon the ground again?

Is there not somewhere a flaw in our exegesis? Simply considered as literature and history, it might well be that the story of Genesis had not yielded up its gem of the ages to our strictest research. Learning, logic, and piety have striven to unfold its secret, and, for all answer, we have only conflict and clashing. It is easier to say what cannot be the true meaning than what the true meaning must be. Certainly an interpretation which contradicts the ordinary notions of sense and justice must have a good deal to say for itself, before it can be received as a veracious history, or a true philosophy, of the ways of God to man. A theory which starts out with the statement, that,

> "In Adam's fall
> We sinned all,"

it cannot be irreverent or profane to question.

If a man in New York or Boston had grown up virtuous, amiable, and honorable, and in his mature years, with a happy family surrounding him and depending on him, should suddenly steal a million dollars from the desk of his best friend, not because he was in need of money, or had any special desire for it, but because a veteran pickpocket had suggested to him that he should, we should say the man had lost his mental balance, that he was beginning to have softening of the brain. If we read the story in the reporter's column of the morning paper, we should say, "What absurd stories these newspapers invent, now that the war and the panic are over!" But Adam had a better character than any bank president; and, where the defaulting cashier brings only his own family to grief, Adam dragged down with him a whole world. The great comfort in doing moral work is, that, once done, it stays done. The United States is not in the smallest danger of lapsing into Druidism. The vices of the freedman and the Indian, we say, are the vices engendered of long years of slavery and barbarism. After a few successive generations of freedom, education, and religion, we shall see that the one is not incapable of self-government, nor the other of civilization. Moral inertia is as strong as physical inertia. No man plunges at once from the heights of virtue to the depths of vice. It is not the man of wise prudence, self-restraint, large views, enlightened conscience, and liberal mind, who slays his opponent, even in a moment of passion. It is the man, who, however fair to far-seeing, is within weakened by self-indulgence. He only falls at a sudden blow, because his props were never well set. The crash of disaster may be sudden; but a long series of secret crimes, weaknesses, and selfishnesses, led up to it.

If, then, our theory be correct, — that Adam was created holy, and that he fell, at the first comparatively slight temptation, into iniquity and irreparable ruin, — it would seem that he must have been very differently constituted from any of his descendants. As vast numbers of his descendants, in their fallen state, do resist many and grievous temptations, and as Adam, in his unfallen state, created in the image of God, in knowledge, righteousness, and holiness, according to the Westminster Catechism, never resisted any, it seems to follow that an estate of knowledge, righteousness, and holiness, is less favorable to goodness than is an estate of sin and misery.

But is not that a conclusion in which nothing is concluded?

There is a theory that Adam was not positively holy, but negatively innocent; that he had perfect moral purity, but not moral strength. That may be; but that makes him a man in physical and mental powers, while morally a baby. If that be the true theory, then it seems hardly fair to have made Adam the representative man of the race. Ordinarily the moral faculty, though opening later than the other faculties, arrives far sooner at maturity. Adam's descendants have usually a very clear sense of right and wrong, long before they have a very correct sense of what is wise or unwise, prudent and imprudent. But, if Adam was created with mind and body fully developed while his moral sense was infantile, he was so different from the rest of mankind, that it is not just to bring them all to destruction because he fell: it is not just that the fate of a whole race, whose moral powers ordinarily keep pace with its mental and physical powers, should be put to the test of the only man in it whose moral power was created organically weaker and tardier than his other powers. A chain is no stronger than its weakest link; but, when we would strengthen the chain, we do not begin by reducing every link to the weakness of the weakest.

If the answer to a question in addition do not "prove," we try it over again. The very number and earnestness of the solutions which have been given to this problem indicate that the answer will not "prove." But the record of an event so august as the foundation of a world has been thought worthy the closest study, the most continuous attention, and is full of the deepest interest.

The story of Genesis can hardly be intended as a literal scientific statement. "The Lord God planted a garden. And out of the ground made the Lord God to grow every tree that is pleasant to the sight, and good for food." But could any one garden contain every kind of tree to be found in every sort of climate, — in torrid, temperate, and frigid zones? "The tree of life, also, in the midst of the garden, and the tree of knowledge of good and evil." What sort of trees are these? What nurseryman has ever had the seedlings? What gardener has ever eaten the fruit? We find ourselves, at the very outset, palpably and unquestionably in the midst of an allegory. Something mysterious and uncomprehended, whether or not incomprehensible, is represented as the tree of life, planted in the garden where man entered upon his active career. In the holy city, the New Jerusalem, whither this world leads and leaves him, the same mysterious tree blooms down the centre of the golden street, and shadows the banks of the river of life, yields every month its teeming fruitage, and offers even its "leaves for the healing of the nations."

Was it a literal plot of land in Asia that bore this tree? And the tree of knowledge of good and evil — does it spring in any earthy soil? Is it propagated by grafting? Is it nurtured by irrigation? Is it blighted by early frost? Does it grow side by side with apples and apricots? We see at once that the idea is absurd. These are allegorical trees, symbolical trees; and, if they are allegorical, the garden in which they are planted, the whole story in which they are found, not only may be, but must be presumed to be, allegorical. It is contrary alike to the laws of literature and of sound reason, that an allegorical tree should be planted in an agricultural garden.

What we cannot fail to notice in the story of Genesis is, that the Lord God said to Adam, "Of the tree of the knowledge of good and evil, thou shalt not eat of it; for, in the day thou eatest thereof, thou shalt surely die." But the serpent said, "Ye shall not surely die; for God doth know, that in the day ye eat thereof, then your eyes shall be opened, and ye shall be as gods, knowing good and evil."

And the serpent was right about it. Adam and Eve ate the fruit, and they did not die, as the Lord God said they would; but their eyes were opened, and they knew good and evil, just as the serpent had predicted. The serpent, apparently, spoke more truly than the Lord God. No wonder the narrative affirms the serpent to have been more subtle than any beast of the field which the Lord God had made. I suspect the serpent himself honestly believed what he was saying. He knew a great deal; but he did not know every thing. Adam and Eve seem to have been like two children, — frank, innocent, ignorant, unsuspicious, fearless. The serpent was far superior to them in intelligence and experience; but, when he undertook to measure himself against the Almighty, he sank into abject insignificance. It looks as if he knew what death was, and he knew what was the tree of the knowledge of good and evil; and he knew what were its apparent, superficial, immediate consequences. But its deeper, more remote, most vital consequences, he did not know. He evidently thought the Lord God was jealous of his prerogatives; that he did not wish Adam and Eve to become like himself in knowledge of good and evil, and so was frightening them off with a warning of consequences which would never follow. But the serpent meant mischief. Out of pure malice, he meant to get Adam and Eve into trouble; or perhaps, in revenge or hatred of the Lord God, he would set Adam and Eve in a more godlike place than their Maker intended. The only death which his sensual mind comprehended, he knew was not a natural result of eating of the tree of the knowledge of good and evil. The result which would follow — and the only result of which he was aware — was a perception hitherto to them unknown, and a perception which the Lord God had not intended them to have, and which, the serpent thought, would thwart the divine plans, and chagrin the Lord God. He himself turned out to be the one who was thwarted and baffled and chagrined; yet he had laid his plans well. His failure was because he only saw things on the surface, and could not pursue them into the depths. If there had not been to death a deeper meaning than he knew any thing about, if there had not been in the knowledge of good and evil a higher life than he could divine, he would have been right. To the short-sighted eyes of wickedness, the far-off truth seems a present falsehood.

One of the most remarkable features of the narrative, one that has received far less prominence than its character merits, and one that seems full of significance, if we could but find the key to unlock it, is the assertion of the Lord God, " Behold, the man is become as one of us, to know good and evil : and now, lest he put forth his hand, and take, also, of the tree of life, and eat, and live forever ; therefore the Lord God sent him forth from the garden of Eden, to till the ground from whence he was taken."

That was precisely what the serpent said. What the serpent said would happen, the Lord God declared had happened. But what was this wondrous change? And why should the Lord God be angry about it, or have forbidden it in the first place? It would seem as if the change was a very elevating and a very desirable one, — a change from a low to a higher state of being. This man was become more like God. But he was made, at first, in the image of God: therefore, we should say, the more he became like God the better. Why should the Lord God object to any act which could make man more like himself? And what was this knowledge of good and evil, of which man had suddenly become possessed? He knew good before; for he had felt it all through his happy life. It can hardly mean that he was to know evil in the sense of doing or suffering evil; for he was to know it as the Lord God knows it, who is incapable of either. And what was that tree of life which once brought immortality within human grasp? The tree had been in the garden from the beginning; and it does not seem that Adam and Eve were forbidden to eat of it. It is, indeed, mentioned as the tree which was in the midst of the garden; and the woman declared that it was the fruit of the tree which was in the midst of the garden, of which God had said, "Ye shall not eat of it, neither shall ye touch it, lest ye die." But, in the direct command of God himself, nothing is said of the tree of life. The prohibition applies only to the tree of knowledge of good and evil. Was it, then, that they had eaten of the tree of life, but that its effects were but temporary; that immortality could come only from continuous partaking of its mystic fruit; that the long lives of Adam and Seth and Methuselah resulted from the fruit of the tree of life which Adam had eaten in the garden, — a fruit whose lingering virtue lengthened out even the days of Abraham and Joseph, but dwindled, and presently disappeared, till the human organization had nothing to depend on but its own unaided force, and finds now its limit at threescore years and ten? It would seem, then, that man was not originally and inherently immortal. He was made liable to death, but susceptible of life. He would naturally die; but, by the use of certain means, he had a frame that could live forever. If he had not partaken of the tree of knowledge of good and evil, he might still have fed on the tree of life, and have lived forever; but he would have lived in that lower estate in which he was created. He would never have been like God, knowing good and evil. Here is where the reverend assembly of divines at Westminster must have been plumply and squarely wrong. They were wise above what is written. They were not content with the simple Scripture statement, that God made man "in our image, after our likeness." They gave no heed to the subsequent modifications, which showed how far the statue varied from its model. They say, "God created man after his own image, in knowledge, righteousness, and holiness." The writer of Genesis does not say one word about God's having created man like himself in knowledge, righteousness, or holiness. The only thing he says about it is, that, in one whole department of knowledge, man was created unlike God; and the only way he got in was by rushing in, in spite of God. His very fall consisted in leaving the estate of ignorance in which he had been created, and trespassing upon an estate of knowledge in which he had not been created. But this estate of knowledge was one in which the Lord God dwelt; and it could not, therefore, have been of itself guilty or undesirable. Adam's fault was, not in being in it, but in going in when he was commanded to stay out. Yet, thrusting himself forward all unbidden, he did not, thereby, wholly forfeit all the advantages of the estate. The fruit of the tree was potent. His eyes were opened, and he did know good and evil, and he did become as God. We have the lowest authority in the universe foretelling that this is what would happen, and the highest authority in the universe asserting that this is what did happen. The serpent knew a great deal more about the tree of the knowledge of good and evil than we know; but there was so much that he did not know, that his knowledge was not of the smallest account. No created being seems to have fathomed the secret of the Almighty.

It does not seem certain, when we look at it carefully, that God was even angry with Adam and Eve for thus clothing themselves with the attributes of the Most High. Their banishment from the garden is alleged to be, not by way of penalty, but of precaution. They were expelled, not for any thing they had done, but for something which it was feared they would do. "And now, *lest* he put forth his hand, and take of the tree of life, and eat, and live forever: *therefore*, the Lord God sent him forth from the garden of Eden." Even the divine unwillingness that man, after his disobedience should eat of the tree of life, and live forever, may have been divine compassion, and not displeasure. An immortality that would have been forever fresh and fair and sweet in the garden of Eden might be a burden too heavy to be borne outside. It is not the least solace of a life whose sorrows are greatly multiplied, and whose toils are often excessive, that its troubles are limited. One man of genius represents death as the poor man's dearest friend, the kindest and the best. Another pictures to himself the consternation that would ensue in the world, if death were suddenly abolished. The woes entailed upon the human race by that mysterious and awful comprehension of good and evil are lifted and lightened by the certain knowledge that the time is short, or, if not by the knowledge, certainly by the fact. Sin cannot grow hoary; for the sinner returns to the dust; and out of the dust comes each living soul with something of primal innocence about it. Suffering does not on earth annihilate the power to enjoy; for aching brow and throbbing pulse find peace and rest in the ever-welcoming grave.

It may be noticed, also, that a very different tone is assumed toward Adam and Eve from that which is assumed toward the serpent. To the latter the Lord God says, "*Thou* art cursed." To Adam he says, "Cursed is *the ground* for thy sake." When Cain afterwards killed his brother, the Lord said unto him, "Now art *thou* cursed. Lamech observed the distinction, and knows no curse upon man, but comforts himself concerning our work and toil of our hands, because of *the ground* which the Lord hath cursed.

It was the ground, and not the man, who was cursed. Nay, the ground was cursed for the man's sake. Is not the phrase, "For my sake," oftener a friendly than an unfriendly phrase? Is not the necessity of industry everywhere and always recognized as the almost indispensable condition of excellence? Is not idleness denounced, and justly denounced, as the fruitful mother, and the untiring foster-mother, of vice? And seeing that man had presumptively, rashly, but really, drawn upon himself the immeasurable responsibility of the knowledge of good and evil, did not God, in love and kindness, curse the ground for his sake, render it necessary that man should toil, and by his toil be disciplined and trained into a fitness for the station into which he had thrust himself, all ignorant, untrained, unfit? That absolute ease and luxury in which Adam lived before he had any knowledge of good and evil did not hurt him. After that godlike knowledge came to him, it would have been fatal. A baby plays with his toes and his toys through all his waking hours; but, when he becomes a man, he puts away childish things.

Nor does it appear afterwards that God was angry with Adam, or alienated from him, or that Adam and his family and friends and descendants fell under God's wrath and curse. And when the reverend assembly of divines at Westminster declare that "all mankind, by the fall, lost communion with God, are under his wrath and curse, and so made liable to the miseries in this life, to death itself, and to the pains of hell forever," they must go far for authority. How they could make such a statement with the Book of Genesis before their eyes is incomprehensible.

For, immediately after the fall, before Adam and Eve were sent out of the garden, the Lord God made coats of skin, and clothed them. He took pity upon their shame; he was touched by their simple, awkward, clumsy efforts to clothe themselves; he did not wait for them to learn by cold and fatigue the insufficiency and fragility of the poor, perishable garments they had stuck together: but he put them himself on the right track. He made for them himself strong and decorous coats, clothes that would stand the rain and storm and toil that awaited them outside of Eden, garments that could serve them till their progress in art and skill should produce better. Does this look as if they were under God's wrath and curse? What could he have done different, if they had been under his pity and care and love?

When Eve's first baby was born, she cried in rapture, "I have gotten a man from the Lord." That is hardly the cry of a woman whose whole nature was corrupt, and who was cut off from communion with God. It seems, rather, as if Eve were still living close to the Lord God, and attributed this new, strange blessing at once to him.

"And the Lord had respect unto Abel." And the Lord talked with Cain. "And Enoch walked with God." "And Noah was a just man, and perfect in his generations; and Noah walked with God." And God talked with Noah, and "blessed Noah and his sons." And all through the book comes a long line of men whom God talked with, and bore with, and labored with, and taught and directed, and blessed and comforted. And the reverend assembly of divines at Westminster, with this long record of love and patience in their hands, could put their heads together, and declare that all mankind, by the fall, lost communion with God, and are under his wrath and curse. Worse than that, if any thing can be worse, in our own National Council that met in Boston, there was not found a man to vindicate the ways of God to man; but " all we, like sheep, went astray" after the Westminster divines, and declared our adherence for substance of doctrine to the faith and order which the synods of 1648 and 1680 set forth or re-affirmed.

As between the theological assertions of the Westminster Assembly of Divines, and those of any other body of divinity, it is doubtless proper to go with the Westminster Assembly; but where the issue is between the Westminster Assembly on one side, and Moses and the prophets on the other, I should go decidedly with Moses. Much as we esteem the Catechism, we esteem the Pentateuch more. The Book of Genesis, whether we accept it as authority or not, is all the authority we have concerning the origin of the human race. That book tells us that continually, after the fall as well as before the fall, God did lovingly and patiently and unwearyingly talk with man, lead him along pleasant paths, and over hard places, rebuke and punish him when he was wicked, praise and reward him when he was even a little good, encourage him when he was weary, strengthen him when he was feeble, and in all ways and places show himself a father and a friend; so that after all these years, in these remote corners of the earth, one cannot read the story without an amazement, almost an incredulity of gratitude; without exclaiming, "What *is* man, that thou shouldst be so mindful of him?"

When any one says, on the other hand, that, after

the fall, man lost communion with God, and fell under his wrath and curse, I ask, with all respect, for his authority. I ask, also, if there is any such authority, why it was not incorporated into the book, — the only book that professes to give a connected and complete account of the creation?

A recent book discusses the story of Adam and Eve from an entirely novel point of sight. It is called "The Rise and the Fall; or, The Origin of Moral Evil." Its explanation is one that I should never have thought of; yet, once presented, it is a theory of which one does not easily become disembarrassed. The book is written in a reverent and rational spirit. It professes as close an adherence to the text of Scripture as to the rules of right reasoning; and the magnitude of the problem to be solved, the unsatisfactoriness of all attempts hitherto at its solution, and the earnestness and intelligence which this writer brings to the discussion, certainly merit for it a fair hearing, and not a summary dismission.

His theory is, that the tree of the knowledge of good and evil was the tree of the knowledge of right and wrong; that Adam and Eve were not originally created with such knowledge. Their mental perceptions, their physical powers, were in full play; but the moral faculty was in abeyance, corresponding to its later appearance in every subsequent individual of the human race.

The probability is, that they were intended to be endowed at some future time — and after whatever necessary training, under whatever favorable circumstances — with this moral faculty; but, at the time of their creation, they were not so endowed. By their disobedience, which could not be guilty (they not being moral creatures), but which was rash and imprudent, they became prematurely possessed of the moral faculty, which, in its and their weakness, became often and speedily prostituted to immorality. Nevertheless, the possession of the moral faculty was in itself a rise, and not a fall. To come into such an estate, even presumptuously and forbidden, was to rise into a higher order of being. The fall was after this rise, when the new moral faculty chose tergiversation rather than frankness, and falsehood rather than truth.

This is but a hint of the gist of a theory which is weak, perhaps, and far-fetched on the face of it, and yet, in body and soul, is not without strength. And as the answer to the great problem is an unknown quantity, and must be represented by some x, y, or z in order to be worked out, the necessarily hypothetic theory which harmonizes the greatest number of facts must, it would appear, be the best one to begin on. This may not be such an one; but we have ciphered, patiently or impatiently, on the old hypotheses with distinguished lack of success; and it can surely do no harm to take a fresh start on fresh ground. This theory may develop difficulties of its own; but many of those which perplex the old dispensation disappear under its light. Especially falls to the ground that monstrous assumption, that all mankind, descending from Adam by ordinary generation, sinned in him, and fell with him in his first transgression; that all mankind, by the fall of one man, for whom they were in no wise responsible, and from whom they involuntarily descended, lost communion with God, and are under his wrath and curse. The law of the transmission of traits, faculties, qualities, is indisputable, though little understood. Adam having, by his own act, become a moral being, all his descendants became, perforce, moral beings. But by that act he did not sin. When he performed the act, he was not a moral being. His first act after that change may or may not have been sinful; but the act itself was not sinful. And each child born is born sinless — sinless, but with tendencies to sin or to purity, according as its ancestors have kept themselves pure, or have lapsed into sin; have consecrated him to God, or left him to be the prey of the serpent. We all recognize the fact that virtue produces virtue, and vice has a tendency to spring from vice. This theory shows it reasonable that moral strength should be, as our experience finds it, cumulative, and gives us encouragement to work for the exaltation of the race.

By this theory we are not dismayed to find ourselves, at the outstart, with a perfect and a perfectly-equipped man, tripping at the first step into the gulf of wreck and ruin. We find ourselves, on the contrary, entering the lists with a progenitor far less perfectly equipped than we, and whose mistake and whose subsequent sins, even if sins there were, were, in a certain sense, entirely natural. We see why the Lord God should pronounce a curse on the serpent who had intermeddled so disastrously, who had tempted the ignorant, innocent man to thrust himself into a sphere for which he was unfit, and which could not fail to bring him dismay and woe, instead of waiting the slow, sweet processes, the pleasant paths, by which the Lord God would have prepared him, and have led him without hurt into the realm of the divine — but should have pronounced no curse upon the man and woman so beguiled. We do by no means lose sight of the horror of great darkness which envelops the origin of evil; but what we do see is clear and pure, and casts no shadow on the great white throne. It doth not yet appear, perhaps it never in this world will appear, that he hath put all enemies under his feet. But certainly, in this guise, he does not figure as a God of wrath and cursing, shutting himself away from the poor, feeble, falling man whom he has just made, but a God of infinite love and condescension and consideration, standing by his puny man "through evil report and through good report," punishing him only when he must, and as little as he can, bending low to his infirmities, promising all sorts of earthly good to him while his soul is not elevated enough to value higher things, and gradually, and with godlike pains and patience, lifting him into a more spiritual life.

It is not to be supposed that the framers of any systems of theology and philosophy have acted from wrong or unworthy motives. Doubtless they have acted from the highest and the best. Our fathers did not mean to make a sanguinary, arbitrary, cruel God, being themselves cruel and arrogant men. They acted, on the contrary, on the sublime and self-sacrificing principle, let God be true, and every man a liar. There is something pathetic, heroic, in their resolution to justify God, even at the expense of every instinct of humanity. And unto them and their offering, doubtless, God had respect. But it cannot be that God *wishes* us to sacrifice our common sense in his behalf, though it is to be hoped he will not wholly condemn us if we do. It must be that he wishes us to bring to the study of himself the same modes of thought and reason that we use in reference to other things; for with these minds has he himself endowed us. If there is something which we do not understand, and cannot reconcile, it is better to let it go uncomprehended and inconsistent than to warp every rule of reason in the effort to explain and combine. It is not indispensable, though it is lawful, for finite human beings to attempt to frame perfect theological and philosophical systems; but it is indispensable that they should not overturn reason and instinct and consciousness in so doing.

It seems, sometimes, to be thought, that, unless we sinned in Adam, we cannot be saved in Christ. But, if we are not saved in Christ any more palpably and consciously than we sinned in Adam, we might as well be lost.

If we are to take Paul verbally, and not argumentatively; if we are to understand his eager, rapid discourse as a presentation of historical facts controverting the original account of creation, and not as a literary and perfectly just illustration to elucidate the thought that glowed within him, without reference to scientific or historical statement,—then we must so take it in all its parts, and to the last degree. To me there is no clashing between Paul's statements and the absolution of every man from guilt in Adam's act. We might, indeed, say that not only sin, but sinners, and every thing else, entered into the world by one man. But Paul is not concerned with any naturalistic theory. He is striving to set forth the unsearchable riches of Christ, to show that salvation is as broad as sin, as wide as death; that man cannot go outside the love of

Christ; that just as truly as all men die by reason of their belonging to a mortal race, just so surely may they live by reason of the life and immortality brought to light in the gospel of Christ. If he does not mean this; if he means that literally all men sinned and died in Adam, without consciousness, or will, of their own,—then we must continue the parallel, and maintain that they live in Christ without any voluntary acceptance of him, or belief in him, or following after him.

THE "BLUE BLOOD" OF CANAAN.

THE "BLUE BLOOD" OF CANAAN.

IT seems sometimes as if God did not care so much about honor and truth and righteousness as the newspapers do. We are convulsed at some flagrant misdemeanor; but the sacred historians take it as coolly as possible. The Bible is full of sound moral precepts, and bad practical examples. You cannot teach your Sunday-school class the lesson of Jacob's ladder, without striking snags in all directions. What a family it was, to begin with! — a doting, partial father, a deceitful, partial mother, and two spoiled children. Isaac loved Esau — because he did eat of his venison. But Rebekah loved Jacob. Whether she had an equally creditable reason for her preference, we are not told. Esau seems to have been a rash, headlong boy; quick-tempered, but generous and forgiving; relinquishing his birthright in a moment of passionate impatience, but capable of lifelong regret; bitterly resentful of his defrauded blessing, yet gentle and magnanimous; a vigorous, manly, and somewhat savage character. No wonder his father loved him. But the mother's pet was Jacob, — a quiet boy, content to stay at home, while Esau was gathering strength and skill from the chase; a docile, stupid boy, without wit enough to plan deceit, or will enough to prevent it, and only just enough of both to carry it out. It was Rebekah who devised fraud upon the blind old father, and then another fraud to save Jacob from the richly-merited consequences; for even the man seems tied as closely to his mother's apron-strings as the child had been. But Esau, too, with all his breezy, outdoor life, was not indocile. He humored his father's ruling passion for venison with as much alacrity as Jacob humored their mother's for deception. He went out for his prey as readily as Jacob went in for his. When he saw that his wives did not please his father, he cheerfully took more wives. Since the daughters of Canaan did not suit, what more natural than to try the daughters of Ishmael? When Jacob came back from Padan-Aram, fearing the wrath of Esau, and deprecating it with crafty forethought, with gifts and servile words, hale and hearty Esau seems quite to have forgotten their little tiff, and to have been entirely at a loss to know what all this ado was for. In short, and speaking after the manner of men, we should say that Esau was far the more agreeable, interesting, and gifted person; and that Jacob — with his sly ways, and his mean-spirited willingness to work seven years longer for the man who had cheated him out of one wife and into another, instead of rising up in virile wrath and love, and taking the one he wanted out of hand, will you nill you, as Esau would have done—was not a man to be held in esteem of gods, or men, or women.

Yet it was Jacob, and not Esau, that God chose for the transmission of his word. Nay, more, it was when Jacob was fleeing from the just and natural wrath of Esau, it was when Jacob had just concluded a most barefaced, unprovoked, and successful scheme of perfidy against his own brother, when he had just made that brother's kindness, and their father's blindness, an opportunity for high-handed cheating, that the Lord met him and said—what? "The blessing that thou didst obtain by sacrilege shall be turned into curses: instead of lording it over the brother whom thou hast cruelly and repeatedly wronged, thou shalt be his servant of servants: what thou hast gained by fraud thou shalt lose by force, that men may know that I am a God hating iniquity, and that I will by no means clear the guilty"? Not at all. Nor did God even say, as Isaac did, with sore regret, "I have blessed him, yea, and he shall be blessed, though he came with subtilty," recognizing the irrevocable word while bitterly lamenting the false pretences upon which it was obtained; for Isaac, at least, never held that fraud vitiated election. It was by treachery of the most outrageous kind,—treachery to an innocent brother absent on an errand of filial love,—treachery to the blindness of a dying father,—treachery in the name of the Most High God. "How is it that thou hast found it so quickly, my son?"—"Because the Lord thy God brought it to me," replies he, whom a newspaper, if it were reporting the case, might call the hypocritical villain. By such treachery had Jacob gained the blessing; and for all Esau's great and exceeding bitter cry,—for all his pathetic entreaty, "Hast thou but one blessing, my father? Bless me, even me also, O my father!"—Isaac could not take back the promised supremacy.

But God did more than this. He met this false, cruel, heartless man on his way to Padan-Aram, with his sins still hot within his heart; and, instead of rebuking, he repeats and confirms and intensifies the plundered blessing. Without even an implied censure, without so much as a reference to his past, he assures the guilty man, "The land whereon thou liest, to thee will I give it, and to thy seed. . . . And behold I am with thee, and will keep thee, in all places . . . for I will not leave thee until I have done that which I have spoken to thee of."

Surely it would have seemed more impartial and fatherly in the Great Father to appear in a vision to poor, cheated Esau, to comfort him. Was it quite fair that Esau should suffer all his life, through all his generations, for one sudden moment of self-indulgence, and that Jacob should not suffer at all, but be cherished and encouraged for a cold-blooded outrage of every honorable instinct and every filial and fraternal obligation? Is yielding to a quick temptation worse than partnership in deliberate vice? At any rate, Jacob's treason seems not to have alienated God from his cause. And in practical, actual life, it is equally true that momentary sins are often more severely punished than lifelong sins. There are sins which in themselves are no sins, which are sinful only by reason of circumstances, which have their root in innocence, and spring side by side with every virtue, grace, and charm, yet in one moment overspread and shadow life. And across the way a fatal selfishness blights every fair thing it touches, and scatters disappointment and misery on all around; yet the selfish man lives with untarnished respectability, and dies at last in the odor of sanctity. Esau's one lapse from virtue forfeited his birthright forever; and Jacob's smooth-faced wile and saintly guile sealed his inheritance, and crowned him with glory and honor.

It has happened to this generation to be disturbed because persons who have retired from public with a shadow upon their fair fame have been received at home with formal respect and rejoicing. Those who believe that the shadow was a stain are indignant that a man's fellow-townsmen who do not believe it should publicly testify their unbelief, and should welcome their respected friends with music and festivity. "What safeguard for public virtue," we cry, "when public opinion and sentiment are thus undiscriminating of right and wrong?" But human judgment is not infallible; and it is to be set down to a man's credit, if the community in which he lives believe him innocent, though all other men speak evil of him. But here is a case which admits of no doubt. Jacob had lied and cheated in the most abominable, the most contemptible, and the most successful manner. Yet it was when he was fleeing from the natural consequences of his unnatural crime, that he had a reception which throws all other receptions into the shade. For the angels came out of heaven to honor him; and the Lord God, who could have made no mistake about the nature of his act, appeared to him in the skies, and blessed him exceedingly. If he had been a hero, saint, and martyr, he could not have been more distinguished by the divine condescension. And in all the comfort and re-assurance was mingled no word of rebuke.

When the divine Being deigned to give a human record of his ways, he, in a manner, challenged human criticism. In the matter of Jacob, he managed very differently from what we should suppose a just God would do; and we naturally cast about for reasons. Was it an occasion where magnanimity was more effective than penalty? Did the divine condescension work remorse in Jacob's heart? Not at all. He was surprised, but not into repentance, still less into restoration. The prudent, discreet man was convinced that his vision was from God; and he vowed a vow, but still with his eye steadfastly fixed on the main chance.

"*If*—God will be with me"— God had promised to be with him.

"And—will keep me in the way that I go"— God had promised to keep him in all places whither he should go.

"And—will give me bread to eat"— None of your glittering and sounding generalities for Jacob! He meant to have the terms of the bargain clearly defined. "Keeping thee" is neither here nor there. He was too wily himself to believe that the Lord God could be trusted with verbal discretion or a liberal rendering of the terms of the contract. "Shall I have plenty to eat and drink and wear?"

"And —raiment to put on?"

"So that I come again to my father's house in peace"— Not harried and hated and hunted by that great, strong, and angry Esau.

"Then shall the Lord be my God."

Truly such worship must be pleasing to the Maker of men.

There is a sort of sublime audacity in the way in which the Bible deals with facts. It not only never palliates, but it never explains. It makes the most astounding statements without a particle of emotion. Its respectable and virtuous men are credited with high-handed villany as coolly as the census is taken. Nations fall at the edge of the sword, and nobody winces. Principles are enunciated, precepts laid down, biography and history written. You are left to work on them at your leisure. You may reconcile contradictions if you can. You may find motives if you choose. You may like or dislike, accept or reject; but you will get no help from the sacred writer. He is absolutely indifferent to your conclusions and opinions, to your creeds and your theories. He marches straight on through his narrative, perfectly calm and composed; and you can take yourself and your hypotheses out of the way, or be serenely trodden under foot. He gives no sign.

Apparently the Creator manages his world on a business basis. We are apt to think of him as intent only on rewarding the good, and punishing the bad. Doubtless, in the end, goodness will be upheld, and iniquity destroyed; but at present, and to our experience and consciousness, it is not holiness, but availability, that seems to be in requisition. God chooses men and nations for his service, not in proportion to their innocence, but their fitness. Just as, in time of war, commands may be awarded, not to the officer of blameless moral character, but of the greatest military genius. Just as, in time of peace, men may be elevated to high station, in spite of known personal blemishes, because they have the knowledge, the capacity, the experience, which the country needs. Their moral delinquency may be a grief of heart to Isaac and Rebekah, a thorn in the side of Rachel; but it may not incapacitate them for handling the public revenues, or caring for the public interests, better than any other man. We say, sometimes, that the people should vote only for good men; but a good man in the wrong place will do as much mischief as a bad man. God does not seem to have been very particular about employing good men.

The divine purpose or object was to choose a nation to receive the Christ for the whole world's sake. For this purpose, it is easy to see that Esau — fearless, adventurous, great-hearted, raiding around the country sword in hand, sacrificing his most valued treasures in a moment of impetuous fatigue, easily placated, but easily inflamed — was far less fitted than the plain and quiet Jacob, dwelling in tents, clinging to his mother, working seven years for his wife, and, when cheated out of her, patiently taking another seven-years' pull at it; not, like Esau, carving out his fortune with his sword, in the wide, wild desert, but whittling it out with his jack-knife, among his sheep and goats. It was not Esau's unsuspecting readiness nor generous forgiveness that unfitted him for the Lord's service, but his impulsive temper and nomadic tastes. It was not Jacob's duplicity that recommended him to God, but his tenacity of purpose. God met him at Bethel, not to encourage him in his wickedness, but to encourage him in spite of his wickedness. Jacob was thoroughly frightened; and it was necessary that he should be re-assured. But, in order that he should be the bearer of the Messiah to the world, it was not indispensable that he should be brave: it was only indispensable that he should live and prosper. Jacob was no better a man for securing his just wages from tricky Laban by a trick, and stealing away from him unknown, when he had the power and the right to march off with flying colors; but that intense love of life and peace and quietness, and that ever-present timidity which made him always and instinctively choose the submissive, peaceable, servile course, rather than the outspoken, resolute, and possibly violent one, constituted him the fit recipient of the ark and the covenant. He failed in grit, but he was mighty in grip.

Probably Jacob was of so mean a nature, that he could not understand the nature of the transaction in which he had just been implicated, nor in the least appreciate the enormity of the crime which he had committed. But a high moral sense was not necessary. There needed only certain mental and individual qualities, which Jacob possessed; and God did not even make the attempt to indoctrinate him into a high spiritual life, or to inspire him with high moral sentiments, but accepted his coarse, mercenary loyalty, and left it to time and circumstances to make a better man of him. Jacob, as an individual, was no dearer to God than was Esau. But Jacob as the founder of the nation chosen for the most important mission of the world was invaluable. Therefore, God met him, and sustained him.

This, also, may have had a place in the divine economy. Christ came to save that which was lost; to call, not "the righteous, but sinners to repentance." As he took upon himself the form of man in order to save men, so it may be that he took upon himself the form of the lowest and least of men to save the lowest and least. Humanity was to be saved, not from its noble, its generous, its manly traits, but from its vile, mean, underhanded tendencies. So God chose out the mean and sly, and made himself of no reputation, but incorporated himself with them, that no one henceforth should think himself, or be thought by others, too mean, too low, for salvation. Christ, in rising up out of this crafty, cruel, wretched family, drew all the crafty, cruel, wretched human family with him. God could have staid in heaven, and ruled the world thence; but, choosing to descend, he showed that it was necessary he should descend, in order, as it were, to get a better purchase. We may, thence, infer, that, the deeper the descent, the more sweeping the salvation.

There remains, of course, always the alternative of denying the reality of the revelation. We may believe that it was only a dream; that God did not appear, but that Jacob magnified his own consequence, and salved his conscience with a trumped-up story. This would be no worse than many things which he is reported to have done. And, when he subsequently told the story of his speckled and ring-streaked cattle to Leah and Rachel, we cannot help suspecting that he drew a long bow. But, besides that he seems to have been too unimaginative a man to have invented such a story; and that the narrative is not given as from his lips, but from the pen of the historian, — his tale of the second vision rather confirms the reality of the first. He could not invent a circumstance so remarkable; but, when it had once happened to him, he was so childish, and so given to deceit, that it was quite easy and natural to him to get up a dream and a vision on slight provocation. It was so very respectable a way to disarm criticism upon any questionable proceeding to say, "The angel of God spake unto me in a dream."

Dr. Robinson makes a remarkably, indeed, I might almost say a startlingly, interesting statement on this subject. In his travels he had reached a slope that looked straight down upon the spot where Jacob must have lain, near the old city of Luz; and there the party halted to rest.

"I remember now how instinctively I found a stone for a pillow. I lay back with my hands over my eyes, but irresistibly peering through them. A long, beautiful valley lay right down before us, so regular and smooth, that it might have been furrowed with a giant's plough. Wonderfully green it was with the first verdure of spring. It stretched away for full three or four miles, rising rapidly in the glade all the time, until it faded into dimness and disappearance on the summit of a high hill. It appeared to be a most fertile land-tract, caught thus thriftily by some industrious husbandman, who, in order further to guard it on either side from the wash of the hills, had *terraced* it all along its length with conspicuous walls of stone. So there below us it was spread, a green oblong of soil, outlined and plain, between two lengths of rude yellow masonry the entire distance. Across the slender tongue of land, at right angles to the rest, the painstaking man had constructed other *terraces* in the same way,— one in perhaps every forty rods, or thereabouts. This was to catch moisture, and prevent the wash in the other direction. But, if I make myself clear at all in the description, it is evident that the appearance was precisely that of a gigantic ladder, — one end close to us, distinct at our feet; the other almost touching the sky. While I was recalling the history in listless reminiscence, it suddenly occurred to me that this was Jacob's vision.

"I started up with an exclamation of surprise that fairly aroused my companions. . . . All our eyes were instantly turned toward the spot. There could be no mistaking it. Here was the faultless natural image, half disclosed as it must have been in the starlight to him, out of which Jacob's ladder grew. I do not say this was what he saw. I only say it was what we saw. We laid our heads back upon the 'pillows,' and the illusion was perfect. Away from us, from earth to heaven, that exquisite structure rose on its background of beautiful green."

If we were not alarmed by the cry of "naturalism," would not this seem to give the story a purely earthly, though a beautifully poetic origin? And, again, why is "mere naturalism" such a *bête noir*? Is not God at the head of this world which we see, just as truly as he is the head of the unseen world? All theological professors admit that only the divine Hand could keep the sun up after nightfall; but it seems to me a pretty divine sort of thing to keep the sun up *till* sundown every day. The doctors of divinity speak as if it needs omnipotence to divide the Red Sea on a particular occasion; but anybody could do it ordinarily. Supernaturalism must be accredited to Deity; but any tyro is equal to mere naturalism. For me, I confess I cannot speak so cavalierly of the creation. To me, God is of this world and in this world, just as truly as he is above this world. It is very interesting to know how he appeared to Jacob; but it is still more interesting to know that he is not far from every one of us. Suppose we reject every supernatural element from Jacob's ladder, and reduce it to "mere naturalism," what harm is done? God is not mocked. The sacred writer is not discredited. He tells us distinctly that Jacob dreamed and beheld. He tells us that God Almighty appeared to Jacob. No one doubts that Jacob dreamed and beheld. No one doubts that God Almighty appeared to him. But there may be, without impiety and without irreverence, dozens of opinions as to what particular kind of a dream Jacob dreamed, or in what particular manner God appeared to him. What we are to do is to study facts, and believe according to evidence. What we are not to do is to set up pet theories of naturalism or supernaturalism, and say, "These be thy gods, O Israel!" If Jacob lay down at Luz, weary, footsore, heavy-hearted, homesick, his last waking gaze fixed upon the lovely landscape, longing for the comfort and consolation of which he despaired; and if, as starving men dream of banquets, he dreamed of heavenly succor, and grew strong thereby, did not God appear to him in the dream? Did he appear to him any the less because he may appear to others in the same way? Is God dishonored because we say that "*every* good gift is from above, and cometh down from the Father of lights, with whom is no variableness, neither shadow of turning"? I see no reason to suppose that the divine Being values supernaturalism more than naturalism. On the contrary, he never acts above Nature when he can just as well act through Nature. And whether Jacob had a natural or a supernatural dream is still an open and a perfectly legitimate question.

The gentleman of Genesis was unquestionably Joseph. "There were giants in the earth in those days;" but the only symmetrical figure was Joseph's. Adam had dominion over the earth; but he attempted to shield himself from the divine displeasure by laying the blame on his wife, which no gentleman would ever do. "Noah was a just man, and perfect in his generations," if you do not mind an occasional fit of drunkenness. Abraham was a fine old sheik, a truly heroic figure, brave, generous, courteous, hospitable, magnanimous. No wonder the haughty Jews loved to remember and repeat that they were Abraham's children. But Abraham had his weakness, and fell before his temptations; and Isaac followed in his footsteps. Of Jacob, perhaps the least said the better, though he maintained his position as head of his family with unrelenting vigor, calling no one master, either son or king. There may have been other men whose life was "without fear, and without reproach;" but their history is unknown to us: their portrait is hardly more than a name. Joseph alone rises up out of that vast, far world, clearly outlined, distinctly seen, simple, saintly, strong, — a perfect gentleman.

Yet we should hardly expect it. His father was a man of double-dealing, and courageous only in extremity. His mother could steal, upon occasion, and lie like a Frenchwoman, and was envious, petulant, and unreasonable. His brothers showed their blood and training. They were not without admirable traits; but they were given to low vices; they were treacherous, cruel, and remorseless. And not only was Joseph the son of his father's beloved wife, the child of long waiting and many hopes; but his mother died in his early boyhood, and left him thus still more at the mercy of untrained and unwise favoritism. Surely Joseph had every prospect of becoming a spoiled child; yet he came out of it all tender and sweet, and pure as the angels in heaven. No one pretends that he ever was disciplined. If there is any thing injudicious and unnatural, it is partiality in parental feeling and treatment. Yet Jacob made no secret that he loved Joseph more than all the rest of his sons. It naturally made the others angry; but

Joseph's amiability of temper and disposition seem to have been beyond the reach of the spoiler. We see, therefore, that even Solomon cannot have it all his own way. If you do not train up a child in the way he should go, he may go there, in spite of you. Love — demonstrative, overflowing everlasting — seems to have done for Joseph every thing that the severest discipline, the most careful training, could have done. Let us take courage. We cannot all be wise; but we can all love.

Life lowered darkly over his dreams when this handsome, spirited young fellow was torn away from his fond old father, and sold into apparently perpetual and hopeless slavery. From being the pet and pride of the house, with great expectations of immense wealth, free, commanding, and beloved, this wandering heir was an alien and a servant, and presently in a dungeon. One would think his heart would have broken — his free, wild soul, bred to the hills and the skies and all the wide wilderness; but he held himself firmly and equably. Servitude and the prison were but his opportunity. There he developed his high executive ability, and honor the most delicate and lofty. It was not supineness, nor even an Oriental submission to fate; for his one prayer was to be taken "out of this house:" but, while he was in it, he lived and learned and labored, instead of pining. How came that grand

and tranquil spirit into the form of the spoiled child? Where, in his nomad, turbulent tribe, did he learn this serene self-possession, this instinctive high-mindedness?

He had a gentleman's spontaneous shrinking from "a scene." When he could no longer restrain himself, when there was no longer need that he should restrain himself, since he had tested his brothers' disposition, and found that those who had sold him into bondage were now ready to assume the dungeon themselves to save their young brother for their father's sake, he sent every man — every officer, servant, attendant — out of the room while he made himself known to his brethren. No stranger should witness that solemn moment. And then how his great heart broke in the anguish of love and tenderness and longing! Recognition, re-assurance, inquiry, comfort, he pours upon them incoherently, impetuously. No tact of a French *salon* could surpass the tender tact of this true-hearted gentleman. Their sin and shame must come up (there is no help for that, his identity requires it); but they come up only to be buried away out of sight and sound forever. He gives his brothers no chance to repent. He takes the words out of their mouths: he would take the thought out of their hearts, if he could. He forgives them so completely, that they never sinned. It was not they that sent him hither, but God. Whitest of all white lies! Whiter and purer and fairer than the truth itself! Sweet lie that deceives nobody, and consoles the remorseful, and succors the fainting heart! And how guileless, filial, and natural is his exultation over his proud pre-eminence! Doubtless he goes in and out before the Egyptians as stately and pompous as any Pharaoh of them all. No look or word betrays the smallest consciousness of purple robe or regal chariot; but with these his brothers, who knew him as a boy, playing among the sheepfolds, he delights to speak of his power; and perhaps the first pure joy in his glory he feels is when he bids them "tell my father of all my glory in Egypt."

And let it not be forgotten, this petted, dreaming boy, this spotless, incorruptible man, this fond, forgiving brother and yearning son, was no milksop, but a great, powerful, ambitious, far-seeing man, premier of Egypt, connected by marriage with the first families, emphatically a ruler in his own right and by his own might. Many boys, and some men and some women, seem to think that to be tender and pure and loving is to be "spooney." Our knowing philosophers are apt to assert that "the good ones aren't smart, and the smart ones aren't good." Bring out, then, your rough-and-ready men, your sowers of wild oats, who are "smarter" than Joseph. Let us see a questionable, unprincipled, or careless life crowned with more even of what the world calls success than this Sir Galahad of old Egypt. The boy dreamed dreams by the water-courses of Canaan; but he was an "adroit politician" in the council-chamber of Pharaoh. He was not an advocate of universal suffrage. He had no love for a republican form of government. He did not believe in democracy. He was a land-monopolist of the worst sort, and his income taxes were enormous. But he ruled with a high hand. His word was law, and his law was final. Pharaoh himself seems to have been but a *roi fainéant*. Whether in the house of Potiphar, the prison of the guard, or the palace of the king, this inexperienced young shepherd, this faithful honest servant, this pure, polite, gentle, tender man, rose by sheer wit and worth to the first rank. And finally, above all political preferment, and all ancestral advantage, and all personal ambition, he became the very head and front of one of the most learned, powerful, and prosperous kingdoms of antiquity. Let vice show a more brilliant career, before virtue is permanently discrowned.

But, if I am ever on speaking terms with Joseph, I mean to ask him why it was, that, during the twenty odd years of his prison and palace life, he never communicated with his father. His brothers deserved no better. But the fond old father was blameless; and it would have been such a comfort to him to know that an evil beast had not devoured the lad!

OUR CHARITIES.

OUR CHARITIES.

AT a late meeting of the American Board in Rutland, a great deal was said about giving to the Lord. The point to be driven in was the duty of supporting the various missions undertaken by the churches which act through the Board. One speaker said, in substance, as reported, that "while a Christian man has a right to accumulate all he needs as a capital with which to carry on his business successfully, and make the most money he can for the Lord, yet, when this point is once reached, it should be a serious question, whether the surplus should not *all* be systematically cast into the Lord's treasury." Another said that one-tenth was a very small part for a rich man to offer to the Lord. A third advocated the system which makes each one ask, "How much shall I give to the Lord?" A fourth told of the man, who, in the loss of his fortune, rejoiced in what he had given away; for "all he gave to the Lord's treasury was *saved*, but all he saved for himself had been lost." And so throughout, and throughout our ecclesiasticism generally, the money which we devote to teaching and extending the gospel is considered money given to the Lord; while the money which we devote to other purposes is money kept to ourselves.

That was the phraseology of the law. But we live under the gospel. When there was a Church and a State of which God was the official and recognized head, the treasury of that Church was the treasury of the Lord; and the offerings which God ordained as one feature of the regular worship were offerings unto the Lord. But that Church and that State government have, by God's own decree, passed away. He stands to us now only in spiritual relations. No one church, no one government, no one person, no one cause, is, officially, any closer to him than any other. He has no treasury apart from our treasury. There is no peculiar people; "but, in every nation, he that feareth God, and worketh righteousness, is accepted with him." Phraseology, therefore, which was once strictly accurate, is now only poetically true, and if used too commonly becomes offensive, and if used too strenuously becomes subversive of the truth, a teacher of false doctrine.

Granting to the establishment and support of Christian missions all the usefulness and importance which their most devoted founders claim, it is still not true that the money appropriated to them is necessarily given to the Lord, any more than the money appropriated to the preaching of the gospel at home. Granting to the pulpit all the power and influence which its friends assert, it is still not true that money appropriated to its support is any more, necessarily, given to the Lord than the money which supports the family. Of every dollar and every cent not spent for an evil purpose, and wasted to no purpose, one may be given to the Lord just as much as another — no more, and no less. "The earth is the Lord's, and the fulness thereof." There is no reason to suppose that he has any pet schemes or any favorite persons. He is simply full of good-will to men; and, wherever man spends money for the benefit of man, he is casting it into the treasury of the Lord. My Irish washerwoman, who is carefully hoarding the few dollars earned by her unremitting labors, and coaxing her hens to superhuman efforts in the way of eggs, that she may make up a certain sum for the savings bank at the beginning of the quarter, for the future education and respectability of her child, is casting her money into the treasury of the Lord just as truly as the rich men who are giving their thousands, and the poor widows who are giving their mites, to the American Board. The man who buys a picture to encourage a struggling artist; the woman who buys a silk gown, that she may be dressed in a manner becoming her position; the girl who adorns her hair with a red rose, that she may be pleasing in the eyes of her lover; the lover who would fain choose the fairest ring out of the jeweller's case to express his delight in her who is wholly fair, — they are all giving their money to the Lord. Whatever it is right to do with money, that is an offering unto the Lord. The woman may be extravagant, the man may be dishonest; but whoever is spending money as it is right for him to spend it, he is casting it into the treasury of the Lord.

God is no tax-gatherer, demanding a tenth part of our income or property, and letting us enjoy the rest ourselves. He does not stand in the way, taking toll of all who pass through his world. The whole world is his; and the whole world is ours. He giveth us richly all things to enjoy; and he enjoys what we enjoy. So far as our missionary effort is benevolent, he, no doubt, is pleased with it. If reason and revelation teach us any thing, they teach us that he, also, enjoys the father's pleasure in carrying home a doll to his little girl, a hoop to his little boy. He is pleased at the housewife's pleasure in her tidy home, at the frugal man's satisfaction in his accumulating wealth, at the energetic man's success in great enterprises, at the poet's happiness in friendly appreciation and world-wide fame. In whatever is generous, self-sacrificing, beneficent, we all agree God is well pleased. But I think, also, that in whatever is innocent, agreeable, pleasant, natural, he is also pleased. Wherever men and women and children are supporting themselves, gratifying one another's tastes, bearing one another's burdens, entertaining each other, making life easy for husband, wife, or child, smoothing roughnesses, levelling stumbling-blocks, meeting annoyances quietly, or resenting offences wisely, there they are doing the Lord's work. We ourselves are the temples of the Holy Ghost; and whatever ministers to the temple of the Holy Ghost is — Corban. We are the servants and sons of the Most High God. Not one-tenth, nor five-tenths, of our income, but all our income and capital — personal property and real estate — belong to him, and are to be used to further the ends which he has in view; and those ends must be the happiness, the education, the highest spiritual life, of nations and individuals. The Lord is not in the American Board, nor in the American pulpit. He is everywhere, — in the shop, by the fireside, at the table. He is to be served by the marketing, as well as by the missions. There is no rule of tenth and tribute. We are to judge by our own reason. We will give to the American Board such and so much as its wisdom and necessities demand of us, but on precisely the same grounds as we furnish our tables, and fill our wardrobes. I see no reason why we should ask the Master of the universe how much we shall give to the American Board, any more than we should ask him how much we shall spend upon a croquet-set, or whether we shall buy a Brussels or an ingrain carpet. He has given us abundant means to find out these things for ourselves; and he cannot be pleased to have us ask needless questions. We know, or ought to know, what our account-books say, just as well as Omniscience knows it; and, if we do not know whether the American Board is wise in its administration, Omniscience will never tell us, so long as the publication of "The Missionary Herald," and "The Annual Report," and the daily newspapers, is continued. A lady from the Board of the Interior urged women to give their jewels for the missionary work. The ear-rings alone, she thought, might prevent the need of retrenchment for a long time. Another lady described a scene in Turkey where this idea was put in practice. From a service with the native women there, she had carried home a handkerchief-full of jewelry given for the building of the mission-chapel. One woman gave a bracelet she had worn fifty years; and they observed that her ear-rings were also gone. "Yes," she said, "those are for the Lord too." The good lady who tells us the story says she felt ashamed of her own ear-rings, though they were only the little ones "John" gave her.

I do not question either the sincerity or the earnestness of the speakers or of the writer. When the heart is wholly set on any object, the mind naturally sees all things in relation to that object. The ladies who have embarked their hopes and their fortunes in missionary enterprises must look upon any failure to support them with the utmost regret and dismay. And, indeed, it would seem to the most casual observer, that failure, or even retrenchment, would not be creditable to the churches. But I cannot think we have reached the point at which gentle and affectionate ladies need be uncomfortable in wearing the ear-rings which their husbands gave them.

Nor do the ladies in question think so themselves. The shrinking possessor of the ear-rings goes *naïvely* over to the other side of the argument with the most winning unconsciousness that she has made a change of base. One peculiarity of the Rutland meeting was the evening reception given to the missionaries in the three church parlors. In one of these was spread a table covered with refreshments, and adorned with pyramids of fruits and flowers.

"Why was this waste of the ointment made?" some one asks; and the moderately bejewelled lady answers, "It was not wasted for those brave soldiers of the cross, any more than it was in olden time, on the feet of the Master. It will be told in memory of the Rutland women." And she is as right as a trevet in this decision; but it effectually disposes of the ear-ring question.

It is not simply a matter of giving ear-rings: it is one that concerns the whole structure of society. If we are to devote our ear-rings to the American Board, we must wholly and radically re-organize our mode of life. There is only one principle on which these ornaments are due to that organization; and that is, that we have no personal right to any thing more than the necessaries of life, until all the rest of the world is supplied with the necessaries of life. If this is Christianity, we are bound to put it immediately and forever into practice. If we are not bound to put it immediately and completely into practice, it is not Christianity.

What would it involve? As there are thousands, and tens of thousands, of persons at this moment in the world, with physical needs unsupplied, and hundreds of thousands with spiritual wants unprovided for, we should sacrifice, not our ear-rings alone, but our silk gowns and our broadcloth coats, our carpets and china, and most of our curtains and sofas and chairs and silver. It means, for clergymen, shirts of the coarsest unbleached cotton, and, for their wives, gowns of linsey-woolsey. It means, in short, the relinquishment of nearly every thing that marks refinement of tastes or habits, or culture in art and science. It means a return to the roughest and most primitive form of social and family life. There is no reason why the lady should give up her ear-rings, that does not apply with equal force to her reverend husband's sleeve-buttons; and even then the "refreshments" of those Rutland parlors should, to use a classical phrase, have stuck in their throats.

As a general principle, this seems wholly irrational and unscriptural. There are emergencies which require sacrifices; but these are local, temporary, exceptional, each separate case to be judged upon its own individual merits. It would be disgraceful, monstrous, for a woman to wear ear-rings while her child, or even her neighbor, was dying of starvation which could be fended off only by those ornaments. But the certain conviction that there are at this moment persons perishing somewhere — in London, or China, or Nova Zembla — for lack of food, does not induce us to strip off the rings from our fingers, the lace from our gowns, the gold heads from our canes. The world is one. The cause of refinement, of civilization, of art, of science, is the cause of God just as much as the missionary cause. He seems to be just as much engaged in polishing the corner-stones as in hewing them out of the rough rock. The Bible, on this point, gives no uncertain sound. There is, relatively, perhaps absolutely, **no more suffering in** the world to-day than there was when the Lord God commanded to overlay the ark with pure gold, to make the mercy-seat of pure gold, and the cherubims of beaten gold, and the ten curtains of fine twined linen, blue and purple and scarlet. Splendor of tabernacle and temple and priestly garb seems to have been ordained as means of grace. The souls of the Jews were to be reached through their eyes. Pomp and circumstance, beauty and ornament, are accepted in the Bible very much as they are accepted in the world, — admirable and valuable when they are the outward and visible sign of an inward and spiritual grace, hypocritical and abhorred when they are substituted for the grace itself.

Even the New Dispensation, upheld by no pomp, endowed only with its own inherent vitality, is adjusted on principles harmonious with the severest code of common sense. When the lawyer asked Jesus, "Who is my neighbor?" he set forth no impracticable scheme of universal relief, but minded him of the duty that he owed to all the suffering with which he came in contact.

There is nothing for it but to use our own reason, reluctant as we are to make that last resort. The Bible abounds in precepts and principles and illustrations; but it steadfastly refuses to give us rules. The men and the women of old time, willing hearted, brought their bracelets and ear-rings, and heaped them up for the service of the tabernacle; but they brought them with equal alacrity for the making of the molten calf. The small, sweet courtesies of life have their part in Christian character as inalienably as its sterner duties. The flowers and fruits, the coffee and salads, of the pleasant Rutland reception, were as legitimate a feature of the missionary work as the printing-press and the colporter. A tasteful and cultivated family-circle is a powerful missionary institution. The king's daughter is not only "all-glorious within," but "her clothing is of wrought gold." The emergencies are extremely rare which make it requisite, or becoming, for her to lay aside this regal robe, and array herself in sackcloth and ashes. The diamond ring may be just as truly consecrated to God on your own finger as in the contribution-box.

Which does not affect the fact, that the churches would fearfully stultify themselves, if, while declaring their belief in Christian missions, they should enforce or permit retrenchment.

We need a more intelligent understanding of the principles upon which all wise charity is founded, whether that charity be directed towards the spiritual wants of the heathen, or the physical wants of our own people. This American people is a people of magnificent generosity, and makes some very splendid failures. In benevolence, as in business, the logic of events is merciless. No matter how innocently we sin, our sin is sure to find us out. If business be not conducted in accordance with the unwritten laws of trade, if benevolence be not conformed to the eternal laws of human nature, no integrity and no unselfishness can ward off disaster, either from the one or from the other.

"The most bungling work society ever did," Mr. Beecher is reported to have said, "was when it tried to be merciful." True, doubtless. Society *is* clumsy; but let it always be remembered, in mitigation of its blunders, that the poor are infinitely harder to deal with than the prosperous, and that the difficulties of the situation are enough to make even society lose its self-possession.

The poor-house is a dreadful place, no doubt; but they are a dreadful sort of persons that live in it. Town-paupers are not above their situation. City poor-houses may be filled with high-minded victims of circumstances; but, in the country, paupers who have fallen under my observation have been, without exception, the offscouring of the earth,—dissipated, imbecile, incapable. They are God's children, I admit; but we are God's children too: and, if his hand made the inmates of the poor-house disagreeable and despicable, the same hand made them incurably repugnant to outsiders. One can no more help being repelled by them than they can help being paupers.

These remnants of society are also a great deal harder to get on with than society itself. Society is discerning, prosperous, and polite: it decorously conceals its displeasure, speaks you fairly, understands you generously, and, if it has any thing to say against you, says it behind your back, where it does no harm. But the remnants scowl in your face, if the porridge you bring them is not quite thick enough: in fact, you must carefully find out whether it will do to take them any porridge, lest you hurt their feelings. In English novels, the poor are grateful and reverential: in American life, they are autocratic. It is always a question beforehand, whether they will hold out their sceptre at your approach. They are quite as likely to be angry at your coming so late, or so early, as grateful for your coming at all. You must keep constantly on the lookout, and tack and veer and haul, or you will speedily come to grief on the breakers. To your equals, you can speak with freedom and force; but the sensitiveness of our high-spirited beneficiaries is something to be admired. I have known a man, who had been for years upheld by the charity of his neighbors, fly into a passion of rage because it was suggested that he should be taken to a comfortable refuge. No doubt, society is clumsy in its attempt to help; but the crankiness and kinkiness and general wrongheadedness of the people to be helped make society clumsy. If you could be natural and simple with them, as you can with your peers, it would be easier; but they are so open to offence, and so ungenerous in interpretation, that you must weigh all frankness out of your words, and give only a measured platitude to satisfy their querulous honor.

By poor people, I suppose we all mean, not those who have greater or less incomes, or who are forced to hard work, but people who are not self-supporting, not independent, — the persons who have to be helped.

The fact of poverty in a country like this is a presumption of defect. The land is broad, food is plentiful, labor scanty and high, government just and almost impalpable. What doth hinder any man from earning his own living? Illness may come: sudden calamity may fall. Against these, even energy may be powerless; but, apart from this, it is to be assumed that he who fails, fails because he lacks wisdom, and not opportunity. And the same weakness which prevented him from grasping the opportunity prevents him from keeping hold of it after it is put into his hand. Once in a while, once in a great while, a timely succor avails in a moment of temporary weakness, or averts the consequence of a mistake; and the man starts ahead at a swinging pace. But, oftener, the results seem to indicate that it is of very little use to help people who cannot help themselves. The kingdom of pauperism is within them. The very causes that made them poor keep them poor. It is not that society bears down hard upon them: it is that they are self-indulgent. If you see a widow and five children shivering over a few embers, you pity them, and you must send them coal; but you cannot help feeling a wrathful contempt at knowing that they all went to the photographer's yesterday, and had their pictures taken, after buying a couple of twenty-five cent brooches, on the way, to adorn themselves withal. The very things that you yourself would hesitate to do, on account of the expense, people who are partially dependent on your charity will do without hesitation. Where you will practise a natural, cheerful, unthinking self-denial, they will practise an equally cheerful and unthinking self-indulgence. The remnants of bread that you dry in the oven, and save for future use, they throw away. The fragmentary vest-sleeve that you fashion into a flat-iron holder, they put into the rag-bag, and buy new cloth for their holders. Where you rise at six, they lie till half-past seven. Where you walk, they ride. Where you pray and watch and strive to do your work thoroughly, they are content with any thing that will answer. That is the reason why people are poor. In this country, any man who is strong, and willing to work, can support himself, and all the family he ought to have. This is not a sentimental or a picturesque view to take of poverty; but, so far as my observation goes, it is the true one. I have been far oftener surprised to see how the will to work triumphs over obstacles than I have to see how obstacles triumph over the will to work. Right and left are women with infant children, incapable or invalid or dissipated husbands, surmounting hinderances, and earning not only a living, but a competence, by sheer pluck, or, if that is not an admissible word, will. I see men with indifferent health, but sturdy self-reliance and creditable pride, by steady industry, buying and building houses, lifting mortgages, growing gradually and surely into prominent and permanent respectability; while others, who started with apparently equal or superior advantages, falter and fail, simply from indolence, or feebleness of purpose. We pity them; but we also despise them. Every healthy mind must despise that trait which permits a man or a woman to prefer ignoble ease to a dignified though hardly-earned independence; which permits the day-laborer to live bountifully on to-day's wages, without laying by any store for the morrow, on which he cannot work. Even the beasts of the field know better than that. Have we been all our lifetime reading the fables of bees and butterflies, of ladybugs and ants, to think now that it is pretty and pathetic, and not disgraceful, for a man to be shivering like a ladybug in the winter time, for which he has made no provision? When I see how improvidently people will spend their money, in the face of possible want, and certain need of economy, I question whether our charities have not their unwholesome side. If every man knew that he must earn his bread, or go without it, would he not be more diligent to earn, and more careful not to waste what he did not want? If a drunkard knew that his children would starve unless he fed them, would he not put a stronger curb on his appetite than now, when he knows they will be taken care of, after a fashion?

Logic says, If the young man will not go West, and feed on the abundant wheat which his own hand raises, let him stay East, and die for want of it. If the young woman will not become a skilful housewife, let her stoop her life out over the needle. If the thriving mechanic or factory workman will not lay up wages when business is good, let him see his little ones perish for lack of food when the mills are closed. There is no way to teach providence, except by letting persons suffer to the full the consequences of improvidence.

If men feel that fate is inexorable, will they not prepare to meet it? It is because they expect something to step in, and shield them from the consequences of their own acts, that they are so reckless of consequences. Mr. Brace gives direct testimony to this end. Men, last winter, disdained labor through all the country-side, rejected fair wages and useful work, because New York offered them bed and board without either. Women disdained service, and used without scruple the funds of charity to enable them to hold out against the demands of trade. Able-bodied paupers refused fifteen dollars a month with "keep." Girls would not work at less than fourteen and twenty dollars a month, and would not go into the country at all. Suffering artisans refused to work at twelve shillings a day. With two hundred idle iron-puddlers on the list of a single soup-kitchen in New York, iron-puddlers had to be sent for from Pennsylvania.

The experiment never will be tried; for nobody is strictly logical, or will see suffering without relieving it, whoever is to blame for it, or is confirmed in his sins thereby: but if charity, while holding out relief in one hand, would give a good shaking-up with the other, it might sometimes be just as serviceable as to paint pauperism always as an interesting and romantic condition.

Without detracting a penny from heavenly charity, or one drop of cream from the milk of human kindness, it is well enough to remind ourselves occasionally, that, in this country of slight government and great opportunity, all pauperism, except that which is caused by innocent illness, or overpowering calamity, is somebody's shame; and every thing that shades into it is correspondingly disgraceful, not to be patted and petted and pitied, but to be got out of, and away from, as fast and as far as possible.

While we cannot say that logic should, in all cases, be carried out to its extreme limit, we cannot read such statements as Mr. Brace's without feeling that it is dangerous not to use logic in charity as strictly as in business. We cannot lay down the law that he who cannot help himself is not worth being helped by others, since that contradicts the law of humanity and of the Sacred Scriptures. But, surely, when men have proved themselves so incapable as to need assistance, the assisting party has a right to dictate conditions, and to enforce upon the weak the rules which have enabled itself to become strong.

It is far easier to give a dollar to a poor man, or a thousand dollars to a soup-house, than it is to inquire into the sources of pauperism, and the modes adopted for its removal; but it is to the last degree unpatriotic and unchristian. When a poor woman begs at your door, it is easier to give her food and clothing than it is to follow or accompany her to her own house to ascertain the truth of her story, to supply her with work, to teach her how to do it, and to put her in the way of becoming self-supporting. If the heedless, busy, or selfish giver is remonstrated with, he says, "I would rather give to ten impostors than refuse one deserving," and hugs himself for a generous and benevolent man. But it is not necessary to do either. The over-worked lawyer, or tired plumber, may not be able to follow up every case of distress that presents itself to him; but it is as easy to delegate that duty to another as it is to delegate to another his charity-soup, instead of brewing the pottage himself. Money and wisdom will organize a harmless and beneficent charity as truly, if not as easily, as they will organize an injurious and unintelligent charity. In Boston, beggary is against the law, and all persons are warned against bestowing money on beggars. Whoever does it knows, at least, that he is doing a work of supererogation, and cannot have the applause even of a darkened conscience.

Unintelligent giving is so hurtful, that its perpetration should be made odious. It is giving pleasure to ourselves, regardless of the injury we inflict on the receiver, or the stumbling-block we put in the way of those who are intelligently seeking his welfare. Suppose a great city trying to elevate its poor, to teach them the first principles of political economy, the painful ways to honest work, the slow, sure rewards of skill, the unerring rules of supply and demand. Charity is at its very best in doing this; and charity it is, since logic would do it only by starvation and suffering. Whatever does it tenderly, without pay, without anguish, supporting while it teaches, is charity. He, then, who strikes across this lesson with some entirely irrelevant offer of free lodgings, or free soup, to all the needy, tends to throw every thing into confusion, and does harm instead of good.

Charity should always couple money with work for the able-bodied. It would be better that it should be useless work than that there should be no work at all. Whoever applies for money, or soup, let him be set to work at shoemaking, or any form of simple work, and paid wages as low as may be sufficient to keep him from want; and, if the revenues of the business be insufficient to pay its expenses, let the deficit be met out of the charity fund; and, if he will not work, neither shall he eat. If we could know the facts, we should doubtless seldom find need of this. In our large country, the supply of labor usually falls short of the demand. What we want is not shops for fictitious work, but, if necessary, the ability to transport and apply labor. It seems, even, that we do not need bureaus to regulate such transportation; for they already exist. The two hundred iron-puddlers sipping the charity-soup of New York were not unneeded laborers, who should have been sent to empty Pennsylvania mills: on the contrary, the New York mills had to send to Pennsylvania for puddlers, while these paupers fed at the public feeding-troughs. Mr. Brace advertised largely that they were ready to send labor where capital was loudly calling for it; but labor refused to go. It preferred to stay in the city, to fatten on charity, and herd with idleness and vice. This being the case, I see no reason why the indiscriminate alms-giver in New York is not a malefactor, large or small, according to the scale on which he works. The real workers of the community are preyed upon by the idlers; and the rich help on their spoliation. The householders are deprived of the help which they ought to have in the kitchen; the manufacturers, of the hands which should guide engine and loom, because outsiders step in to drown the natural regulations of supply and demand in a swash of free soup.

If the kind-hearted and the benevolent, the great majority of our self-supporting population, would either turn their gifts into the established channels of charity, or acquaint themselves thoroughly with the persons whom they wish to relieve, they would do all the good, and feel all the pleasure, which they now do, without impoverishing themselves, without injuring the poor, and without deteriorating society. It would no longer be possible for "able-bodied paupers" to prey upon the industrious and self-respecting. That "able-bodied paupers" should exist in and be supported by a city where girls refuse thirteen dollars a month besides their board, and where men refuse nine shillings a day, is a burden upon the worthy poor and the honest rich too great to be borne. Let Charity be wise as well as kind. Let her help the incapable, and not pauper the lazy, or encourage the stubborn. As it is, this flower of our civilization shows a bad tendency to become a weed, and to overrun, and overshadow with its rank mischief, the ground which should be occupied by growths that are pleasant to the eye, and good for food, and to be desired to make one wise.

We have allowed matters so to adjust themselves, that "tramps" are getting to be a distinct and dangerous class. They were always a nuisance; but now, from an annoying, they have become a menacing, nuisance. In ancient days an "old straggler" produced a sensation in a village. The school-children scented him from afar, and, with swift heels and scant breath, reported him to their comrades, huddled into the schoolhouse, watched him by, behind barred windows and bolted doors, and followed him, retreating, at a safe distance. At the rare and hospitable farmhouses the "old straggler" called, modest, and "sensing" the situation. He never drank: he had no thirst for intoxicating liquor, but was generally a prey to some disease for which "a little saleratus and cider" was the sovereignest thing on earth; and I doubt not many a bearded man remembers the curiosity with which he watched the wayfarer's eager hold, rapt eyes, and negligence of breath, as he pressed the cider pitcher upside down to his longing lips, loath to lose one drop of possible delight. As we have arrived at man's estate ourselves, we have seen the "old straggler" coming thicker and faster; but he is not so old as he was. He is shabby enough; but he is usually a young fellow, able-bodied, out of work, and travelling to Portsmouth. Sometimes he is fierce and Spanish-looking; but oftener he is sandy-haired, sunburned, and freckled, ill-favored, but not brigandish. He seldom asks for money, but is perpetually hungry. If you give him a remainder biscuit with an apology, he accepts gratefully, with the assurance that it is "firs'-rate," while, if you proffer a generous slice of squash pie fresh from the oven, ten to one but you shall go out to find it dashed against your garden wall. I do not so much mind the wasted viand, though that grieves me to the heart; but the *spretæ injuria formæ*, the slight put upon my cooking, for all the neighbors to see, — that I never will forgive. Nor do we, like them of old time, invite these wayfarers to the kitchen to warm their frozen fingers by the glowing hearthstone. A seat on the sunny side of the door-step is the most cordial invitation they receive, and that with locks and bolts well secured; for their humility and harmlessness seem to be deserting them. They come no longer singly, but in squads. They have ceased to beg: they demand. Their tramp has become their profession. Their spare money they evidently spend in clubs, knives, and revolvers. We scarcely take up a newspaper without reading of some outrage and violence perpetrated by a tramp. They rob, burn, murder. They attack men and women and children. They travel in couples and quartets, evidently dividing up the houses among themselves. Some of our laws seem especially made for their nurture; or is it that our American institutions are so flexible, that the tramps easily bend them to their own advantage? Every town is obliged, by law, to find lodging and food for wayfarers: so the tramps are assured of bed and board; and if the landlord or landlady secured for them be of congenial spirit, the gypsies live in clover. A little village of eight hundred inhabitants is so generously disposed toward the poor, that its chronic paupers have been distinguished for the elegance of their dress; and twenty-five dollars have been paid for a single night's lodging of the vagabonderie. Of course, these nomads know when they are well off: so they " cut and come again." I have seen parties of four and six walking back and forth on the outskirts of the village, waiting till it was dark enough to make their request for lodgings legal. And so great is their liking for their hospitable quarters, that they are sure not to go so far off that they cannot return at nightfall. This is, perhaps, a good way to prevent crime, since the scoundrels have all they want, and are not tempted to violence; but it is also an excellent way to nurse vice. And it is, it must be confessed, a little burdensome to the proud and haughty, who prefer not to beg, and who are therefore forced to work.

Vagabondage, if it be not made a crime, should at least work forfeiture of freedom. If tramps are to be supported by honest men, honest men should at least have the power to say in what manner the tramps shall be supported. It is unfair for the farmer to work hard in the hot hayfield all day or the shoemaker in his little cramped-up shop, and then be obliged to take a part of his small earnings to feed and lodge a lazy fellow who has been lying under a hedge till sundown, and who will break into his house, and steal his goods, and murder his wife, if he gets the chance or the provocation. Responsibility implies authority. As long as a man is obliged to support his children, he has authority over his children. If a grown man is not self-supporting, he should not be self-directing. Some towns have borne all the burden they feel disposed to bear, and are arresting tramps in all directions, determined to test their liabilities. Public sentiment will doubtless approve their course; but, unless public sentiment formulates itself in common law, these local measures will but increase local distress. If one village, by village law, arrests tramps, and the next village does not, the second village will be but a receiving-tomb for the decayed humanity of the first. These vermin, driven out of the one town, will take refuge in the next; and the last state of that town shall be worse than its first. It should be a recognized State law, if it be not now, that any person asking alms from door to door thereby forfeits his liberty. In surrendering the self-support of manhood, he surrenders also its self-control. The community that feeds him shall restrain him. If he will eat the bread of beggary, it shall be behind a barred gate. He shall not walk up and down, seeking what and whom he may devour; but he shall have keepers, and be made to work: he shall lie down, and rise up, and march to table and field and workshop, at the voice of the bell. He shall have abundance of wholesome food, but no squash pie to bespatter stone fences withal! He shall not batten longer on the toils of honest men; but he shall eat his bread in the sweat of his own fat face; and the only difference between his fate and that of his thrifty brother shall be, that, while the latter goes home to wife and child, and vine and fig-tree, the former shall have neither ownership nor accumulation. If a man find that he must work as hard for bare walls and coarse food as for home and family, and all social solace and standing, it would be but an evil choice for him to make. Let us take off the premium from vagabondage; let us make the tramp's life as stern and severe as that of the honest citizen; let society close upon him, short, sharp, and decisive, and either make a spoon, or spoil a horn.

All of which does not mean that the honest and industrious but unfortunate laboring-man out of employment shall be treated as a tramp, or that the tramp shall not be considered as "a man and a brother." Constraint and labor are means of grace to the man who spurns both, and preys upon his neighbors; while the honest man out of work has no worse foe than these lazzaroni, who drain a community of the sympathy and succor which ought to be bestowed upon those who need help, but not alms.

Physicians tell us that the great stone hospitals on which we latter-day saints pride ourselves, as embodying the last results of sanitary science, are, of all establishments, the most pernicious. The seeds of disease are sown in them from year to year, and are ever springing up in a fatal harvest. With all our knowledge and all our money, the best kind of hospital is the cheap wooden barrack, which can be torn down every three years, and thus prevent the storing-up and distribution of disease, to which the enduring stone building is always liable. Is it not possible that some similar necessity exists with regard to our great charitable institutions?

There are soldiers' homes scattered over the land. This is a form of charity as little offensive as it is possible for charity to be. Indeed, I do not know that it should be called charity at all. Surely, if debt can exist between man and man, it is incurred by the nation toward those who have perilled life and limb in her behalf. So the nation does well to provide a home for disabled soldiers. She rears a lofty and imposing structure, lays out grounds with taste and elegance, keeps every thing in admirable order, receives all poor and wounded and invalid soldiers who knock at her door, feeds them, clothes them if need be, furnishes them pension for pocket-money, lays them under no grievous restriction, and imposes no labor. If you drive to their retreat, you see them sauntering along the gravelled walks, reclining under the trees, lounging upon the piazza, or perhaps engaged in some light work. But, after all, it is a most dreary place, — a mockery of home. You are struck by the absence of life. There is no interest, no animation, no vitality. All is lounging and listlessness. I have been told that soldiers enter these homes with reluctance, and leave them with alacrity. There is no complaint of ill-treatment, insufficient food or care: it is simply that their dreariness is insupportable. Can we wonder at it? Think of fifty or a hundred men living together in a perfectly comfortable house, with nothing to do! They have no care, no responsibility, no occupation, no society but each other. As soldiers, they have had stirring, active, eventful lives. Doubtless, at first, the quiet, the rest, is delightful; but when wounds are healed, and life flows once more in all the channels that are left, how these human hearts must long for the variety, and even for the vexations, of humanity, for the activities of manhood, the attraction of womanhood, the amusement of childhood! In every establishment, ought we not to take the family as the model? So far as our institutions depart from the family type, are they not on a wrong principle? Is it practicable? And, if practicable, is it not better that the fifty soldiers should be distributed through the community, to live in, and become a part of, separate homes, rather than live together in a monotonous and unnatural club? They need not be "town-poor," but national pensioners, honorable, though dependent; receiving their support from the country, not as a gratuity, but as some attempt at an equivalent for services rendered. Many, perhaps most, of them, though partially disabled, are not incapacitated for light labor, and would be all the healthier and happier for its performance. They may not be able to do man's work; but they could be exceedingly useful in doing what is too often added to woman's work. There are thousands of farmhouses where these men could amply pay their board by doing " chores " that now fall to the lot of overworked women. Many families who could not endure the incumbrance of a boarder, nor afford the outlay of hired service, would be greatly relieved by such an addition to their staff. The man would quickly work into a pleasant and profitable position, and join in the wholesome life from which the far more splendid surroundings of the home completely shut him out. It may not be immediately nor entirely practicable; but can we not hold this end in view?

There is an insurmountable repugnance in the minds of many poor people to technical places of refuge. It is not independence; for they will receive without flinching, in their own miserable homes, an amount of assistance at a cost of trouble, thought, and care far greater than would be necessary to support them comfortably at the poor-house, or, as we have taken to calling it, the " home ; " though we do not succeed by our euphuisms in deceiving our victims, who draw back from the " home " as decidedly as from the poor-house. We are at great expense to provide an asylum for old men, a home for aged and indigent females; and the old men throw their cane at you, if you propose to take them there; and the aged and indigent females grow young and rich in the vocabulary wherewithal they declare their determination not to go. This means something. Of course, we can make them go if we choose. Society is a giant, and can use its strength giant-wise, to be strong against the weak. But it is not pleasant, even when it is necessary: how much less when it is not certainly necessary! Perhaps the weak are right, and, haply, we shall be found to fight against God. Instead, then, of giving all our energies to the preparation of a house, why not devote a part to the accumulation of a fund whereby these poor, who so profoundly dislike the more public forms of charity, may be supported in private homes? There are many families whose income would be materially improved by the small sum which would be payed for the support of a woman incapable of self-support, but not needing any especial care or nursing. A board of overseers, or a ladies' committee, could still supervise affairs, keep track of all its beneficiaries, watch over their interests, look out for their comfort. And the old ladies themselves would often be far happier in the humble but more cosey, more sociable, more natural, if more narrow, home, than in the spacious, abundant, but public and unfamiliar " refuge." Beggars should not be choosers perhaps: still, if we give, we may well give wisely. The poor may be unreasonable; and their poverty is often their own fault. But, after all, we would a thousand times rather be ourselves, with the annoyance of their unreasonableness, than to be the poor, with all their dictation. In the general distribution of traits, we are glad those fell to our share which enabled us to be independent, though at the cost of much hard work and self-denial. We are thankful that we can work, that we can turn away from the present pleasure to avert the future disaster. I would make pauperism as odious as possible; but I would make the helpless victims of pauperism as happy as possible. We cannot be too careful not to loosen the foundations of self-respect, not to make it seem easy and pleasant and natural to depend upon others, instead of helping one's self, not to make this false life of leaning too closely resemble the true life of uprightness. Yet, on the other hand, there is so much wretched dependence springing from age, sex, infirmity, calamity, the error and the crime of other people, that one cannot be too careful in applying even just rules, — too gentle, too wise, too considerate in guarding from additional pain those who are already sore wounded and vanquished in life's hot battle.

If our modes of disbursing our charity funds need to be carefully looked into, so, also, do our modes of gathering those funds. The old type ideal of charity is a quiet, modest, retiring, and gracious lady, searching out the abodes of suffering, ministering to the sick, teaching the ignorant, giving of her substance, but always unobtrusive, never letting the left hand know what the right hand doeth. The real Lady Charity seemeth to be somewhat of a brazen dame, sedulously seeking her own pleasure in the name of the poor. She institutes a charity ball, whither she goes dressed in all the silk and lace and jewelry of luxury, or, worse still, in calico fashioned in such fantastic shapes, that neither rich nor poor can make any use of it afterwards. She dances all night; she devours creams and cakes, salads and coffee; she breathes the fragrance of flowers, and moves to the music of a band, and in all things disports herself like a lady bent on her own amusement; and is altogether satisfied and satisfactory because it is a charity ball. The few hundreds that may be left after the thousands are paid out for dress and flowers, and lights and music, and supper and hall and carriages and attendance, are given to the poor; but charity has only the crumbs that fell from the table. The table itself — the bulk of the expense and the effort — was in the entertainment. I do not say there is any thing wrong in this, except the name. If persons find their account in weeks of preparation, and much sounding of the tocsin, and soliciting of patronage, for the sake of an evening's pleasure, who shall gainsay them? Doubtless there are some, perhaps the originators and organizers of the ball, to whom it is really a labor of love; but, in all its length and breadth, let us not call it charity. To the deserving and suffering poor, to the invalids, the widowed, the orphan, who know not to-day what they shall eat on the morrow, it must be a strange sight indeed, — this of men and women rushing together to expend on a single evening's gratification for themselves, and in various forms of luxury, an enormous sum of money in order that a small sum may slip through into the outstretched hands of want. If, indeed, the small dole can be entreated from the rich in no other way than by bribing them with a *fête* for themselves; if the pleasure of blessing be not enough, but must be sweetened with the pleasure of receiving; if giving have no grace, and money must bring to the donor money's worth in marketable values, — then, perhaps, we do well to make a feast, and call in the rich and prosperous to make crumbs for the poor and the maimed, the halt and the blind; but this is not charity. When the Philistines ask, "What meaneth the noise of this great shouting in the camp?" let no man have the effrontery to say, "It is because the ark of the Lord has come in." It is far more like the song of the worship of the golden earrings. Nine parts self-indulgence, and one part charity, may not be an iniquitous compound; but it is certainly not the elixir of life. The clangor of our benefactions does not mark their increase, but their diminution.

In connection with this public hue and cry comes a spirit of dictation, a virtual coercion, which it seems offensive to resist, and hypocritical to accept. It is to be expected, that, in the rattle and clatter of machinery, all the ancient delicacy of charity, both on the part of giver and receiver, should fade away. When men scatter their largesses from the housetops, with bells ringing, and flags floating, they lose every pretext for blushing to find it fame. They are far more likely to redden with rage, if they do not find it fame. We appeal for charity, not to the necessity of the case, to the conscience or the pity of the beholder, but to his vanity, his pride, his self-interest. A church debt is auctioneered from the pulpit on Sunday. "I will give a thousand dollars," says A to B, "if you will give a thousand dollars." But what has A's purse to do with B's? If the case is a worthy one, or, in any case, why should one man's help be conditioned on another man's? A knows, or ought to know, the condition of his own finances. He knows nothing of B's. If he can give a thousand dollars, let him give it. He has no right to dictate the direction, or the amount, of B's gifts, or to subject him to the necessity of refusing, or of giving reluctantly. Benevolence is no justification of impertinence. What is ill bred and improper, dictatorial and rude, does not become polite and gentle and Christian, because it is done in the name of charity. There are some forms of charity which seem to do more harm to the soul than good to the body. They injure the manners of the givers more than they benefit the lives of the receivers. All such charity is suspicious. The true charity blesses him that gives, and him that takes. The true charity is as strong in its reflex as in its direct influence. It shines all around, and not in one straight line alone. It is marked by the most instinctive reticence, and a constant courtesy of demeanor. It represses the forward, and encourages the timid, and respects the self-respectful, and tries to infuse into the shameless a sense of shame. It reverences the dignity of humanity, and the rights of the individual, and never encroaches upon the poor or the rich. It assumes no power of inquisition into the lowliest cottage, the shabbiest hut, any more or any less than into the houses of the great and strong. It is not bars, or bolts, or servants, or force, that guide or guard its entrance anywhere, but its own innate, unerring, ever sinuous sense of propriety. And, while it is thus cautious of imposing itself on the reluctant, it is equally solicitous to win the confidence of the silent and forlorn. It aims to do good, rather than to excite gratitude; to give the feeble a start, rather than to make a stir in society. It would rather help a man to help himself than to make his own exertions unnecessary.

I believe we are mistaken in supposing that this kind of charity would be less heartily supported than the festive, luxuriant, and selfish charity. Men may be reluctant to put a new carpet on the parish church; and it may be necessary to cajole them with a tea-party. But, towards human want, human nature is apt to be generous. The carpet is not a necessity. But men will not willingly let a family suffer for want of food. I do not believe the community exists in America, that is not willing and able to provide for all its needy without an atom of fanfaronade. When Portland and Peshtigo and Chicago are burned, and Louisiana drowned, and the valleys of our own New England overswept by sudden desolation, there is no waiting for balls and theatres. The money does not wind through fairs and fashions, diminishing as it goes, to fall, at last, a feeble, and sluggish stream, into a thirsty soil that drinks it up, and gives no sign. It rushes straight from purse and till, — an impetuous, sustaining, and sufficient flood. Great occasions bring great enthusiasms; and, for ordinary occasions, the enthusiasm of humanity is enough. If wisely appealed to, it seldom fails to respond. The beating of gongs is as unnecessary to secure the desired ends as it is offensive to good taste, and obnoxious to good manners. A charity that is indelicate in its methods is a proper object of suspicion. So far as possible, all the processes, and all the recipients, of charity, should be guarded by a profound and sacred privacy, that self-respect be not wounded, character injured, nor truth destroyed.

Miss Cushman, with characteristic independence, good sense, and good feeling, has entered a protest against this system. The occasion was a request, which had been made, that she would give a gratuitous representation for the benefit of local charities in, let us say, Venice. In response to this protest, one of her rejected addressers says, "No actress in the country has been more generously and heartily rewarded in Venice than Miss Cushman. She has always been a favorite here, and been always treated with uniform courtesy and kindness. We will not say that she has not, in a measure, by her genius commanded all that has been accorded to her: but, at the same time, we believe that there are certain relations of good-will and friendship which should always exist between actors and the public; and that, if any one in the country in her profession is under obligations to a community, Miss Cushman is to Venice."

All of which may be true, without, in the smallest degree, militating against Miss Cushman's position, that she is under no "especial" obligations to any community in which she does not live. The people who go to theatres and concerts, who buy bonnets and gowns and shoes and sugar, are often spoken of as patrons of the singers and players and grocers and milliners; and so they are, but no more so than are the grocers and milliners the patrons of those who buy their goods. You go to the theatre for your own amusement, and not in the least to oblige Miss Cushman, or Mr. Jefferson, or Mr. Boucicault. If they play well enough to please, you go again: if they do not, you stay away, regardless of their feelings or their purses. If they play so well, that high admission-fees may be profitably charged, you pay the high admission-fee, still not in the least to profit Miss Cushman or Mr. Boucicault, but because you cannot get in on a small fee. No one thinks of patronizing an inferior actor from motives of benevolence; and it is pure absurdity to say that one is actuated by benevolence in enjoying the personations of a master of his art. Why, then, should an actor be obliged to you for pleasing yourself? Why should the shoemaker be obliged to you for the money whose lack would make him less uncomfortable than you would be in going barefoot? If there is any obligation, it is as much on the one side as on the other. Venice is just as much bound to help Miss Cushman's charities as is Miss Cushman to help Venice. The family ought to be quite as grateful to the butcher and grocer and milkman who feed it, as ought they to be to the family which pays them money. But did Miss

Cushman ever imply that Venice owed her any thing? or did Venice ever recognize any such relation? She is reported to have met with much pecuniary and other trouble. Did Venice ever concern itself to ascertain, remove, or relieve these troubles? Did it ever make any inquiries as to Miss Cushman's necessities, or pensioners, and ask to bear a part of her burdens? I have pushed no researches on the subject, and, of testimony, know nothing whatever about it; but I hazard the assertion, without fear of contradiction, that, whatever of trouble Miss Cushman may have met, she has encountered it without asking or thinking of help from Venice; that her connection with the city has been purely one of business; and that whatever money she has received has been in exchange for goods sold at their market-value. At the same time, such are "the relations of good-will and friendship" existing between her and the Venice public, that if, by some sudden turn of the wheel of fortune, she should be known to be ill, destitute, and suffering, Venice, no doubt, would take up a generous contribution, and send it to her with such warm admiration and delicacy as would fill her with rejoicing. So, I doubt not, if Venice were suddenly smitten with overwhelming disaster of fire or flood, Miss Cushman, with her great generous heart, would give abundantly for its relief. Great emergencies bring "especial" claims; but that

Miss Cushman should come down from Boston, or that Venice should go up to New England, to help out the ordinary duties of every-day life is — not reasonable.

"There is another point in this five-hundred-dollar-a-night business," says the disappointed applicant. "Does Miss Cushman really think that she earns it? She gets it; but we beg to remind her that she wrings it out of the managers, under the villanous 'star' system, and at the expense of the poor and humble in her own profession, who, in a large degree, contribute to her success, and who are not paid as much in a year as she is paid in almost a single night. She enforces her five hundred dollars a night, demands her pound of flesh; and they must take what they can get. Miss Cushman looks at the matter from a thoroughly selfish, heartless standpoint."

It would not be easy to crowd more erring philosophy into a single pronunciamento. Miss Cushman, doubtless, being a woman of unusual grandeur of character, looks at her business-engagements from a thoroughly business standpoint; and business is and ought ever to be thoroughly heartless and selfish. To make it any thing else is to embroil and despoil it. To mix sentiment with business is to profane the one, and to demoralize the other. But business is heartless and selfish etymologically, not morally. It is heartless precisely as mathematics is heartless. You might as well blame a problem in Euclid for its lack of pity, as to blame business for a similar deficiency. The one principle of business is to buy in the cheapest, and sell in the dearest, market; and it is a thoroughly just and legitimate principle, and thoroughly compatible with generosity and magnanimity in the man who acts upon it. Indeed, there is no other principle on which business could be successfully and satisfactorily conducted.

Miss Cushman, in demanding five hundred dollars a night, is but doing what every merchant does in demanding an extraordinary price for an extraordinary piece of Gobelin tapestry; or a milliner of rare skill, in charging high prices for her bonnets; or Mr. Evarts, in taking a ten-thousand-dollar fee in one lawsuit; or Mr. Beecher, in receiving his twenty-or-so-thousand dollar salary. Does Mr. Evarts imagine he earns his enormous retainer? He gets it; but we beg to remind him that he wrings it out of his clients, and at the expense of the poor and humble of his own profession, who are not paid as much in a lifetime, perhaps, as he is paid in a single month. Mr. Evarts enforces his pound of flesh; and the poor pettifogger must take what he can get!

You might just as well reproach a diamond for costing more than a Scotch pebble as to blame Miss Cushman or Mr. Evarts for being more expensive than their "supes." We pay for things in proportion to their rarity and to the pleasure they give us. The "star" system may be vile; but, when it is superseded, it will not be because it is vile, but because it is unprofitable. Miss Cushman's high demands not only injure no one, but benefit many. The managers, on the whole, find it for their interest to be wrung out by Charlotte Cushman rather than cast their play without her. No one forces them to employ her. It is only, that, if they do employ her, they must pay her price. So far from injuring the poor and humble of her own profession, it is she, and such as she, who give them any profession at all. Who would go to a theatre to see the pitiful mouthing and ranting and strutting, the wooden, lifeless performances, of the lower class of actors? "Can't you say it *so?*" said Edwin Forrest, instructing one of his "supports." "Confound you!" cried the poor fellow, in admiring despair, "if I could say it *so*, do you think I would be pegging away here at ten dollars a week!" It is because Forrest can "say it so," that we listen patiently to Tom, Dick, and Harry all around him, saying things in quite another way. Miss Cushman is far more necessary to her poor supporters than they are to her. When she reads absolutely alone, she draws crowded houses. How many crowds would they draw without the allurement of any superior talent?

Miss Cushman, in enforcing high prices for her performances, is doing more for her sex and her profession than she can do in any other way. No one can excel in any calling without diffusing the benefit of it down through the very lowest stratum of that calling. His genius and skill raise the average, help to make the calling honorable. It goes much "against the grain" to pay twenty dollars for a bonnet whose material cost five dollars; but the milliner has a perfect right to charge fifteen for her skill and taste. She may overshoot the mark; and the just result is, that her bonnets are not sold. But these things arrange themselves on the everlasting principle of supply and demand. It may be very sad that the poor sewing-girl gets but starvation wages, while the mistress grows rich. But poor sewing is as the sands of the sea for multitude; and artistic sewing is like the diamonds of Golconda. Moreover, every new prime sewer and fashioner creates a demand which gives employment to the poor and plodding. The "star" has given to its brilliancy care, time, and culture, of which the clod knows nothing, and for lack of which it has only itself to blame. But also the "star" had an original endowment denied to the clod, for which the clod is not to blame; but neither is the "star." Is there wrong with the Most High?

Since writing this, a remarkably apt illustration has

been given of the obligations which Venice considers due from the public toward those actors who have entertained it, whatever its views may be of the obligations of actors to the public. Mr. J. M. Bellew, the reader, being sick and poor, has applied for help to the public. Venice says, through her press, that he " is certainly the most genteel beggar that has yet appeared. Being sick, and nearly out of funds, he sends telegrams all over the world, stating that he has no prospects of getting better very soon, and would be thankful for any assistance that may be rendered him. Who wouldn't feel overjoyed at receiving aid and succor through such novel means? In case the responses are heavy and full, we would advise Mr. Bellew to engage a clerk to acknowledge the receipt of remittances. There are plenty of young men out of employment in England who would be glad to secure such a position."

I do not see why it was a more genteel beggary for Mr. Bellew to telegraph to the world for charity than it was for Venice to telegraph to Miss Cushman. Certainly her response was not half so scornful, and, I suspect, not more unproductive.

When Miss Cushman said, " You simply ask of me that I should give from four hundred dollars to five hundred dollars to your poor," the seeker replies, " We did not ask Miss Cushman to do any thing of the kind. We asked her if she would give an extra performance, and did not propose to interfere in any way with her regular engagements. . . . Perhaps she is right, and that we were wrong, in asking her to give a few hours of her time to a charitable object."

This illustrates a very common mistake made by persons in whom goodness of heart, let us say, outstrips clearness of head. They have a certain desirable object in view; and, to promote it, they will, with the most cheerful and unhesitating frankness, ask you to give, not money (they would shrink from that), but things which represent money to you, which bring money to you, and which will bring money to them — and think they are doing the whole duty of etiquette. Ask Miss Cushman to give us five hundred dollars? Not we! We simply ask her to give a representation which always brings her five hundred dollars, and to hand over the proceeds to us, instead of putting them into her own purse. Ask her for money? Nothing was further from our thoughts! We did but ask a few hours of her time. Ask her to give us one of her regular engagements, and so diminish her income? Not in the least! We did not interfere with her regular engagements, but desired her to grant an extra performance.

But lives there a man with soul so keen as can explain the difference between five hundred dollars in money at high noon and a performance that brings five hundred dollars before midnight? What is the saving clause that makes a regular performance a part of your income, and an extra performance no income whatever? An actor, during the season, makes, undoubtedly, as many engagements as his nerve and the public purse will stand. If an extra one comes in, he must make extra outlay of personal power, or withdraw an engagement elsewhere. But, however that may be, if he can earn the money, the money is his; and, if it is bestowed upon the poor, he bestows it, and nobody else.

I say nothing of the nature of the actor's calling, since it has no bearing on the case. We may approve, or disapprove, of theatrical representation. If we disapprove, the impropriety is even stronger than if we approve. It is bad enough to make unwarrantable claims upon money honestly and honorably earned; but it is startling indeed, if we may oppose an actress in the performance of her art by every form of moral resistance, and, when she has earned the money in spite of us, we may levy upon her to sustain our own scheme.

Does the artist give only a few hours of her time? If so, then suppose you select the three or four hours that she is taking a railroad journey. Let her contribute the proceeds of the three hours that she is making morning-calls, or indulging in a siesta. Those are the hours of her time as truly as the hours during which she is performing on the stage. But those hours bring no money. So it is not that she gives simply three hours of her time. She gives time that is filled to the brim with her gifts and graces. She gives you all the native genius, the control, the hard study, the assiduous practice, the vital power, the travel and self-control, the fame and glory, which make her three hours of time worth more in hard money than three years of the kitchen-maid's. Her empty time is worth no more than yours or mine.

You go to the lawyer for advice, which he condenses into an hour, and for which you pay five, twenty, a hundred dollars. It is not for his hour's time, but for the three years of preparatory study, and four years of college, and three years of law school, and days and nights of laborious research and continuous application, that make him capable of answering your question, and make his answer worth to you a hundred times what you pay him for it.

The grocer, who would be considered munificent in giving you five dollars, is churlish if he will not give five dollars' worth of flour to your charity, and niggardly to the last degree, if he refuses to sell whatever you want at cost price. The doctor is expected to make out no bill against his poor patients. The editor sends his newspaper to clergymen at half-price. The author is asked to send fifteen or twenty dollars' worth of books to a remote society, whose money donors average a dollar and a half apiece; and the *feuilletoniste*, to contribute a twenty, thirty, or fifty dollar article to the "paper" of some unknown fair, edited by citizen amateurs, whose services in that capacity would not bring fifty cents in any known market. If a knot of young men in Omaha desired to form a reading-club, they would not dream of asking the proprietors of a newspaper for five dollars to pay room-rent; but if Messrs. Proprietors have not been repeatedly requested to send their publications free, by way of encouragement, to incipient and impecunious reading-clubs, their experience is different from that of most publishing-firms whose ways I have known. Beggary of goods seems a very easy Christian duty and worldly pleasure to people who would count beggary of money a thing improper, and deleterious to self-respect.

None of these requests are unkindly meant, though a refusal is sometimes rudely met. They spring from a forgetfulness, or unacquaintance with the fact, that whatever is worth costs; that labor and products are as valuable as the money for which they could be sold; that to ask a man to give that by which he gets his living is just the same as to ask him for his living. If the butcher choose to give meat, instead of money, that is his own affair; but to ask him for meat is precisely the same as to ask him for money; and to ask him to sell meat at cost price is the same as to ask him for all the money which constitutes his profit; and, if he refuse to give meat, you have no more right to call him selfish or heartless, than he has to call you stingy because you do not have beefsteak or veal-cutlets every morning for breakfast. You have no more right to dictate a man's charities than you have to dictate his courtship. Especially have you no right even to pass judgment upon the stranger that is far off from thy gates, — the stranger whom you do not know, whose life is remote from yours, with whose circumstances, and daily surroundings, and personal connections, you are utterly unfamiliar. To hold up such an one to opprobrium, because he declines to contribute to a distant charity, is to hazard the reputation of your own judgment. No one can say whether another is, or is not, justified in withholding alms, until he knows all the sources of that other's income, all his channels of outflow, all the circumstances of all his family and acquaintance, all the system of his life, and all his plans for the future. On the whole, the lesson is so hard, that he would probably employ his time to more advantage by pushing his researches in other directions.

Many of us who would never think of dictating the charities of others are yet never weary of inculcating, and even practising, economy, that money may thereby be saved to bestow upon the poor; and think we are doing God service.

Economy has a good sound, a very innocent and even virtuous sound; but how are we to economize? and who is to economize? and what are we about to economize for? and at whose cost shall the economy be? I should say, first, that if the winter is to be a hard winter for the poor, if it is to be scanty of labor, and meagre in wages, the first duty of all persons is, not to retrench unless they are obliged to retrench. Charity is apt to be unwholesome and demoralizing. Let us see that it is clad in its least offensive forms. The rich man whose income is not seriously affected, or at least not reduced to the demands he makes upon it, ought by no means to reduce his style of living. If he make occasion, from the dulness of the times, to dismiss three of his six servants, is he not adding to the general distress by throwing three unemployed men upon the community, already staggering under the weight of its unemployed force? If a woman who would ordinarily have four new suits for the winter content herself with two, is she not helping to withdraw from circulation money which would help to diminish friction? Women are proposing to make their own gowns, and do their own housework, not in the least because they are hampered by the hard times, not because they are not just as able to hire labor as they ever were, but because of the example. They say, conscientiously, that many persons will be obliged to curtail, and that it will be all the easier for these if they see others, possibly their superiors in social station, doing the same thing. This is friendly and kind; but is it not mistaken kindness? It is foregoing a positive for an imaginary service. Two women, let us say, live side by side. One is rich: the other has a moderate fortune. The first is not seriously affected by the state of the money market; that is, her income is less, but it is not sufficiently lessened to touch her style of living. The second woman finds herself obliged to cut off several expenses. She dismisses her seamstress and her second nurse. Now, if the first woman, to encourage and sustain her, does the same, we have two nurses and two seamstresses thrown upon the already overstocked labor market. One may be inevitable; but the two are not. Most likely these two have others dependent upon them; and so, for a mere sentimental and problematical object, the circle of want and distress is enlarged.

I think, moreover, that we overestimate influence. The thing which it is right and proper to do is generally the thing which will have the best influence. It is pleasant to reflect that one is not singled out by fate for hard knocks. There is a certain satisfaction in feeling that your poverty is not the result of your own folly or error exclusively. But, however your drudgery over broom or needle may be softened by the thought that your bosom-friend is reduced to the same drudgery, there is very little mitigation in seeing your millionnaire friend pretending to be under a similar necessity. Grown people ought not to be so babyish; and, if they are, it is much better to reason them out of it than to give in to it. The people who are to be first considered are not those to whom retrenchment means a little more or less feeling, pride, or work, but those to whom it means perplexity, struggle, despair. To spare the sensitiveness of one woman at the expense of another woman's dinner is a very unreasonable way of setting a good example. If circumstances enforce retrenchment, let people retrench "without fear, and with a manly heart." But let not those who are not obliged to do it diminish aught of their expenditure. Especially let them, in every possible way, purchase labor. No woman who can afford to buy should herself do a stitch of sewing or any household work. The cooking, the waiting, the sewing, which she hires, may be the very life of those to whom retrenchment means starvation. "It will not be disastrous to me," said the manager of a dressmaking establishment to a customer who was proposing to sew her own dresses. "I am sure of work enough for myself for the winter. But I employ twenty girls, not one of whom is independent, not one of whom but has some one or more to be helped by her earnings. As fast as sewing diminishes, I shall dismiss these girls; but what is to become of them?"

Others say that they must curtail in expenditure in order to have money to bestow in charity. This, too, is wise if it be wisely done. But can money be better bestowed in charity than in the purchase of labor? A great point is to arrange our charities so that they shall neither wound nor lower the self-respect of the recipients. There are manufacturers who are running their mills at a loss, because of the large suffering that would ensue from stoppage. This is not business: it is charity. The loss is so much money given to the poor. But it is given in the least offensive way. It is given in connection with a regular life, with stated work, with industrious habits, and, in many cases, to the recipient, wears the aspect of wages; so that he is not demoralized thereby. Many a woman would not consider twenty, or fifty, or five hundred dollars an enormous sum to contribute for women and men who were starving in her neighborhood. Let her, then, distribute it, so far as possible, in the form of reward bestowed for service rendered, and thus prevent starvation and suffering, heal the feud between rich and poor, and avert social confusion and dismay.

And what is applicable to the rich may also be applicable to those who are hovering on the borderland of wealth. Such a winter as is foretold might be doubly a "means of grace" to many women,— to those, for instance, who are a little doubtful as to whether it would be prudent to "keep help," or to add another servant to the household staff, but who would exceedingly enjoy and improve the leisure which such assistance would permit. Let charity give to them, and to some needy woman, the benefit of the doubt, and let the overburdened housewife rest from her labors, and refresh herself with social pleasures, with outdoor exercise, with family diversions, with reading and music, and all possible gratification of taste, and enlargement of culture, solacing herself continually with the added satisfaction of knowing, that, in ministering thus to her own joys, she is ministering also to the more imperative wants, and the greater need, of a poorer and more helpless woman.

When Mr. Charles Kingsley wrote in the young lady's album, —

"Be good, sweet child, and let who will be clever,"

it answered every purpose for poetry; but, in the

conduct of life, it seems almost as necessary to be clever as it is to be good.

And poverty is not without its comical side, even in our serious, self-governing country.

Any person who has travelled in Canada will have vivid recollections of the lively little beggars who swarm in all its streets and highways. Not only in the cities, but along the country roads, some dragon's cub's teeth seem to be springing up as merry alert children, ever on the *qui vive* for *un sou*. Wherever a penny is, there will the beggars gather together in numbers so perplexing, that you feel the sole safety is withdrawing into your shell, and relinquishing specie payment altogether.

The only place in the United States where I have found any thing like this is Washington; and there it is wholly unlike it. Independence, thank Heaven! is the characteristic of our countrymen. The towheaded, freckled-faced, bare-footed children of a New-England village would no sooner think of asking money from the passing traveller than would the president and his cabinet; and, if you wish to give a cast-off garment to a soldier's widow, you must approach her with as many moral *salaams* as if she were the *cadi* himself. Long and long and long may it be, or ever we shall lose our honorable pride in this regard!

But we have changed all that in Washington. Whether it be from some abnormal element in the social atmosphere, Washington seems to have more than its due share of the mendicancy of the country. It is true that you will occasionally find a mature beggar at some Northern street-crossing (I never did, though I have heard of them); but they are generally foreigners: and occasionally a demure boy, with a world too much pathos in his melancholy voice, will implore you to give him a few cents to buy a loaf of bread for his sick mother, or a pair of shoes to enable him to appear at the Sunday school; (the precocious little hypocrite!) but these are sporadic cases, and hardly more than emphasize the general rule of American self-respect. It is in Washington alone that our native but elsewhere latent talent for direct beggary has found the conditions of development; and the result is such as a patriotic American must ever view with feelings of pride. It may, at first sight, seem a rather extreme case of extracting sunshine from cucumbers; but herein is genius. To be first in war, first in peace, and the rest, is easy enough; but to be first in begging requires a rare combination of qualities: and nowhere does the ingenuity, the high spirit, the creative power, the fertility of resources characteristic of our countrymen, show more clearly than in the manner in which they have lifted beggary out of the gutters of Washington, and set it among the high and fine arts. Some in rags, and some in tags? Not a bit of it! The rags and tags, the bandaged arms and blinded eyes, the shipwrecked sailors, and all the hackneyed machinery of the professional beggar, are haughtily and completely abandoned. They may well enough serve the purposes of the effete despotisms of Europe; but America plants herself on the rights of man. Rags for the peasant, tags for the serf, but, for the free American citizen, black coat and clean dickey forever! And, if your American woman takes to begging, be sure not one hair of her chignon shall fail, nor shall her overskirt miss a single puff, or the regulation ruffle be wanting from her walking-suit, with gloves and parasol to match.

Your door-bell rings before breakfast; and your servant brings you the card of Rev. Dr. Adams. You are hardly in visiting-humor before breakfast; but, if it is the gentle and scholarly pastor of Portsmouth, you would not for the world miss seeing him. And perhaps it may be Rev. Dr. Adams of Madison Square: who knows? You give the last touch to your crimps, and a slight adjusting shake to your flounces, and go down with your best face. A single glance shows you that it is not the Portsmouth clergyman; and, though there is a white cravat and a black coat, an indefinable something convinces you that it is not Dr. Adams of Madison Square.

Dr. Adams rises to meet you, and bows with dignity. You return his bow with dubiety.

"Mrs. Smith?" inquires the doctor blandly.

You assent, stiffening slowly each instant.

"I have called," pursues the doctor, "in behalf of a brother-clergyman who has been obliged to retire from the pulpit on account of ill health, and who is thus left without resources. He is a very respectable man: I have known him for a long time, and can vouch for his character."

> "The River Rhine, as is well known,
>   Washes the city of Cologne;
> But, oh, ye gods! what power divine
>   Can ever cleanse the River Rhine?"

"He is in great need of help; and any assistance you may be able to render him" — But here you take up the parable, like any heathen man and publican; and Dr. Adams departs, unconsoled for his brother-clergyman.

Mrs. Karl begs the favor of a few moments with Mrs. Smith. It is little to grant to a woman and a sister, and you go down. Mrs. Karl is a woman who has seen better days. She owned, in New York, a farm worth twelve thousand dollars. War, sickness, and misfortune came: they lost their property, farm and all. She is very desirous of getting it back. To do so, she proposes to set up a bakery. This bakery once established, she is confident she can recover her farm in a year. The bakery building is already taken; but as it was formerly a barrack, or hospital, or something of the sort, her claim to it can be secured only by congressional action: of course, this involves delay. Meanwhile, could she borrow of you money enough to buy a load of coal? She will pay you in baking, when her title-deed is secured, and her barrack made over into a bakery. She will send it to you in bread or cake, as you may desire. She has a very accomplished daughter, and has no doubt of her success.

You are less sanguine; but is it not an heroic plan? You give her five dollars. Three months pass, and the barrack still remains unmolested; nor have you any proof of the spelling-book assertion, that

"Bakers bake bread and cake."

An English lady has called to see Mrs. Smith. The English lady is short and stout and ruddy, in a rusty black suit, with double rows of ruffles, with a spotted black veil parted here and there in the meshes. She brings herself to your recollection as a woman who has formerly applied to you for sewing. She then brought you a note of recommendation from the ambassadress of her British Majesty, who had often employed her. The ambassadress has now left town, and can give her no more assistance. Her daughter is apprentice to a hairdresser. Her time will be out in two weeks; and then she will begin to receive wages. Meanwhile, would you be willing to have the daughter come to your house every day to lunch, at precisely eleven o'clock? She does not wish you to lay yourself out on the lunch: any thing will do. She is particular only that it shall be at precisely eleven o'clock. A very kind gentleman in one of the departments has hitherto given her her meals; but he has now gone into the country: hence this requisition upon you.

You compromise by giving her two dollars, assuring her that that will provide her daughter with lunch for a week. And, while I am writing these words, the Englishwoman has returned, after a month's absence, and asks for a little money, just to keep her over Sunday. I cannot, for the life of me, see why she should want to be kept over Sunday more than any other day. If you are to starve on Monday, you may as well starve on Saturday, and be done with it. But my lady looks the farthest in the world from starving: even hunger can never have come unpleasantly near that ruddy face and rotund form. "Fee-faw-fum! I smell the beer of an Englishman." I have even grave suspicions of gin. But what can you do? The voice is tremulous. Compromise, always compromise. You do neither one thing nor another. Fifty cents is neither here nor there; and then she asks you if you will not use your influence to get her a place in the treasury. If she could have a place in the treasury, it would yield enough to supply all her needs. As it is, all their money goes to pay the rent.

It is hardly hypocrisy to say you will mention it, as you would probably have far more difficulty in deceiving her than she would have in deceiving you; and, before the door has closed upon her retreating alpaca, a little girl trips up the steps, and informs you cheerfully that the baby is very sick, and cannot live, and, "if it does die," ma has not money enough to buy a coffin. You invest ten cents in that hypothetical coffin, with an alacrity which does no honor to your heart, and which will be very far from appearing on the credit side when your account is made up.

Mrs. Henderson calls before breakfast to see Gen. Smith. Gen. Smith, scenting the battle afar off, cowardly but piteously implores Mrs. Smith to go to the front. What exigency is too great for woman's devotion? Mrs. Smith goes—and is covered with confusion. Mrs. Henderson a beggar, with gay bonnet and spruce walking-suit? Not she! What is this? Two five-dollar bills held out to you! the genial McCulloch-face shining up at you from its home of dingy green as sweetly as if no war nor battle sound had ever been heard the world around. You put your hand to your head, almost like Mr. Twemlow, fearing a softening of the brain. But Mrs. Henderson explains that this is money which Gen. Smith was so good as to lend her some time ago. She has called to pay it before; but the general was out. She has tried again and again to find him at the Capitol, but failed. You take the money with unresisting, and even with unthinking, innocence; but she does not go. She lingers, hesitates, tells you they are still very poor. She has just received a letter from her sister in Virginia, to whom she had written, to know if it were worth while to come home. Her sister told her by no means to come; that there was nothing for her to do, and their poverty was extreme. Her sister is a girl of education and accomplishments. She should like to read you the letter, that you may see in what condition they are: whereupon she unfolds the letter, and stands in the window to read it; you, by the way, standing, all the while, to redeem what time you may. Father, it seems, has borrowed twenty-five dollars from Cousin Tom; and, "just think of it!" comments Mrs. Henderson, "of the leetle, leetle money that poor girl has been able to earn, he has borrowed five dollars, and even of me five!" and she resumes her letter with its tale of woe, till she comes to "we don't even have"— and there she stops short, saying, it just relates to the dishes on the table which they do without: she will not read that. Could the force of genius farther go?

She has too much delicacy to enter into those minute details, yet manages to convey to you the pith of the whole catalogue. You express your regret; and the thought dawns upon you, that, perhaps, you ought not to keep the money. How can you take ten dollars from a table where they don't even have? — The more you think of it, the tighter you clutch the bills. Why should she read such a letter to you, a perfect stranger? Why did she bring the money, if not to pay the debt? Wretch that you are, thus to take the pound of flesh so scrupulously proffered! But you do not let go the bills; and you do let Mrs. Henderson go. You report proceedings to the money-lender. Oh, yes! he remembers Mrs. Henderson. She came to him, representing herself a Virginia woman, who had somehow got a place in the treasury. There she proclaimed her "secesh" views with a violence which lost her the situation; but she appealed to Northern Republicans, in season and out of season, till she was restored. From the same gentlemen she had also borrowed various sums of money; and to one of them, a senator, she had afterwards gone, saying that she had a great desire to attend Mrs. Secretary's reception, and begged him to escort her. Unhappy Mrs. Henderson! Ill-timed honesty! Had Gen. Smith obeyed her summons, she would doubtless have retained her little bills with the pleasant McCulloch face; but a woman has no sentiment about a woman, and takes her dues as coldly as the frosty Caucasus. Let a woman pray Tennyson's prayer, "O God! for a man," if she designs to do any thing in the way of wool-pulling.

Mrs. Forrest sits in the hall, patiently waiting opportunity to see you. She is dressed in a perfectly plain mourning calico, and black, broad-brimmed straw hat, trimmed with a single ribbon. Her voice is low, her manner quiet, her words well chosen. She was the daughter of a Maryland farmer, and was reared without affluence, but in entire comfort. Her husband is an invalid, bed-ridden. She has five children. They have had absolutely nothing to eat since three o'clock the day before. They live out in the country, — a pleasant evening drive after dinner, but a weary, weary way for this poor woman to drag herself in on a sunny Washington morning. Yet again and again has she made the toilsome tramp in search of something to do. She is willing to sew, she will take service, she will work by the day, — any thing that will bring food for the helpless family. She has worked one day at Mrs. Evans's, assisting the ordinary household staff through an entertainment. For her day's work, she received fifty cents.

"But you should have asked a dollar. That is the usual price for a day's work of that sort."

"I did ask it; but they refused to pay it. They

said fifty cents was all it is worth; and," she added quaintly, "the spunk has all gone out of me."

Back and forth, from one department to another, had the poor woman sought employment. She had thought herself very near getting the washing of the towels at the post-office; but it had been given to another person. She had just heard of a woman who had got a place in the treasury, and had been told that she might, perhaps, secure one, if she could get a letter of recommendation from some influential person. What could she do in the treasury? Any thing but write. She could be a messenger, a porter, — any thing that does not require education. You give her a little money (which, no doubt, perplexes her with the necessity of spending it twenty ways at once) and, perhaps, a very little hope, which is, after all, more than you feel yourself; for what is her waning strength among so many wants?

Enter Mrs. Bainbridge, representative, in her own person, of the oldest and most aristocratic family in the Carolinas, and, in her husband's person, of the next best. Thus Mrs. Bainbridge. A gentleman told her that Gen. Smith used to be in the Carolinas, and recommended her to come to him. Her husband died in the Union army, and she is entitled to a pension; but she has never received it, and, in fact, does not know how to go to work to get it. She was well educated;

but her accomplishments have become rusty through disuse. She had, however, brushed up her music, and earned a little money by giving lessons. Her son obtained a place in the folding department, where he worked by the piece; and, as he was very ambitious, had earned sometimes as much as thirty dollars a month. Indeed, she has kept him at it so close, that he scarcely knows how to read and write. "You would be surprised, Mrs. Smith, to know how little we can live on. Two sandwiches a day from the market is very often all we have." But her boy's arm, owing to the intensity of his toil, has become paralyzed; and he is completely disabled. She has now the offer of a little school at Richmond, which she would take at once if she could but get money to pay her fare. She has been to the railroad authorities to beg them to take her free. They refused, but would take her at half-rate. That would be seven dollars and a half. She has pawned all her clothes, except what she wore. Mrs. Montgomery, who used to know her, had given her a fan and parasol, saying, "Mrs. Bainbridge, you are so reduced, that you must keep up your spirits and self-respect by being well dressed, or you will go down entirely."

Very much shaken in mind, you ask her why she does not apply to the gentlemen from her own section, rather than to the representatives of the frozen North.

She says they are Democrats, and would not do a single thing for her. There is Mr. Lang, a gentleman from her own town; but it would be no use at all to go to him, because he is a Democrat. You think better of the Democrats than that, Red Republican though you be. You do not believe the man lives, North or South, who would refuse to help a suffering woman because of the political creed of her dead husband. But it is a pitiful case on the face of it. If it should be true! You go scrambling around in your mind to catch an impartial view of the situation. She is a Randolph, let us say, by birth, and a Bainbridge by marriage. Why does she not appeal to the extant Randolphs and Bainbridges, if they belong to her, instead of exposing the family poverty? But you have heard that the Randolphs and Bainbridges have a large and impecunious family connection; and this may be one defective link in the rusty chain. Why did the unnatural mother sacrifice her son's arm and education so ruthlessly? A Yankee mother would sooner have lost her own life. And why did they send to market for sandwiches? It would have been cheaper to make their own bread. But, bless me! if a woman is faint and hungry, there is an end of it. There is no use in arguing that it is her own fault. "The poor ye have always with you," so long as the fools are three out of four, in every person's acquaintance, according to Lady Mary. Yet, if she should be an impostor, and this merely a way of getting a living! You remember that your friend and neighbor kept the tally of all the beggars for a month, taking the name and address of every one, and sending her son, or a trusty servant, to investigate each case. Of thirty applicants, only one proved to be honest. The god of this world whispers over your left shoulder, and you give five dollars, telling the distressed relic of the first and second families that no doubt the railroad company will carry her for five dollars. All day you are haunted, at intervals, by an uncomfortable feeling that you may have been a grudging steward of the Lord's estate; held in suspense by an almost equally uncomfortable suspicion, that you will be laughed at by the lord of the earthly manor for having again been duped by a gay deceiver. So far as peace of mind is secured, your five dollars is as poor a venture as was the bow which Silas Wegg invested in Mr. Boffin.

Mrs. Nott's card comes up to you perfectly *comme il faut*. Long experience has made you suspicious of strange names; but this may be a visitor proper. You descend to find Mrs. Nott a quiet, ladylike-looking person, as non-committal as her card. To beg, or not to beg, is a question which must be left to answer itself.

"Have I the pleasure of knowing you, Mrs. Nott?"

"I have never seen you before, madam; but I have called in behalf of a lady of my acquaintance who is very needy, and wants assistance."

"What is the name of the lady?"

"Oh! you would not ask me to give her name, if you knew her: it would hurt her feelings so much!"

"Surely you cannot expect me to give blindfold."

"Oh! I do not expect a great deal from any one place; but twenty-five cents here, and fifty cents there, make a great deal in course of the day."

"Do you find it agreeable to go about from house to house asking alms?"

"On the contrary, it is the most disagreeable work I ever did. I do not mind being refused; but some of the ladies refuse so harshly! If they would only refuse me kindly, I would not feel so badly."

You mentally thank the Jew for teaching you that word, and refuse her with the very honey and cream of kindness.

You are sitting, like Father Abraham, in your tent-door, *anglicé* bay-window, in the cool of the day, listening to the wandering minstrels. No beggars they, no vulgar organ-grinders, with grinning monkey, hardly less hideous than themselves, but an Italian troupe, olive-skinned, dark-eyed, pleasant-voiced, decently-dressed, — a young man with a harp, a younger man and young girl with violins, who play "Norma" and bid you good-evening; or go quickly away without playing at all, if you do not appear at the window at the touch of the first few notes. They are not mendicants, but ministers to your pleasure, harbingers of the millennium, honest earners of honest money. The mendicants are the two able-bodied young men coming up the door-steps, who, seeing you convenient, tell their moving tale without further parley. The thunderbolts of fate have smitten them sore. One has lost his wife, and one his betrothed, — " his only friend, to whom he was to have been married." Sisters and brothers followed in rapid succession. "Give me some money for them," says the general.

"I won't," says the colonel in flat insubordination.

"Fifty cents?" pleads the general. "Haven't you any heart?"

"I haven't fifty cents in it."

"A quarter, then. Lend me a quarter."

"I won't: you will never pay it."

And the hapless afflicted, seeing the case going against them, proceed ruthlessly to slay father and mother, till they stand alone in the world, a pair of helpless orphans.

"There!" says the general, "now they've killed them all off. Give them ten cents, colonel, and let them go. Don't be stingy."

"No," says the colonel. "Now I won't give them any thing," as if he had meant to settle a handsome pension on each; and the bereaved young men march away, unfriended, melancholy, slow.

A buxom Irishwoman sends up an earnest appeal from the kitchen for permission to see you a few minutes. She has been unable to keep the wolf from the door, except by pawning her clothes. She shows you the pawn-tickets. She has two dresses and a shawl which she is exceedingly desirous to redeem from the gentlemen of the three balls; and she solicits you to advance — mind, I say, to advance, not to bestow, — eight dollars for the purpose. Remuneration is to come to you in the shape of spring chickens for your table, if Providence smiles upon her poultry-yard. Your servants know nothing about the woman. No one knows any thing about her; but the general, who hears of her story, thinks it is better to be on the safe side, and give her the eight dollars. Observe the superior sagacity of the superior sex. Women give hesitatingly, fearing imposture on the one side, and ridicule on the other. Man, the tyrant, having nobody to fear, gives with a high hand, assumes imposture in the first place, bestows his alms in spite of it, and defies fate. A young man accosts the general at the Capitol, tells him he is from his own State and city, and gives his name. He has been on duty at Fortress

Monroe; has received news that his mother in Ohio is very ill; and has obtained leave to visit her. Coming up the Potomac on a steamer, his money is stolen; and he finds himself in Washington, penniless, unable to go forward or backward. Thus appealed to, what can the general do, but lend him thirty dollars for his sick mother's sake, "hoping for nothing again," — a hope, it is needless to add, which does not fail of fruition.

To the same general comes another young man, representing himself to be the brother of a friend of his in New York. He, too, in Washington, has fallen among thieves at the hotel, who have stripped him of his money, and reduced him to the necessity of begging for a loan of twenty dollars, for a week at the longest. And the general looks him in the eye, and knows he shall never see his twenty dollars again, and gives it to him; and is careful to buy his own horse-car-tickets by the package, to save a cent or two a year. So complicate, so wonderful, is man!

But one of these adventurous young knights was foiled, though "more by hit than any good wit." A gentleman, a member of congress, served on a committee, several years ago, with another gentleman, who used frequently to refer certain questions to him, saying, half jocularly, that he was the only business-man in the house. Not long ago, a young gentleman, of pleasing person and address, called upon him, stating that he was the son of his former congressional friend; that he was returning from a trip to the White Mountains, in company with his two sisters; that on the road his purse had been stolen, and that they were now at their hotel in a very embarrassing position. He knew no one in the city to whom he could apply; but he remembered this gentleman's name as that of a friend of his father's, of whom he had often heard his father speak as the only business-man in the house. He had, therefore, ventured to call upon him, and begged to know if he would furnish him with a hundred dollars, on receipt of a telegram from his father saying that it was all right. The gentleman, very much prepossessed in the young man's favor by the combined frankness and dignity of his demeanor, and perfectly recollecting the phrase which his father had been in the habit of using, hastened to assure him of his readiness to assist him in every way; and was about to add that he would give him the money on the spot without waiting for the telegram, but thought better of it, and asked him, instead, whether he was at all familiar with the city. The young man replied that he was not, never having been in it till that morning.

"Then," said the gentleman, "as my carriage is coming immediately, I will telegraph to your father myself, and save you the trouble; and the money shall be ready for you when you call."

The young man thanked him, and took courteous leave. The telegraph brought, from the gentleman appealed to, the reply, that he had no grown-up son; that all his children were small, and all were at home with him.

The young gentleman never returned for his hundred dollars.

There is another class, a sort of cross between beggars and work-people,—women who ask to do washing for you, and, when they have spoiled your laces and muslins, will take no pay for it; but if you will get their boy a place in the department!—merry, hearty women, who will accept any thing, and inveigle for more before your very eyes.

"You know that coat you gave me," says one of these jolly beggars. "I ripped the tails off, and made a jacket for my man. People say, 'Where did you get this nice coat;' and I say, 'Why, the Hon. Judge Smith gave it to me.' (The Hon. Judge Smith never having been inside a court-room in his life.) 'Look at this cloth,' I say to 'em. 'See how fine it is! You wouldn't catch the Hon. Judge Smith wearing any thing but fine cloth.'"

To such adroit compliments can you refuse an old waistcoat, even if the Hon. Judge Smith must wear his coat close buttoned to the chin in consequence?

Sometimes they sue for sewing. They always come

with verbal recommendations from Mrs. Admiral This, or Mrs. Secretary That, or Mrs. Minister Tother. The plain Mrs. Jones, Brown, and Robinson receive scant courtesy from these dames of the needle. In an experimental, or a quixotic, or a philanthropic mood, you suddenly take one of them at her word, and introduce her to your happy home. She has just been two months at Mrs. Senator Irving's, can cut and make all sorts of children's clothes, can run a machine, and will rent one for you at five dollars a month, and just finish your whole season's sewing at one smart swoop. Her buoyancy and confidence are contagious; and you meditate a general clearance of the sewing-room. Alas! the very first overskirt gives signs of woe. The waist is a total wreck. Puffs swell awry; gaps yawn tremendous; seams close untimely. Material for two is swallowed up by one, and that a failure. Still she cuts and sews, and sews and cuts, like one possessed with an evil spirit. The sewing-machine becomes a hungry monster, gobbling up dry-goods with insatiate maw. Your one object is to get this Witch of Endor out of the house before you are quite stripped of your possessions. At the end of three days, by force of hard money and soft words, Sindbad frees himself from his old man; and you stand in your sewing-room, which looks as if a whirlwind had swept through it, feeling that you would gladly pay the money over again, if you could but be put back to the place whence you started, yet thankful that any thing has escaped from the general wreck.

Next day there comes in a bill of fifty-five dollars for a sewing-machine.

Separate from all these is another class, — the real poor, the poverty-stricken, maimed, halt, and blind, deformed children, squalid children, ragged beyond the verge of decency, dirty, famished, pitiable, — "creation's blot, creation's blank." You cannot help them. You can only give to them as they come, from day to day, tiding them over from one wretched hour to another. Whence they come, or whither they go, you cannot divine. Must they not burrow in the ground like moles? Out of their ranks, I fancy, come the newsboys, who seem to be a more miserable, filthy, and forlorn set of boys than are ever seen elsewhere. Their pinched old faces, apparently, lack the humor that enlivens the Northern newsboys; and any thing more hideous is seldom heard than the laugh which accompanies the Washington newsboys' proffer of a paper.

Ingenuity, hypocrisy, deception, one does not look for in these unhappy creatures; yet I would fain hope they are less unhappy than they seem. Painful to the eye, hopeless to the heart, they, and such as they, are the insoluble problem of the world. Making every possible allowance for that power of becoming used to things, which, according to Plato, is a gift of the gods, and which needs must soften their hard lot, rendering less sharply bitter what nothing can make sweet, it still remains, that unconsciousness of evil is the last, worst result of evil. And, for a life so harsh, nothing can atone, — nothing in this world; but, in some of the pleasant stars that go shining through the sky, may not the Father of all have prepared a clean and wholesome place for these neglected little ones? — some pure and perfect world, where light and love may find them; where all the defilement of earth shall be cleansed from them, and all the abasement of earth shall vanish away; where, in the ministrations of unwearying care, and the unfolding of repressed tendencies, all memory of degradation shall fade into a dim far-off dream, whose only power shall be to lend an ever-keener joy to the happiness of their ever-brightening home?

But I do not set the Rev. Dr. Adams on that star; at least, not yet. Late may he return to those skies, and never until he has cast off his black coat, and torn off his white choker, and turned into a retired clergyman, whose sands of life shall henceforth run out honestly. For him no shining star, but a lonely journey on the melancholy moon, and on its dark side too; for all home, a crag in that worn-out world, a sharp coal-peak on that burnt-up cinder, companioned only by the ghosts of dead generations, where he may bemoan himself for the brother-clergyman, who lived only in his own wicked heart; since, doubtless, nothing short of the moon will bring this obdurate and decorous sinner to repentance.

RELIGIOUS BEGGARY.

RELIGIOUS BEGGARY.

THERE is no such thing as religious beggary. All beggary is irreligious. A "converted Jew" walks through the country village, asking the hard-working farmers to help him prosecute his studies, preparatory to going back to Jerusalem, and converting his brethren. He presents on a paper the names of several neighboring clergymen, by way of indorsement, some one of whom has also given him a list of the persons upon whom it will be worth his while to call. I survey him, — an able-bodied young man, lounging across the country in a decent coat, daring to ask alms of men who toil from sunrise to sunset in shirt-sleeves, — a strong man, with muscles in his arms, daring to ask bounty of women; and I think the Jews might as well stay unconverted. A self-supporting Jew is better than a beggarly Christian. Why will clergymen countenance such riff-raff? Why will they bring conversion into contempt by making it a vagabond's profession? What is it that causes clerical and ecclesiastical mendicancy to be honorable, while social and secular mendicancy is disgraceful? Can beggary be baptized into the name of Christ? Does the abnegation of self mean the abnegation of self-respect?

A little while ago, while walking home from church on Sunday, we were assailed by a decently dressed beggar-boy, asking money to send the gospel to the heathen. One might have supposed it was an ingenious species of fraud, adapted to church-goers: but the boy declared that he was no impostor, that his Sunday-school teacher had just given him his commission; and he produced a paper, showing that he had actually been sent out into the street as a common beggar, on the sabbath-day, with some trumped-up story about the heathen. This country, not long ago, entertained a company of heathen for several weeks; and it is safe to hazard the assertion that not one of them was guilty of a misdemeanor surpassing this. Such Sunday-school teachers are corrupters of the young: such Sunday-schools are nurseries of vice. They tend to all manner of craft and cunning. Let Sunday-school teachers go and stand themselves, hat in hand, at the corners of the streets, if they like; let them bandage their arms, or blind their eyes, and adopt a dog and a string as additional persuasives to early piety; or perhaps a hand-organ and a monkey might bring more money into the treasury of the Lord from the pockets of church-goers: but let them do this beggar's work themselves, and not tamper with the children. The worst count in the indictment against Jeroboam, the son of Nebat, was, not that he sinned himself, but that he made Israel to sin. Ecclesiastical Fagins may even pick pockets with what dexterity the service of the sanctuary seems to them to require; but we do not care to have even our work'us boys turned into Artful Dodgers.

Speaking of pickpockets, once there was a church that wanted a new bell. If a cotton-factory were in a similar predicament, it would take its own money, and buy a bell, or go without. But we change all that when we experience a "change of heart." Accordingly, this church took the more excellent and ecclesiastical way, of going around with a subscription-paper among the "outs" and the "ins," Christian or infidel (all is fish in which can be found a piece of money); and, having mulcted the community in a goodly sum, this enterprising church changed its mind, broke out into a local honesty, appropriated the money to pay its debts, and, after a while, started on another tour of bell-wringing.

"Half-pence and farthings
Say the bells of St. Martin's,"

calling to the worship of Mammon.

"Leave is light," thought another church which applied to Demetrius, the silversmith, for his aid in replacing their old communion-service with a new one, although Demetrius confessed another creed. Demetrius being a generous man, with the instincts of a gentleman, and as yet unhardened by ecclesiastical practices, asked how much money was required, and, to prevent the necessity of further begging, offered to furnish a new service, and pay all the cost, beyond what the proposed sale of the old one should bring, out of his own pocket. In due time the work was done, at an outlay considerably larger than the original estimate; and the gift was received by the church with the grateful and pleasant suggestion, that, if Demetrius chose to bear the whole cost, the money arising from the sale of the former plate should be devoted to replenishing the Sunday-school library. In the world, this would be called greed and grossness; but, in the Church, it is only that "the zeal of thine house hath eaten me up,"— hath, at least, eaten out of me the unregenerate virtues of delicacy, modesty, and propriety, the sense of Christian and even of Pagan courtesy, and made me, instead of a self-respecting, high-minded Christian gentleman, a bold and shameless beggar.

Motive does not affect such deeds. Bad manners in the world do not become good manners by "joining the church." Brass in the street is not gold in the pews. The whine of a beggar is not music, because played on a Jew's-harp. You might just as well ask your neighbors to put a piazza on your dwelling, as neighboring churches to put a bell on your meeting-house. I have my own heathen constituency: it is an impertinence to ask me to look after *yours*. We inveigh, justly enough, against political corruption. We do not believe that all the money which is raised for elections goes to circulate documents, or transport voters, but that many a stream deviates into dishonest pockets. The raising and the managing of church funds may not be open to the same objections; but, considering the higher plane of Church than State, they are equally unsatisfactory. We have departed as far from piety as politics from honesty; and it is not unquestionable that we have always saved honesty intact. "Let not thy left hand know what thy right hand doeth," says Christ; and we send a subscription-paper around the parish, with every man's gift against his name; the big figures at the top, to be seen of all, the little ones following suit in a pell-mell of publicity. "Whosoever is of a willing heart, let him bring it, an offering of the Lord," was the divine way of building churches. And "they came, every one whose *heart* stirred him up, and every one whom his *spirit* made willing." We do not trust a man's heart to stir him up, nor his spirit to make him willing. If there is a church to be built or rebuilt, or a debt to be paid, we engineer it, from the first stage of reluctance to the last announcement of success. We have private conferences, and well-selected committees, and public meetings, minutely prepared for well-manufactured, spontaneous enthusiasm. It is edifying to read in the religious newspapers, that the Church of Sardis has, by a freewill and united offering, removed the heavy debt under which it had been suffering since the erection of its new house; so many members coming forward with five thousand dollars, so many with three thousand, so many with one thousand, cheering the heart of their pastor, and reviving the faith of the saints. But it is not edifying always to hear the remarks the saints make at home, touching the manipulations and manœuvres by which they have been forced to volunteer. If the freewill offering of the Israelites were like many of ours, Bezaleel, the son of Uri, and Aholiab, the son of Ahisamach, must have heard some pretty plain talk.

In the Protestant Church we have abolished priesthood; but mendicancy, prevented from concentrating itself in a single order, has become diffused through all orders. It is not strange that the lay mind becomes confused when clerical views are vague. "If golde ruste, what shulde iren do?" The laborer, whether clergyman or farmer, is worthy of his hire; but the clergyman and the farmer stand on entirely different grounds. The farmer sells a bushel of potatoes, a ton of hay, and receives the price agreed on; and that is the end of the matter. The clergyman receives his stipulated one, two, five, thousand dollars a year, but is never let alone. Somebody, generally a woman, is evermore perambulating the parish, gathering dimes and dollars to buy the minister's wife a set of furs, or himself a silk gown, or a carpet for their parlor, or, in a general way, to make them a present, or get up a surprise-donation-party, till ministers have lost somewhat of manhood. Something sturdy, self-reliant, independent, upright, and downright, has gone out of the profession. Ministers will permit, will even invite, what other men would resent. The merchant in a city, the shoemaker in a country village, would feel disgraced by a contribution-paper going about town to collect money to buy himself a coat. The lawyer's wife would rather wear calico all her life than levy tribute on the parish for a silk. But the minister and the minister's wife will wear the contributed clothes, and make a note of it for the religious newspaper. The school-teacher surveys his district, builds or buys such a house as he can, and, if not able to do either, rents a tenement, or boards, and betters himself as soon as possible. Ministers are willing to be accounted a feeble folk, for whom houses should be provided, without responsibility of their own; and this unmanly self-surrender loses its sting by christening the house a parsonage. The carpenter who wants to take his wife on a summer-trip to the White Mountains waits till he has earned enough to do so at his own expense; but some rich deacon, or "active brother," is expected to take the minister, and pay the bills. And the minister not only suffers these things, but takes pleasure in them that do them, and sometimes feel aggrieved if they are not done; and sends a note to the religious newspapers, suggesting or affirming that they should be done. A minister of æsthetic tendencies has his rooms frescoed by a painter who has recently joined his congregation. After waiting a reasonable time, the painter sends in his bill. The clergyman returns an injured-innocence sort of note, saying that he had not expected to be called upon to pay; but he will settle the bill as soon as he can, though not immediately, as he shall have to save the money out of his salary. The painter, being a gentleman, immediately sends him a receipted bill; and the minister, being a — minister, accepts it. But upon what ground should he expect to be frescoed for nothing? Why is it a grievance for a minister to pay his bills out of his salary? What else is his salary for? The blacksmith never asks his neighbor the mason to give him money to buy his wife trinkets, or to treat him to a pleasure-excursion. Why is it better manners for the minister? The little boy is taught that it is very impolite to go to a companion's house, and ask, or even hint, for plum-cake. Why is it polite for his father to ask in the religious newspaper, or hint in any way, that his companion should join hand in hand to give him the plum-cake that his soul longs for? But the religious newspapers blossom with hints and downright exhortations to parishes to make presents to their ministers, to take them on journeys, to pay their expenses to national councils. There is often a certain space devoted to a record of the presents thus made; for indelicacy has come to such a pass, that donors do not sometimes neglect to stipulate with the *donee*, that their donations shall be given the publicity of print; and, on the side of the clergy, the argument is unblushingly used, that the facts are bruited for the sake of stirring up other parishes to make similar presents to their pastors. The resources of ingenuity are exhausted in devising pleasant and playful metaphors to describe the presentation; and sometimes the statement is as formal and crisp as an advertisement. Donation-parties are occasionally made the object of a little gentle satire; but it is not because they are donation-parties, but because the donations are not big enough. "According to the ecclesiastical almanac," says a religious paper, " now is the time for ministers to ' look out for donation-parties ; ' which, in the words of one of their number, ' are cheerful gatherings, when a clergyman's flock overwhelm him with bead watch-pockets, and eat up about one hundred and twelve dollars' worth of his winter provisions.' "

Here is a good text for the religious journal. An excellent sermon could be preached upon donation-parties in general, — the evils from which they spring, the evils which they engender, and the propriety of their discontinuance. But the religious journal only draws the very mild moral, " Nevertheless, a good donation-party is a good thing. Try it, flocks, and let the ministers see." It is not that flocks break into the parsonage with their cumbrous fleece: it is that they only rub up against it, leaving bits of stray wool. If they would shear close enough, there would be no fault found. Indeed, the amount of fleece left is getting to be the measure of grace received. I read in a missionary report, that " Our associates, Mr. and Mrs. S., are meeting with great success among the natives of N. During the seven weeks we were absent, they received more presents from our people than I had for eight years. And Mr. S. had made such progress in the language, that he occupied the pulpit three sabbaths, discoursing in the native language. This is a most hopeful beginning for the missionary work." Most hopeful indeed. "Rev. A. B. C. and wife," we are told, "were favored with a very pleasant visit and valuable gifts from his people, on the tenth anniversary of his marriage. Great harmony prevails; and a gracious outpouring of the Spirit has been enjoyed."

Grace and greenbacks are the two horns of the altar. A "precious revival," and "a purse of money and other gifts, amounting in value to seventy-five dollars," enjoy the honors of the same paragraph. A gifted young brother preaches to the heathen in their own tongue, and draws more money out of their pockets in seven weeks than his less eloquent predecessor had done in eight years. The power of the gospel is seen in a whole parish's coming together in the vestry to present the minister's wife with a thimble, and the minister himself with a gold-headed cane — as if the kingdom of heaven were to be taken by violence. The number of young converts gathered into the church, and the market-value of the beef and cheese contributed by the old converts, are reported with equal precision; and it is counted for distinguished disinterestedness, if the minister looks around upon the dried apples and salt pork left by the receding donation-tide, and exclaims, with tears in his eyes, "Not yours, but you!"

"Let every church," says the religious newspaper,

"whether rich or poor, contribute, of such as they have, to form a fund to enable their pastor to take such journeys as are expedient. By his attendance on the associations, conferences, and conventions, — meetings so closely allied to the best interests of the Church, — he will be so stimulated and refreshed, that the enriching which his people have bestowed on him will be returned to them fourfold. This fund may be called 'The People's Relief-Fund,' or 'The Minister's Travelling-Fund.' Let the people try this; and, certain it is, that they will be relieved of a dull minister."

They will be relieved of him while he is gone to his county conference; but they will be surprised to find how short the time seems before he is back on their hands again. To hire a dull minister, and then hire him to go away, is burning your candle at both ends. Would it not be cheaper to hire a bright one in the beginning? The notion that a dull minister is to be sharpened up by conferences and conventions is preposterous. They are far more likely to fritter away an able man's power. Doubtless, for certain purposes and to a certain extent, conference is useful; but the multiplication, in our day, of associations and consociations, of convention and council, is any thing but conducive to intellectual or moral vigor. No doubt suggestions are sometimes made, and thoughts elucidated; but we are oftener reminded of Mr. Weller and the alphabet, and ask, "Is it worth while to go through so much to get so little?" Any thing like a mental shock is studiously avoided. The questions which are really questions are left outside, or represented only by persons of our own faith; and what is admitted is that which is, in the main, universally assumed. Our National Council in Boston may have been greatly productive of good fellowship and good feeling, and, so far, a good thing; but as an exponent of religious belief, as a simplifier of theological creed, as an organism of faith or polity, did not the mountain bring forth a mouse? The great object of the council seemed to be to keep hands off. The great aim was, how not to do it. But why come up from the ends of the earth to declare our adherence to the articles which our fathers set forth or re-affirmed? That goes without saying. Life and thought have changed since the days of our fathers; and, if we want to know any thing, it is how we stand affected by this change. To say that we are not affected at all is to say that we have a name to live, and are dead.

The chances are, that the association, the conference, the convention, will travel around in the same orbit, and on the same plane, as the dull minister. He will be stimulated and refreshed to pursue, upon his return, the precise path which has already led him to failure. If the People's Relief-Fund would send him to a political caucus, to the gaming-tables of Hamburg, to the Derby Races, to the Louisiana legislature, to a travelling circus, to a French assembly, or a London dinner-table, — to places where men are in deadly, if wicked earnest, or places where he will be dashed out of his grooves, and into new contacts and courses, — the People's Fund might, indeed, afford relief.

But, apart from the wisdom of any mode of applying a relief-fund, why should the suggestion of a relief-fund be made? Why should the farmers and the shoemakers and the day-laborers of a poor church take their hard-earned money, and give it to their pastor, to send him anywhere? They have already paid him his salary. Why must they give him gifts? They need their surplus earnings as much as he. Their lives are more limited than his. Their wives stay at home from year's end to year's end. If they have any money to spare, let them take their own little trip, and enlarge their views to broader horizons. If the rich merchant choose to give money to his minister, and his minister choose to take money as a gift, it is their own affair. But for an educated man to take the money of uneducated men and hard-working women, and spend it in pleasure and recreation; for religious newspapers to urge or to hint that the hard-working men and women should thus devote their money, and praise them without stint when they do thus devote it, — seems not high-minded, seems mean and mercenary.

A parsonage is a good thing in many respects. Very few ministers, perhaps, are able to buy or to build houses; and it is desirable that they should have a fixed home. If parishes should feel that the parsonage was as much a part of their responsibility as the church, that they could no more expect a minister without the one than without the other, I should not object. We should all be better, if ministers were so able that they could dictate their own terms. Whatever the parish in its own interest, from a business-point of sight, chooses to proffer, it need not be unmanly for a minister to accept. But is it manly for him to ask people to provide him a house? Is it even proper or necessary? As ministers come and go, there are very few parishes where they cannot hire a house for as long a period as they are likely to stay. Why should one man in a town be freed from the need of care and thought by the care and thought of other men? Is it that he may be the more free to pursue his spiritual calling? Come, then, the celibate clergy of the Roman Catholic Church! Let us have either one thing or another, — either a celibate priesthood, without entangling alliances, wholly devoted and subject to the Church; or a man taking care of himself and his wife and children, precisely like other men.

A woman spends her prime in teaching the children of her native town at a third, or a half, or a quarter, what the minister receives; and boards in her father's house, or wherever she can find shelter. No one ever thinks of building her a house, or giving her a quit-claim deed on a single apartment in anybody's house. The person who teaches your children six hours a day for five days in the week has, apparently, a greater influence on the next generation than he who preaches to grown-up people two hours a day once a week. That person needs, just as much, freedom from material care; and, if a woman, she has immeasurably less chance for securing such exemption. But the women of a parish, who never think of providing a domicile for their townswoman, will meet at each other's houses to knit toes and heels to coarse woollen stockings, at seventy-five cents a dozen pairs, to provide a house for an able-bodied man. I should not think *a man* would like to live in such a house. It cannot be a pleasant thing for a man to look around upon his wainscots and windows, and reflect that a dozen or twenty women, by "working smartly," finished a dozen pairs of stockings in three evenings, and, with the seventy-five cents therefor received, built up painfully the roof that shelters him. It is a reform against nature. If ministers will not let women preach, neither should they let them build. If they do not want women to become men, they should play the man themselves. It is certainly no more unwomanly to occupy a man's pulpit than to rear a man's house. But a woman in the pulpit sets a whole presbytery to cackling; while a woman may build a Presbyterian parsonage from turret to foundation-stone, and not a clergyman of them all will move the wing, or open the mouth, or peep.

"Who says that we have no 'plain speaking' in the pulpit, these days," asks a religious newspaper, "when the Massachusetts preacher can be named who uttered the following in a recent sermon? —

"'Some of the ladies of the —— Church may say, that, if they lived in Christ's time, he should have made their house his home, nor suffered for the lack of any hospitality they could furnish. But I think he would have gone homeless for all you would have done for him. And here is why I think so: you allowed me to pay the hotel-bills of every minister who supplied the pulpit while I was in —— a few months ago.'"

If a teacher hire a substitute during his absence, does he expect the committee to pay that substitute's hotel-bills? If a treasury clerk put his brother in his place during his extra furlough, does he expect the government to pay his brother's board? Why should the church pay the hotel-bills of the substitute any more than the butcher's bills of the regular preacher?

At the outset, the church agrees to pay so much salary. It is no more incumbent upon the church to entertain the preacher's guests, be they substitutes or exchanges, than it is incumbent on the minister to entertain the deacon's son-in-law, or the merchant's aunts and cousins. Yet this preacher has the profaneness, the vulgarity, the assumption, to say, that, because his church did not pay the hotel-bills of his hired man, they would have rejected Christ. The religious newspaper calls this "plain speaking:" I call it brutality. The minister who can so defile his pulpit as to use it for such purposes is not fit to be admitted to any lady's house.

Again: the same paper says it hears of a "minister, who lately astounded his congregation by reading 'out in meeting' an account of his receipts and expenses for the year. The only item to the credit of the richest member of his flock was 'one apple-pie.'"

This seems but a smart joke to the reverend recorder; and, no doubt the reverend reader thought he had scored one against his congregation : but it is such things as these that lower the clergy in public estimation, and inspire the laity with disgust. Why should a minister be going over his accounts on Sunday, any more than the merchant or the banker? Why should he bring his private affairs into the great congregation, any more than the milliner or the cook? If he is dissatisfied with the bargain which he made with the people, or if they do not fulfil their part of the contract, there are places and times when it is proper for him to enforce his contract, or to secure better terms. But to take his account-book into church, to preach his groceries for the gospel, to feed his "flock" with stale bread and scanty steaks, makes his pastorate dear, even at the price of one apple-pie.

What is the quality which suggests such a paragraph as this? — "As a St. Louis preacher was leaving the church last Sunday, an appreciative parishioner slipped a hundred-dollar-note in his hand as a reward for his excellent sermon. Perhaps, if there were more such parishioners, there would be more excellent sermons."

Is it, indeed, only the voice of malice and all uncharitableness that calls ministers mercenary? I have quoted nothing from foes, only from ministers themselves. Think what a sermon is represented to be, — the message of God to man by his appointed and anointed ambassador, the application of saving truth to souls sore-wounded and shot at by the archers of sin, light to them sitting in the darkness, salvation to the lost. And a man, an ambassador of heaven, will preach Christ and him crucified with more fervor and unction, if a hundred-dollar-note awaits him now and then in the pews below!

Benighted and blind leader of the blind! Thy money perish with thee, because thou hast thought that the gift of God may be purchased with money. Thou hast neither part nor lot in this matter; for thy heart is not right in the sight of God. Repent, therefore, of this thy wickedness, and pray God, if, perhaps, the thought of thine heart may be forgiven thee.

I do not join in the outcry that the clergy are mercenary. As a class, they are not mercenary. They give largely in proportion to their means. In a very large diocese of clergymen, I know not a single one who is miserly, or who is even charged with being mercenary. Yet the responsibility of the charge rests chiefly with themselves. It is because clergymen set up a standard for themselves different from the standard of other men, that they are differently judged. They are ridiculed, not for exchanging a low for a high salary, but because they insist on calling the higher salary a louder call. No one says aught against the country school-teacher who goes to the city schoolhouse, or the author who sells to the publisher that pays the best, because these are reckoned as matters of legitimate business. But the clergyman assumes that the question of salary does not enter into his profession. He is concerned only to put himself where he will do the most good. Ministers are on precisely the same ground as writers and other clergy. An author is entitled to sell his books to the highest bidder. But the author who lets the consideration of money into his writing, — the author who would write better for ten dollars than he would for one dollar, — the author, who, at any time and for any purpose, does less than his best, is mercenary, and unworthy to be an author. The minister may lawfully, manfully, and religiously go where he may receive the highest salary; but no consideration of salary or hundred-dollar-notes may ever slip into the fountain whence his sermon springs. And, in view of such paragraphs as this, it may be questioned whether the same public sentiment which forbids a bribe to a judge, which has taken away the moiety from internal revenue collectors, which frowns upon the fee to waiters, should not, also, investigate the system of gifts to the clergy. But, however this may be, there can be but one opinion, — that it is more manly, more apostolic, more devout, to settle the question of salary in private, and in a business-like manner, than it is to disclaim pecuniary considerations because Christ had not where to lay his head, and then stand up in the pulpit to flout at hotel-bills, and whine over an apple-pie.

If the minister's be a peculiarly sacred calling; if he devote himself to the salvation of souls; if he have sacrificed all hopes of making a fortune, all prospects of personal advancement, to the cause of Christ; if it be proper that extraordinary means should be employed to assist him, because he has performed an act of extraordinary self-abnegation, — what then? If he have only shifted the burden of providing himself with luxuries from his own shoulders to other people's, what sort of self-abnegation is it? A minister is expected to live, and generally does live, in as good style as the majority of his people. I think it is safe to say, that the average minister occupies as high a position, has as many of the comforts and luxuries of life, and perhaps as much money to spend, as he would have done in any other occupation. But be that as it may. A minister adopts his profession, either as a business or as a consecration. It may, and rightly, be both; but it must be one. If it is a consecration, then this talk about parsonages and donations is not only idle, but it borders on the profane. Jesus Christ had not where to lay his head. Must those who call him "Master," not only have a place to lay theirs, but have it secured to them by title-deed, hung with satin paper, carpeted from Brussels, and stocked with winter provisions? To go cold and hungry for the good cause is a sacrifice; but to sit still, and hint to other people to haul in coal and flour and sugar for you — what sacrifice is that? To turn away from costly books and fine pictures, the desire of the eyes, and the pride of life, for Christ's sake, is the act of a devotee; but to buy your books and pictures, and have your church come in at the year's end, and pay your debts — is that devotion? I say that the man who does it follows no more closely the footsteps of the Master than he who goes into the "cotton trade and sugar line," and pays his own bills.

Of course, it is absurd and unjust to ask ministers to suffer privations. Therefore, it is absurd to put these matters on other than a business-ground. A theological student may be never so conscientious and consecrated; but he chooses his church on common business-principles, as it is proper he should. The only unwisdom is in talking as if he did not. He never remits a cent of his salary because he calls his parish a field of labor. When he leaves that parish for another, he says God has called him to another field of labor; and the dismissing council says, Amen. But all it really means is, that the people are tired of him, or he of them; or his salary is too small; or the house is damp, and the situation unhealthy; or he wants to live in a city; or preach his old sermons; or have a wider scope. God calls him to go just where the minister thinks, on the whole, he would rather go. If one or the other candidate should be defeated at the next election, it would be God calling them to another field of labor. There is no reason to suppose that the Deity is not just as much concerned with the shoemaker who moves from Lynn to Boston, in prospect of higher wages, and better lectures and concerts, as with the minister who moves from Boston to New York. God calls us all, and in only one way, — by the use of our own reason; and it would be just as pious, and a great deal more savory, if we would speak of it in a reasonable, and not in a supernatural way. We may be perfectly sure of our motives: we are not perfectly sure what God thinks about it. If people will not come to church, or will not pay their minister's salary, that is something tangible; but precisely what attitude the divine Being assumes toward it is another thing. When the religious newspaper says that one of the members of a church in Chicago "planned a large addition to his dwelling; but, after the cellar-walls were completed, the work ceased for about one year, — the reason for which, it was said, was, being president of the board of directors of the Chicago Theological Seminary, and seeing its pecuniary wants to be so pressing, he concluded to give up building, and appropriate the money to the relief of the seminary," — we are ready to receive its testimony, because it testifies of what may have come within its scope. But when it goes on to say, "And, as another proof that God loves the cheerful giver, his place of business was the only one belonging to the church which was not consumed," we are constrained to enter a demurrer. Was the president of the board of directors of the Theological Seminary the only member of that church whom God loved? Was there no cheerful giver in all that burnt district, but him who gave up his new dining-room above the cellar-walls? Is not the fact that Mrs. O'Leary's house and barn were the only ones in that quarter not burnt, an equally conclusive proof that God loves the woman who does her milking by a kerosene-lamp? Considering that Jesus has said that "no man, having put his hand to the plough and looking back, is fit for the kingdom of God," and that "whom the Lord loveth he chasteneth," it is quite as reasonable, and quite as scriptural, to say that God hated the president for having begun to enlarge his house, and not being able to finish it, and punished him by leaving his shop standing amid desolation. And if the fire had induced Chicago to remove its business-centre, and the president's property should thus have depreciated, Madam President would be perfectly just in saying to her husband, "I told you so. You ought to have finished that kitchen while you were about it, and have been burned down like the rest, and so have reaped all the advantage of taking a new start."

Is the work of God injured by a clergyman's prosperity? "A minister," says a high clerical authority, "whom the question of money or fame could influence to desert a more useful post for one more lucrative or more honored, is unworthy of that Saviour, who . . . 'made himself of no reputation,' and became exceedingly poor, to . . . accomplish man's salvation. He who toils and suffers like Christ, in obscure places, where frowns are thicker than smiles or applause, shall, like him, and with him, be at last exalted; and every being in the universe shall know and acknowledge the excellence of his motives, and the success of his obscure toils. Christ says, 'If any man serve me, him will my Father honor.'"

It is true that the gist of this remark is the exact opposite of what it is supposed and intended to be. A minister is not to be influenced by fame, because — fame is one of the strongest motives to which Christ appealed. It is unworthy, and a shame, to care what others say about you. Stay where you are, and every being in the universe will presently applaud you. The writer does not see that this is not laying aside the question of fame and honor, but putting a small and immediate fame against a remote and world-wide renown. Leaving that matter, however, the point to be observed is, that the useful and obscure place is set off against the more lucrative and more honored post, as if lucre and honor were separate from usefulness. But do not the very characteristics which make a ministry lucrative and honorable, by that token make it more capable of usefulness? We cannot, of course, bring a mathematical certainty into moral forces; but is it not generally considered that usefulness increases with the enlargement of one's circle? The man who is known by six men may be just as good as the man who is known by six hundred; but, other things being equal, is not the man who helps six hundred men out of difficulty more useful than he who helps only six men? On what other ground does the same journal from which I have quoted say elsewhere, "Who believes the usefulness of a laborer who raises a hundred bushels of corn a year to be as great as that of a village pastor, who, by his teachings, and the daily beauty of his example, 'allures to brighter worlds, and leads the way'?" The laborer may be just as sweet-tempered, just as self-denying, just as devout and benevolent and blameless, as the village pastor. That, no religious newspaper or religious teacher will deny. As to the quality of his work, the production of food is universally admitted to be the one occupation that lies at the very foundation of life. Nothing can be more important than this, because, without this, no other occupation could exist. The superiority of the pastor, therefore, consists in certain qualities, in certain powers, which have been cultivated in him at great cost, which command money, and which enable him to touch life at many more points than the laborer is able to do. The church which calls him away doubles his salary, and promises him a "larger field," — promises, that is, more listeners, more men and women to learn of him, to criticise his statements, to stimulate his intellect, to disseminate his views. All these are advantages; but the increased salary is also an advantage. The larger the salary, the larger may be the life. An ample income is no more to be despised than good eyesight or great strength. If a man has qualities that command money, he has the same right to use them that he has to walk, or ride or row, for his health. A man is just as mighty to the upbuilding of Zion with five thousand dollars a year as with five hundred. He is no more mercenary in receiving ten thousand than he is in receiving one thousand. He may benefit his kind just as much on a salary of twenty thousand as on eight hundred and hints.

The minister is on the same ground as other men. Only let him occupy that ground manfully. He should discard, once for all, the notion that he is a peculiar people. The nineteenth century knows neither priest nor Levite, but holds every laborer worthy of his hire. A minister has only to be simple and natural, to propose or assent to terms, to enforce promptness, and pay his debts like other men; and ninety-nine out of every hundred will uphold him. But what we cannot uphold is the grotesque commingling of sacred and profane things. What we cannot endure is the substitution of a man for the Lord Christ. What we will not away with is the idea that the gift of God may be purchased with money, if a clergyman act as auctioneer. Yet to such straits as these are ministers reduced. They profess to be ambassadors of God, successors of Christ and the apostles. They are not money-makers. They cannot buy and sell, and get gain, as other men do, because their calling is holy. And under this sacred banner they will do and say things which violate the decorum of the world, shock the sensibilities of sinners, and bring a blush of shame to the cheeks of many a man who has been stolidly buying and selling all his lifetime.

Do ministers like the *rôle* that has been assigned them,—not quite a woman, yet but half a man? Do they like the semi-charity which has tampered with their business-relations? Do they like to have their homes invaded, their carpets chosen, their coats cut, let alone bead watch-pockets and winter provisions? It is a matter that lies entirely in their own hands. It is man's own free will, and not divine sovereignty, that inundates his house with bead watch-pockets. Parishes will never give their pastors donation-parties, if pastors decline to accept them. For the sake of the good ones, they are willing to put up with the poor ones. It is the hope of a fruitful harvest that lures them into the disappointment of empty wains. If they would stand on the same footing as the lawyer and the farmer and the merchant, they would have no disappointment to bear. The people who flock to their minister's house, and give him useless trinkets in return for his bread and meat are precisely on a level with their minister. It is no more mean to go to a man's house for what you can get than for him to receive you for what you will give. It is barter on both sides. It is a travesty, and a profanation of hospitality; and whichever side is worsted in the scramble deserves no sympathy.

Donations — the ecclesiastical term for gifts — are defended on the ground, that, without them, the minister has not a sufficient salary. His people will pay twelve hundred dollars. They will not pay fifteen; but they will give the minister presents "amounting in value to three hundred dollars," so that he will receive and report a salary of fifteen hundred dollars. But this three hundred dollars has to do double duty, — as gift and salary. The people have the genial glow which arises from a generous act, and the calm content which springs from justice done. "What do you pay your minister?" asks the foreigner. "Twelve hundred dollars is the nominal salary; but really it amounts to fifteen" is the satisfied reply. But let the minister leave for another "field of labor;" and the aggrieved comment is, "Should you think he could, when we had just made him that handsome present?"

If a people can give their minister fifteen hundred dollars, they can pay him fifteen hundred. If he has earned it, it should be paid as wages, not doled out as charity, or bestowed as affection. It is for the minister himself to decide how large a salary he will claim, or with how small a one he will be content. If he agree upon five hundred, let him take his five hundred, and say no more about it. If he find himself mistaken, he can ask a higher; and, if it be not granted, he can withdraw. But he can make it known from the beginning that his salary is salary, and not sentiment. Nothing is easier than for him to nip in the bud donation-parties and subscription-presents, and all such makeshifts, by a simple announcement. A bargain between clergyman and parish is as practicable as any bargain and sale; and the dignity of his office is no way infringed upon by proceeding on the principles of ordinary bargain. It is sadly infringed upon by the course which at present obtains. In what attitude appears the clergyman who complains that his flock overwhelm him with bead watch-pockets, and eat up his winter provisions? What becomes of his sacred office, while he is ridiculing the small-type Testaments which his donation-party has left in his parlors? Apart from the vexation and uncertainty which he brings upon himself, the minister injures his people by permitting them to flatter themselves that they are generous, when they are not even just. If they pay him a sufficient salary, he has no reason to complain of meagre gifts. If they do not pay him sufficient, he wrongs them by letting them feel as if they did. He should train them to discrimination. He should make a contract, and keep it, like any other man. He ought not to complain that his salary is small, or that it is not promptly paid. He should stipulate for a larger salary, and enforce its prompt payment, and thus keep his business out of the pulpit. If his parish decline, the world is all before him where to choose. If he have no choice of places, he cannot dictate terms. He must view himself as a commodity which has small market-value, and must go for what it will fetch. Ministers with four or five thousand dollars' salary will stand in their pulpits, and complain, that, if they die, their children must go to the work-house, as if that were a fact in which the parish is concerned. The only question is: Did the minister agree to five thousand dollars? and does the parish pay it? If so, their responsibility is over, and the place of his children's death is impertinent. If he cannot live on five thousand dollars, what doth hinder him from going where he can get ten thousand? It would be just as apostolic for him to do that as to stay, and grumble.

Anecdotes are in circulation "illustrative of the close-fisted meanness of certain rural congregations in dealing with their ministers." If lions wrote history, it would be found that there is a "congregation side," as well as a clerical side, to the close-fisted meanness of the rural districts. To Parson B——, the story says, the parish agreed to pay four hundred dollars; yet they fell short seventy-five dollars, and, when reminded of the deficiency, suggested that "ministers should not be greedy of filthy lucre." After continually falling short, and excusing themselves, and leading their pastor a life of anxiety, till he grew old, infirm, and unable to do clerical duty, they at length took him to the alms-house, where he yielded up his life.

This is a very mean way to treat a minister, but not half so mean as the minister who would permit himself to be thus treated. A man who cannot make any more headway than that against greed and avarice is dear at any price. A minister who preaches all his lifetime to a people, and cannot bring them up to the point of common honesty, has certainly mistaken his calling, and should be thankful that he is permitted to die peaceably in the alms-house. A man who will permit his congregation to cheat him year after year, who has not power enough to convince them of sin, nor nerve enough to leave them, may be a sincere Christian, and receive his reward at the judgment-seat; but he certainly has not earned his salary in this world. He has helped to demoralize his people, instead of uplifting them. He has made the gospel a " savor of death unto death."

It may seem cold-blooded and mercenary to discuss such matters on such grounds; but nothing can be more mercenary and cold-blooded than for a minister to sneer at the gifts which his people bring him, and the greed with which they eat up his winter provisions. We have well-nigh lost the divinity which should hedge a gift; and no class of persons have contributed more to this result than clergymen. The ideal gift is spontaneous, is useless, is private and sacred. It is the blossoming of assured love, or the timid outreaching of a love that craves assurance. We give diamonds the most enduring, flowers the most fragile; and love knows no distinction. In love, it is the giver who is uncertain, who is obliged: it is the receiver who confers obligation, and approves affection. It is only a long course of the most complete harmony, of the most profound and unwavering confidence, that justifies a man in being careless about gifts, and bestowing, in the matchless freedom of inviolable friendship, what is the ordained prerogative of charity.

In the hands of clergymen, the gift has fallen from its high estate. They have solicited it; they have proclaimed it; they have computed and bruited its money-value, and mocked at its insignificance. They have debased it into the payment of a debt, confounded it with the discharge of a duty, profaned it by association with a grudge. They owe it to the congregations they have tampered with to sit for a generation in sackcloth and ashes, — sackcloth of their own buying, and ashes of their own burning, — and, with tight fists of integrity, to reject and repel the false gifts of tight-fisted meanness, of uncomprehending carelessness, while with uplifted voice they teach their people the eternal distinction between a tax wrung, a subscription badgered, a compromise effected, and the spontaneous offering of brooding and delighted love.

HEAVENLY HEATHENISM.

HEAVENLY HEATHENISM.

TANDING amid the ruin of a great disaster, and seeing on all sides the ungainly relics of stately edifices, while one building, apparently no better and no less endangered, remains unharmed, almost untouched, one instinctively inquires, "How could it be that this did not burn with the rest?" Says a pretty pietist in reply, "A kind Providence protected us. God did not mean that this store should burn. That is the way I account for it."

A little farther up, out of the desolation, but close upon its brink, rises some such institution as an Emigrants' Aid Savings-Bank, with a placard arched over the sign, to the effect that "God has protected the savings of the poor;" from which we are to infer, I suppose, that the Emigrants' Aid Savings-Bank has not gone out in the flame.

Far be it from me to attempt to dissociate man from his Maker in ever so small a measure. Nothing is more wholesome, more heartening, than the ever-present consciousness of an ever-present God, interested in his children, co-working for their good, watching over them with unceasing love and care and wisdom. But let us not, on that account, discontinue the use of our reasoning faculties. When a young girl, untaught either by books or by life, inexperienced, and without responsibility, utters a saintly sounding but senseless sentiment, we accept the saintliness as an omen of good, and hope the sense will come with years and exigencies; but when mature business-men — men who hold other people's property in trust, bank directors and proprietors — publicly placard the divine favor as a reason of their exemption from disaster, it is time for stockholders to look into the books.

> "God moves in a mysterious way
> His wonders to perform;"

but he is in no proper sense a bank director, nor a fire-insurance company; and it would seem as if even his divine patience would be taxed with our petty attempts to glorify him by attributing to him their functions. For look you, fair philosopher: a kind Providence protected you, you say; and your shop was not burnt. Was it an unkind Providence, then, that refused to protect the shop across the street? or did not Providence care, one way or another, and just let it burn? Does God love Hovey, and hate Holbrook? Is he kindly disposed toward Bigelow Brothers, but hostile to Palmer and Bachelder? When Shreve, Crump, and Low succeeded in removing their goods to a place of safety, did they elude an angry God who had planned to burn them? Do you really think that God cares more for Jordan and Marsh than he does for Stevenson? Are Boston and Portland and Chicago any less dear to him than New York and Baltimore and Cincinnati? If God saved one house, did he set fire to the others?

Hard-headed money-man, when you say that God protects the savings of the poor, what do you mean? Did he protect the poor people of Peshtigo, who rushed from their burning houses to swift death by flood and flame? Did he preserve the savings of the poor in Chicago? Does he have more regard for the five cents which the sewing-girl puts in the bank than for the sewing-machine by which she earns it?

And why should God care for the savings of the poor any more than for the savings of the rich? He (according to this philosophy) desolated whole tracts belonging to the rich. He swept away in a night the savings of years. Men who had grown rich from poverty grew suddenly poor from wealth. Was it the hatred of Deity? Many of them were men who feared God, and honored him with their substance. The churches of Boston did not minish aught of their Thanksgiving contribution to the poor, though they had been fearfully marred by the fire. Does that indicate a quality that would be likely to incur the divine displeasure? The burned-out merchants of Boston are, so far as human eyes can judge, as worthy a class of people as the emigrants who come to us from abroad. They are as honest, as upright, as humane, I think I may say as devout. Compared with emigrants, one would say that God could have nothing against them but their wealth; but, if he disapproves of wealth, it must be that he disapproves of the qualities that produce wealth. These are more likely to be sagacity, industry, prudence, integrity, than greed and dishonesty. They are far more likely to be those traits which in combination we call virtue, than those which we call vice. But when a man, using the talents of which he finds himself possessed, and the opportunities which are presented to him, becomes a rich man, a supporter of the churches, a patron of the arts, a promoter of education, does he pass thereby under the ban of Deity?

Our piety needs a stiff breeze of common sense blowing through it. We need to remember that God is no partial parent, caressing one child, and chiding another, but impartial, loving all, through evil report and through good report. The saved and the lost, the murderer and his victim, are alike children of one Father. The little barefoot boy is as dear to his Maker as the dainty lady in her silken attire; and the silken lady is as beloved of God as the barefoot boy. God is angry with the wicked every day; but below the anger dwell love and untiring compassion, working always for repentance and reformation in the guilty but beloved child.

God no more saves a shop or a bank than he builds them. He does both, for he is the source of all things; but he builds houses by the architect, and he saves them by the fireman. It has pleased him to enact that a nail shall go where it is driven; that mortar shall harden in air, and clay by fire. We discover these laws, and build houses, and live in them with great delight; but we do not say that God built them. He has enacted that wood shall consume, and granite crumble, and water turn to vapor, and air to wind, by the action of fire; and our houses burn,

> "Our spirits consume,
> Our flesh is a flame:"

but to say that God did it in any other sense than he does every thing is to outrage reason, and exasperate justice. It is good to be religious; but it is not good to make God capricious. A great conflagration is kindled and fanned by natural causes. Its lesson is one of logic. We should aim to discover what produced it, what increased it, what the duties it devolves upon us in attempting to prevent its recurrence, and to mitigate its consequences; but to overleap all these possible and comprehensible steps, and mount up into heaven, and define what part the Deity took in it, is a work of supererogation, of utter inconsequence and fatuity. The only legitimate way of finding out God is through his word and work, not through conjecture. The lazy fatalism of the Mohammedan is in no way allied to the intelligent trust of the Christian. God is as much dishonored by our attempts to fasten upon him our puerile ways of thinking, our feeble modes of acting, as by denying his existence altogether. An inscrutable God may still be God; but an inconsequent, capricious, unreasonable God is — Atheism. The divine name is not a talisman for security, a charm against evil: it is the sign of one existence, the great I Am of the universe. What we can comprehend, that we know. Beyond this, let us not wildly and profanely assume, but wait in reverent silence.

And let us sometimes worship in reverent silence. A devout writer wishes to " combat the idea that God can be worshipped at Boston and Chicago, but must be ignored during the thirty-six hours of travelling between Boston and Chicago." His idea of worship is the Jewish and Samaritan, not to say Gentile idea, that there is no worship but the external ceremony performed in this mountain, or in Jerusalem, or in Delphos. He, apparently, never heard that the hour cometh, and now is, when neither in this mountain, nor yet at Jerusalem, but in spirit and in truth, anywhere, shall true worshippers worship the Father.

"A company of Christian workers," he says, "journeyed to Chicago, and beyond. Christ was with them at all times while journeying." He speaks, it will be observed, as coolly and confidently as if Christ were a Pullman porter, ticketed through without change of cars. A good many of us believe in Christ's help and comfort, know that there is such a thing as the full assurance of hope and of faith, and feel, sometimes, what seems to be a real and elevating communion with the divine Being; but knowing, also, the vanity, the impatience, the indolence, and selfishness which so easily beset us, we should shrink from asserting, and almost from believing, that Christ was with us in any other sense than that in which he is always with his children, — the poorest, weakest, most wayward, as well as the stanchest and wisest. But to assume Christ's peculiar presence with a whole company for a whole trip, at one clip, seems rather more like assurance pure and simple than like the assurance of hope or faith, or any other Christian grace. But, "moreover, he was seen by others as with them;" and this is the keynote of the whole performance. This Christian traveller has, or at least expresses, no other idea of Christian travelling than to be seen of men. He wants the Bible to be as freely used, and as fearlessly perused, as a travelling hatter takes out his pass-book for an order. He has no other, at least he presents no other, conception of Christian travelling than saying your prayers, and studying your Sunday-school lessons, on the train. When the twilight of the first evening came, one of them (I venture to say it was the very man himself) remarked to his fellow-travellers, — not simply of their own party, but of the whole car, — that, " as this was their usual hour of worship at their family altars, they knew of nothing that should prevent them here," and accordingly fell to. It seems not to have occurred to them that the peculiarity of family prayer is its being offered in the sacred privacy of the family, and that what is sweet and tender and devout by the fireside may become ostentatious, conceited, and displeasing in the noisy publicity of a promiscuous, rattling railroad-car. The next thing they wanted was a state-room in the Pullman car to study their next Sunday's lesson in Mark. Why they should have wanted a state-room, it is difficult to surmise, as the Christian traveller takes special pains to inform us, that during all the singing, praying, and studying, " the door was left wide open." To be sure, Christ implies and assumes, that, when we enter into our closet, we shall shut the door; but these Christian travellers could not afford to have so much piety shut up in a state-room. They were altogether too economical to waste thus the odor of sanctity; and they left the door ajar, that it might be wafted through the whole car. It is true that Christ says, " When thou prayest thou shalt not be as the hypocrites are; for they love to pray standing in the synagogues, and in the corners of the streets," and in the Pullman cars, "that they may be seen of men." But we have changed all that. Christ was not a Christian traveller. To be seen of men is the very essence of Christian travelling. Its only trait in distinction from profane travelling is being seen of men. Not a word is said about behavior, — honesty, kindness, politeness, promptness, neatness, unselfishness, good-nature; nothing at all of any thing but public appearance.

The disgust and derision excited by his ill-breeding and self-conceit are recorded by this *naive* Christian traveller, without the smallest suspicion of their nature. He probably, to this day, never dreams that he played any thing but the man. One good old gentleman, indeed, afterward placed in the hands of some member of the party at Niagara a paper recording his love for God. But what of the official in charge, who, in spite of their family altars, replied afterwards to their request for a state-room, with a knowing wink, and the remark that they "could have a nice time playing euchre"? The wink and the wit were lost on the impervious Pharisee who evoked them; and he "frankly informed" the ungodly official, "that the next sabbath's lesson in Mark was to be studied, as there would be no other opportunity." Equally wasted upon the Christian traveller was the sarcasm of the Episcopal clergyman, that "he took them for actors, performing their parts." Hands off, Episcopacy! You have got your chasubles and your maniples, and I know not what of incomprehensibilities; but you are not to monopolize the theatricals of the church. We also, we Congregationalists, have our cap and bells; and if any choirs of yours can jangle longer and louder than these Christian travellers, speak now, or else hereafter forever hold your peace.

"Now this," says my martinet, "I call commonsense travelling." I thank thee, O God, that I am not as other men are, — devout at heart, silent, reverent toward God, respectful to man, not obtruding my personal views and habits on strangers, shutting my closet-door to pray to God in secret. I thank thee, O God, that I do not count religion any thing, unless it be seen of men. I believe nothing of right living, or true thinking, or of worshipping thee in the spirit, but only in perpetual talk, — talk to, talk at, and talk about. I thank thee, that, rattle the railroads never so noisily, I can rattle louder still. Conductors may wink, and clergyman frown; but my pachyderm is impenetrable. I am that kind of fool, that, though thou bray me in a mortar among wheat, with a pestle, yet will not my foolishness depart from me!

But it is this sort of thing which gives us faith in Christianity, in spite of right-hand fallings-off and left-hand defections. Only a divine institution could withstand such advocacy, and remain respectable.

There are a good many persons who are not dead in trespasses and silliness, but who yet are influenced by such sentiments. They are well disposed, busy about other matters, and rather apt to adopt views without discrimination, especially if they have a religious tinge. But it cannot be too strongly urged that such teachings as these, so far as they have any influence at all, are utterly destructive of simplicity of character. He who talks about reading the Bible freely and fearlessly in the railroad train has fallen from grace. He is not thinking about things, but appearances. He is not thinking about divine truths, but of how he looks reading them. He is not thinking of the Bible, but of himself. A man has no more occasion for fearlessness in reading the Bible in a car than in reading a newspaper or a novel; and, if he thinks he has, it is only because he is swollen with conceit and self-importance.

And, if he is a Boston Sunday-school teacher, the best thing he can do on his way to Chicago and Oregon is to leave his "International Sunday-school Lessons" behind him. He will see little enough, if he keeps his eyes out of the window the whole time. If he rides through Michigan studying his question-book, he might as well have staid at home. The very object of travel is change. The Sunday-school teacher abroad should put his Sunday school as far out of mind as possible, and lay open heart and soul and mind to all new and strange scenes. If a man in his vacations cannot get on without the machinery of religion, that machinery is of little use to him, is likely to be of harm. If a man cannot feel comfortable at twilight, without standing up in a Pullman car, and praying aloud before the passengers, he has prayed to little purpose before he stepped into the car. I do not say, that, among the group which assisted at this spectacular performance, there were not sincere and trustworthy Christians; but I do say, that their reporter has succeeded in setting them in a singularly ridiculous and offensive light. And I venture also to add, that — outside of the artificial atmosphere of technical professional religionists, in the real instantaneous and solitary application of principle to action, without fuss or formality, or the observation of men; in the strenuous wear and tear of life, — the religion that is silent and simple and modest, cherished in the sacred and secret depths of the soul, self-mistrustful, and not overbold, is more to be depended on than that other religion, which, however sincere, is ever patent and blatant, ready, like a Jack-in-the-box, to spring up into your face at the slightest touch, and which, fed by vanity and supported by admiration, is likely to have neither courage nor discretion left for the real emergencies of life, that come without warning and without witness.

Is it Christ, or Apollo, that said, " Not every one that saith unto me, Lord, Lord, shall enter into the kingdom of heaven; but he that doeth the will of my Father which is in heaven "?

When Chicago was cast down in dust and ashes, the whole world went out to her with compassion and succor. There was no solicitation. All hearts swelled with a passion of sympathy, whose only solace was a swift and eager giving. The most orthodox of our pulpits found itself exclaiming, " Who could read the telegrams last week, without a choking in his throat? Who could think of this great outpouring of compassion and bounty, without feeling that love is mightier, after all, than selfishness; that the new commandment is, indeed, the highest law?"

But *is* love mightier than selfishness? Then must not all things follow? Love is the law of heaven. Selfishness is the law of hell. If heaven is the stronger, surely heaven must prevail.

We believe in original sin and total depravity, after a fashion. Indeed, in the midst of the falsehood, the slander, the malignity, the recklessness, the shamelessness, of a political campaign, we believe in it after a very sturdy fashion. Somewhere in the human heart there seems to be a fountain of sin, which is easily unsealed, and which sends forth bitter waters. But what if, close alongside, lies a fountain, as accessible, of original purity, of total goodness? You touch the chord of selfishness, and man grasps and jostles, and turns neither to the right hand nor to the left. You smite the chords of love, and he stops in his gain-getting, flings all his eagerness into helpfulness, and becomes as a god. Never were our growing, hot-headed cities more bent on making money than they were on giving it away when trouble came. Never was their intelligence, their sagacity, their experience, their activity, more swiftly and imperatively summoned for their own advantage than for the succor of a suffering neighbor on one memorable morning. Which is the fact, then, on which to base our creed? Why predicate total depravity, unless we predicate, also, total goodness? Are we any more sure that men will sin than we are that men will save? May we not count as confidently on human generosity as on human greed? Does human nature any more quickly fall before temptation than it rises before opportunity?

Has it not an aptness for good as strong as its aptness for evil?

To which is it, in the long-run, and sometimes in the run that is not very long, safer to appeal? — the good, or to the evil passions? Who is the more influential leader of his kind, he who assumes that men are corrupt, immoral, dishonest, tricky, or he who assumes that they mean to be honest, just, and candid? Why do men, in speaking to their fellows, always try to maintain the appearance of right, unless it be because there is still in the human breast an unspoiled appreciation and approbation of the right?

Right thinking is not, indeed, right doing; but it is the first step which costs. And is there not, on the whole, more right doing than wrong doing? Sin in the mass is odious; and the mass is immense. It is noisome and noisy: it is against wind and tide: it makes outcry, and attracts attention. Innocence and virtue and holiness are quiet and natural. Their voice is not heard; but they are pervasive, and one might almost say, overpowering. The honest, generous, worthy people in almost any community outnumber the thieves, the misers, the worthless. The fathers and mothers, the brothers and sisters, do many more good deeds to each other than evil; say many more kind words than harsh ones. But the ninety and nine respectable and exemplary families figure far less before the public than the one litigious and quarrelsome family. The one hasty word of the good husband stays longer in memory to harass and annoy than the twenty kindly and comfortable words to soothe. The little children play in the sunshine for hours, and nobody minds them; but one howl of displeasure speedily rivets all the attention of authority. The mass of vice is immense; but the mass of virtue — is it not, also, immense and immeasurable? Where, then, is total depravity? and what is total depravity?

Shall we say that generosity and benevolence and sympathy are but natural traits, have no moral character, are destitute of holiness, and will not avail in the general summing-up? that there is in them no more saving virtue than in the playfulness of the kitten, or the timidity of the lamb? But is it not the best thing possible to be said of Nature, that its unforced, spontaneous traits are noble? It is, surely, far better to be kind simply, naturally, unconsciously, than to be forced to make a fresh resolution every time there is an opportunity for kindness. To be, without thinking, what, with your hardest thinking and strongest determination, you would wish to be, ought not to be counted a disadvantage. The strongest condemnation we can pronounce against any sin is, that it is unnatural. In that do we not pronounce a eulogy on Nature?

And if kindness and benevolence have no moral character, are simply temperamental and insignificant, shall not unkindness and malevolence come under the same head? If a man's good deeds to his neighbor shall go for nothing in the general judgment, because he did them, not from love to God, but simply out of a naturally kind disposition, shall not his evil deeds be equally set at nought, because he did them with no hatred, and no thought of God, but only out of that temper which his mother gave him?

One child is so rooted and grounded in love to his father, that he never thinks of disobeying him; never thinks of the household rules as law, more than of the sun rising. Another rebels and revolts; and it is only after a hard struggle, and much inward discussion, that he conforms to the household authority. Shall his submission be counted to him for righteousness, while the other's blameless walk, which is not submission, but harmony, counts for nothing?

Sin is a terrible blot on the world's page; but perhaps it is a blot, and not the page. For me, I am amazed at the amount of quiet, stolid, unswerving goodness that does not know itself for goodness, but thinks it is simply supporting the family, or paying the taxes, or training the children, or doing the fall sewing, or electing the candidate, or minding its own business generally, — goodness that rates itself too low to imagine that the Deity could take any cognizance of it, but which *I* imagine to be an offering of a sweet savor unto the Lord, — goodness which wears no phylacteries, and flaunts no banners, nor ever thinks itself meet to enter even the outer court of the sanctuary, but before which, I fancy, the inner doors will one day part, on golden hinges turning.

PRAYER.

PRAYER.

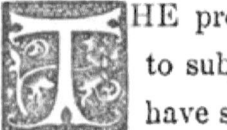HE proposal of Prof. Tyndall, or his friend, to subject prayer to scientific tests, seems to have somewhat shocked, not to say angered, the religious world. Possibly, that is what the gentlemen wanted. Perhaps, however, they were sincere in their desire to ascertain the efficacy of prayer; or perhaps it was less to show their own disbelief than to convince the world of its unbelief. It is surely unnecessary to assume that they were actuated by unhandsome motives. Even if they were, would it not be wiser, and worthier the truth, to ignore that fact, and treat them as if they were simply mistaken, and sincerely inquiring, rather than attempt to cast odium upon them, to call them Sadducees, and their proposal a trap?

Why must it be a trap? Why is not the test they propound just as fair as that named by Elijah to the prophets of Baal, to which we never raised objection? James said, "Is any sick among you? Let him call for the elders of the church; and let them pray over him, anointing him with oil in the name of the Lord: and the prayer of faith shall save the sick, and the Lord shall raise him up." If we believe that James meant to state a truth of literal and universal application, why are the philosophers unreasonable? If we do not believe it, what do we believe?

To say that God will not answer a prayer that is a challenge, or prayer that proceeds from a doubt as to the efficacy of prayer, and that Christ always refused to give a sign, is hardly fair to Prof. Tyndall, and is not beyond question. Christ would hardly refuse to give a sign which was precisely what he had himself prescribed. If the prayer of faith shall save the sick, how is one to know that it is irreverent to ask all the faithful to pray for the sick? Elijah's proposal was a challenge of the most defiant sort; and the priests of Baal showed, at least, the sincerity of their belief, by accepting it. We may, indeed, say that the challenge was not given to the true God, but to the false god. But we cannot place the divine Being in the attitude of proposing what he would decline to accept. He surely showed conclusively that he was not offended by being subjected to a material test. It was not, indeed, scientific; but it was purely popular. Gideon, in great doubt and fear, sought an arbitrary sign from Heaven; and it was granted him once and again. Christ did refuse to give signs, but not when something was asked in direct conformity with his directions. Elijah had great faith; but Gideon, apparently, had little. If it does no good for any person to pray who does not believe in prayer, if prayers have no effect except when offered by persons who have no doubts to set at rest, alas! would not the lips of the world be well-nigh sealed? I have not so learned Christ. It seems to me that God is so abundantly and immeasurably kind, considerate, and helpful; he is so eager that we should confide in him, and love him; he is so anxious to put us into communication with himself, and yet so unable to do it without our concurrence,—that he clutches at a straw as it were. He comes out to meet us while we are yet a great way off. He catches the first glance turned toward him, even though it be of gloom and doubt. He accepts even an unreasonable and arbitrary challenge. He is glad to hear us say, "Lord, I believe: Lord, I believe," even though we contradict ourselves in the next breath, and cry out, "Help thou mine unbelief." He will hear and answer the prayer that is offered with halt and hesitancy; that has scarcely a stronger hold on the soul than has the spider's web on the tree from which it trembles.

Does not the question, after all, turn on the nature of prayer, and, by implication, on the proper objects of prayer? The Bible certainly seems to teach, that prayer for direct, personal, material objects, will be literally answered. We who have grown abstract and philosophical are inclined to reject the theory, and say that the only prayers to which we ought to expect literal answers are prayers for spiritual gifts. We may pray that our friends recover their health, but with the proviso, if it be God's will. So, then, if our friends die, the prayer is not lost. We pray that we may be of forgiving temper. That needs no proviso, because we know it is the will of God that we should be forgiving. Such prayer, then, will surely be answered. But, says the scientist, "if the disease be an incurable one, all the prayers of all the world will not cure it. Filth brings fever. Prayer cannot interpose." And we admit the force of the statement. But law has no more force in the physical than in the moral world. The heart is just as truly, if not just as directly, under the sway of logic, it is just as subject to cause and effect, as is the head. God cannot make me good without my concurrence, any more than he can make me healthy. I must take just as reasonable and definite measures against malice, envy, and uncharitableness, if I have a tendency that way, as against rheumatism and typhoid-fever. A forgiving temper is as much within my own grasp as physical vigor, and as unattainable outside of certain conditions. God as really desires I should be well as he desires I should be good. I pray him to enable me to forgive my foe; and I at once turn about, and speak peaceably to him, and help him bear his burdens. I pray God to conduct me safely on my journey; and I take care never to step upon the train when it is in motion. But if I am weak, and fall into revenge; if I am late, and fear to miss the train, and, in each case, come to grief, — is prayer unanswered, and of no avail?

Reason does not forsake the spiritual to control the material world. The two worlds are one, — subject to the same law of cause and effect, ruled by the same sovereign. The Lord our God is one Lord. If the little geological hammer shivers the efficacy of prayer for material blessings, it annihilates with the same blow all prayer for spiritual blessing. If science will not permit God to refresh the thirsty earth with falling showers, in response to the prayers of the saints, neither can it permit him to refresh their thirsty souls with the dews of divine grace.

I do not believe any theory of prayer can be framed which will satisfy either the believer or the unbeliever. There is a whole universe to rove through, and we know very little about it all. It is not only that the stars in their courses fight shy of us; but we are living every day in close contact with forces, of whose nature, origin, and ends, we are almost totally ignorant. It is not only we, the people, who walk "in a vain show;" but the scientists hold their knowledge by the most insecure tenure. The learning of one generation is the rubbish of the next. "God cannot contravene his own laws," says the philosopher. "Why pray that he should?" But tell me, O my philosopher, what are God's laws? Once it was a divine law that heat was caloric, a latent substance in all bodies: now it is divine law that heat is no substance at all, but a mode of motion. Once the law bade the sun go around the earth: now it sends the earth spinning around the sun. Once the law made light to be the emanation of matter from luminous bodies; then it was the undulation of ether, pervading all bodies: now it looks as if light were decreed to be the vibrations of the molecules of matter itself. Once the law made sharp and essential distinctions between mind and matter: now the correlation of forces transmutes bread and butter into thought, and philosophy is but phosphorus on the brain. Surely the condemnation of Christian devotion is premature. Further investigation may yet discover prayer, too, among the secretions.

Indeed, the philosopher's refusal to recognize prayer as a possible force seems to me eminently unphilosophical. After long and elaborate treatises to prove that muscular power is correlated with nerve-power, and nerve-power with will-power; that mental operations are directly correlated with physical activities;

that external material force may become a mode of internal consciousness; that emotion may be converted into movement, — they turn around, and affirm that one special form of emotion cannot be converted into movement, a certain mode of consciousness, a certain exertion of will-power, one especial form of mental and moral operations, can have no influence whatever upon physical activities. Our magi are ready to swear to the correlation and conservation of forces; but they must select the forces.

Learned and logical Herr Professor, we believe in you profoundly. Whether you go down into the darkness of the under-world, or up into the very brightness and substance of the sun, we follow you with unequal steps, but with reverent eyes and delighted hearts. Many things which you say we must take on trust; but the results of your difficult and occult processes we receive gladly. But if you put prayer outside the pale of cosmical forces, if you demonstrate that it is only a name, and nothing more, we may not refute your argument, or resist your action; yet, all the same, not one single believing heart is shocked one hair's-breadth out of its position by your flawless argument. This is one of the facts you must build on, and it is as indisputable as an alkali. We pray, not because it is reasonable or logical to pray, but because we cannot help it. Does

Mr. Galton say that "prayer is but a signal of distress, the outcry of the hare in mortal terror of the hounds"? Why, even thus he concedes every thing. It makes prayer organic, natural, real. Admit that prayer is what it seems to be as truly as is the cry of the hunted hare, and we need ask no more.

We know well that typhoid-fever is generated by ignorance and negligence. We are ready to believe that the germs of disease have a fatal affinity, so to speak, with certain living tissues; but, when the child of the house is prostrate and tossed with fever, all the treatises in the world would not keep the father and mother from pushing to Heaven constant and earnest implorings for his recovery. In the early morning, as you stand at your window, looking over the green world, all sparkling and dewy, all alight and alive, your soul rises to God in praise and exultation, — not by a mental causation, perhaps, but upborne by a no less powerful moral instinct, which is, also, not without the line of causation. If you come to that, you may resolve the dew, and the brightness, and the fertility into vapors and suction and absorption, the blind workings of Nature, the simple procession of cause and effect, for which no one has any especial call to be grateful. But we *are* grateful. We do praise the Lord for it. All nations, in all ages, have ascribed glory to God. Find room for that fact in your system of philosophy, or your induction must be incomplete.

We are ready to relinquish our philosophical theories whenever you speak the word. We are not indissolubly wedded to the syllogism. We shall never make any fight against the convertibility of forces, or the indestructibility of matter. In the heavens and the earth, and the waters which are under the earth, in the solar system, and the whole boundless universe, you shall have every thing your own way; but suffer the little children, and forbid them not, to say, "Our Father which art in heaven, hallowed be thy name."

And except ye become as little children, and until ye become as little children, and in as far as ye do not become as little children, I do not see but you will have to wander forever in the outer darkness of your molecules and your imponderables, your dynamics and your transmutations, and never enter into the warm, loving, certain kingdom of heaven.

No doubt, at heart, the philosophers are far better Christians than they make themselves out to be. They have a profound trust in protoxides, and a simple faith in the spectroscope, which promises to keep bright their power of faith and trust. And if they do seem to remit the Deity to the further end of the chain of causation, and allow him no part nor lot in the affairs of to-day, nevertheless, he is not far from every one of us, and, haply, they feel after him, and find him, even in a chemical experiment or an astronomical observation.

Nor are we, Christians after a sort, such hypocrites as they fear, although we do not readily accept their suggestion of concerted and concentrated prayer. The reasons that we give for our refusal may not be coherent or consistent; but the one unanswerable reason is, that we do not like the idea. It is repulsive. If you cannot see why, O philosophers! never mind. The fact remains; and it is an insurmountable objection, just as truly as if it bristled with premise and conclusion.

> "The reason why I cannot tell;
> But I don't like you, Dr. Fell."

And Dr. Fell would have been no more completely rejected if he had been a villain, and therefore rejected. Somebody, who apparently believes that the Deity is of the Chinese persuasion, and will hear a clash of gongs, when he would be deaf to a "still, small voice," proposed, that, when the blare of trumpets should have died out of the Peace Jubilee House, a world's prayer-meeting should be gathered there from all quarters of the globe. The suggestion fell flat upon the public ear, and was never heard of more; but it was not in the least because Christian America does not believe in prayer. We are bad enough, Heaven knows (and it is a great comfort that Heaven does know it); but, amid all our dissensions and distractions and inconsistencies, the one thing on which we are most closely united, the one thing in which we believe both instinctively and intellectually, is prayer, not distinctively in social prayer, in public prayer, in formal prayer, but in the unforced, spontaneous, irresistible outflow of the human soul to a personal, sympathizing, all-comprehending God, in whom we live and move, and have our being.

It seems to me, learned and beloved Prof. Tyndall, that if you would only say the Lord's Prayer every night, reverently and really, as such a man as you must needs say it, if he say it at all, the problem of prayer would soon solve itself. And it is worth while to observe, that, while there are prayers and prayers, the Lord's Prayer seems to cover the ground. All the good in all the world is comprehended in those simple, succinct formulas. They are relegated largely to children and Episcopalians; but adults have not outgrown them, nor have even Congregationalists devised any thing better. I cannot think of a blessing to be desired, an evil to be averted, which is not included in the Lord's Prayer; and we are expressly warned not to lay stress on much speaking. Still, if the soul wishes to go outside the form presented by our Saviour, and voice its wants in its own words, I suppose the Lord God will still be attent.

Shall I give a little narrative that proves nothing, and may go for nothing, but is, nevertheless, not unconnected with our theme?

Said my friend, a simple, unlearned woman, " I wanted a servant. My house was in order; and I was ready to set up housekeeping. I went to the intelligence-offices. The same shabby benches of shabby women, rough, untidy, repulsive. My heart sank within me at the thought of organizing a home on such a basis. It occurred to me, would it do any good — in fact, would it be right — to pray over it? If good servants are not to be had, God himself cannot bring me one. Moreover, the supply is extremely limited, and the demand very great. I was not in sore need. There were a great many other women to whom a competent servant meant health, peace of mind, content with life: to me, it meant only freedom from annoyance; and I was so rich in happiness, in comfort, in occupation, in satisfying friendships and natural life, that it seemed selfish to be craving the good servant which other women needed so much. And with it all was a doubt whether God ever intended us to throw such things on him. Having given us ability to help ourselves, would it not be like indolence to ask him to help us? And, ignorant as we are, is it ever safe to set our hearts upon any thing in particular? Still I wanted the right one so much, and did not in the least know how to get at her. So, all quietly, and with never a thought of breathing it to any one, I made a little arrangement with the good God, that if it could be done without depriving any one else of assistance, and if it were not a thing so much my own business that I had no right to trouble him about it, and if, in addition to all the rest of my satisfactions, he could afford to let me have the satisfaction of a good servant, why I should be very glad and grateful. But I stipulated expressly that I would not presume on an affirmative answer, and that a negative answer should apply only to this particular case. If nothing came of it, I would, perhaps, be more backward about trying again; but I would not promise not to try again.

"On my way to the intelligence-office, it came into my power to attempt a good service for an absent acquaintance. It would cost me two or three hours of time, a good deal of discomfort, and interruption of my present pursuit; and the woman in question had showed herself entirely unappreciative, not to say resentful, of previous favors. I had a thousand minds not to go; but it occurred to me, that here was I asking a doubtful favor for myself. I was not sure I was on legitimate ground there; but I was quite sure in doing a kind act. Was it rather bribing the good God? Perhaps so. But I knew he could not be bribed: so there was no harm done. My errand over, I went to the intelligence-office. Immediately a young woman was presented to me, so pretty, modest, and ladylike, that I thought she could not be a servant; but she was. I put several questions, which she answered so satisfactorily, and her whole appearance was so prepossessing, that I was taken aback, and actually sat and stared at her. I don't know what the poor creature thought of me; but I was thinking over and over again, 'I wonder if God did send you.' It seemed just like the Old Testament. And yet it seemed, also, somehow, as if God was making fun of me, you know. But there was nothing to do but take her home. On my way home, it came into my power again, by taking some trouble, to do another small kindness to certain good friends. I was just as uncertain where I stood as before; but I said, 'If there is any such thing as putting God under bonds, I will do it. He shall have no excuse for not obliging me in my indisposition to oblige others.' Well, I have not got over it yet. Here is my pretty handmaiden, neat and trim and tidy, intelligent, capable, sweet-tempered, quiet, respectful, modest, — a girl that I can really love, not with what theologians call the love of benevolence, but with the love of complacency, — a servant who is in her place a lady. Now, as she moves about the house with noiseless footfall, as I see the brown hair put smoothly back from her delicate forehead, as I mark the varying flush in her round cheek, as I look into her deep, earnest eyes, it is not simply that a helpful, healthful Scotch lassie is making life pleasant to me; but I say over and over again in mute apostrophe, 'I wonder if God did send you.' It is such a perfect answer, that it does not seem as if it could be an answer at all. But, if it is not an answer, should you think God would let it happen so?"

Wise men of the East and of the West, this is not argument. It is hardly illustration. It is only a specimen of the way in which the minds of the unlearned work. You know perfectly well that God had nothing to do with it, but that it was simply the result of long trains of Scotch history and American politics. But political and historical scholars are few; while the men and women are many in the world, who, not with gong and trumpet, in the open squares, but silently, in their own hearts, in a thousand modes and forms, are putting God to the test. "There is no speech nor language. Their voice is not heard." They can give no physical nor metaphysical formula that can for a moment resist your logic; but it is borne in upon them somehow, that God stands the test; and against this solid, deep-seated, lifelong conviction, believe me, you will never make any headway.

TEA-PARTY SALVATION.

TEA-PARTY SALVATION.

THE problem of saving young men from moral destruction in large cities is of vital importance to the Church, and perhaps an incident . . . may help to solve it. For two evenings in succession, one of the elders of" [a certain] " church had noticed two young men in the lecture-room, apparently strangers in the city. Entering into conversation, he found that neither belonged to any church organization, but both were favorably disposed in that direction. In response to a question, one of the young men said, that it was the first time in seven years " [they had been that time in ———] "that any Christian man had spoken to him about his soul. The elder invited the young men to take tea with him at his house, which they accepted. The sequel was, that both young men became regular attendants upon the sabbath school and church; and both are now converted and active members of the church. The incident has a moral and a sermon in it."

The incident has two sermons in it. The one more

commonly preached is to church-members, to the effect, that, if a young man loses his soul, it is rather their fault, in that they have not "spoken" to him about it. The other was preached, many years ago, to the young man himself: "If thou art wise, thou art wise for thyself; but, if thou scornest, thou alone shalt bear it."

It is not to be denied, that the problem of saving young men from moral destruction is of vital importance to the Church; but it is also undeniable, that it is of equally vital importance to the young men. Selfishness, indifference to our neighbor's weal, and neglect of his claims, are sins; but the warmest Christian interest in another's welfare is always to be cherished in deference to the requirements of good breeding and good sense. Much of our religious talk seems to proceed on the assumption that a young man is a moral infant, who must be kept from hurting himself by ecclesiastical petting. There is strength in association; but, if association is to relieve a grown man from the necessity of standing alone, it cannot be too soon dissolved. The object of combination is to utilize, not neutralize, strength. Strength is to be turned into force, not into weakness.

Here is a young man who has been seven years in a church-going city, — himself a church-goer, — and says this is the first time any Christian man has spoken to him about his soul. What does he mean? There are churches in that city: there are young men's Christian associations, to which every young man is again and again, and in many ways, welcomed. There are ministers who every Sunday are honestly and earnestly trying to point out to their hearers the way of life. Every word spoken was intended for these young men. They had, moreover, the Bible and all the institutions of a Christian city. Every avenue to the kingdom of heaven was as wide open to them as the clergy and the church could open it. No elder of any church can tell them how to become a Christian, any better than they can tell themselves. The Bible is his source of information; and a New Testament can be bought anywhere for twenty-five cents. Instead of censuring the neglect of the churches, I censure the egotism of the young men. It was not that no Christian had spoken to them about their souls, but that no one had taken notice of their special personality. No one had flattered their vanity by addressing them as Mr. Smith and Mr. Brown. They would not join the church until they had been invited to tea.

Many years ago, a half-witted negro, called Pompey, was to be hung for having murdered his master. The Sunday before his execution he was taken to church, and sat, the sermon through, on a stool in the broad aisle. The minister prayed for him fervently; but when he was returned to his cell, and asked if he heard the prayer, he asserted and insisted that the minister had not prayed for him at all. "He never said, 'Poor Pomp' once." The good clergyman was informed of Pompey's incredulity; and in the afternoon he prayed with renewed and real fervor for "Poor Pomp" by name, to Pompey's great edification and consolation.

Young men in this age and country have no more reason to charge neglect upon church-members for not speaking to them about their souls than had Pomp to charge neglect upon his pastor. All their grievance is, that the deacons do not say, "Poor Pomp." They have not been invited to tea. I do not say that the elders shall not, for Christ and the Church, invite them to tea, and talk about their souls. If they have no power to reason, if they have no original thought, if they have no conviction and no principle, perhaps there is nothing left but to work upon their emotion. If "poor Pomp" is helped by the mention of his name to reach feebly up to God, it is a small thing — and yet not small — to name him. But I do say that the young man is egotistic, self-conceited, and, as yet, very shallow, who brings this forward as a reason why he has not joined the church. That is a question for himself to decide. Either it is his duty, or it is not.

Society furnishes him with every opportunity of enlightenment on the subject. No man has spoken to him about his soul? But has he spoken to any man about his? The church-member has no more responsibility for the young man's soul than the young man has for the church-member's. Whatever the pulpit says to its elders, it ought ever and ever to say to the young man: "If thou art wise, thou art wise for thyself; but, if thou scornest, thou alone shalt bear it." What the State and the Church want, is, not the surging and swaying of the populace, not the blind force of an unreasoning multitude, not people who go as they are led, but strong individual character, — young men and young women who think for themselves; who unite with the church, or remain outside, from intelligent conviction, from well founded principle, — men who can give a reason for their hope and their action; who can reject error without becoming disgusted with truth; who can resist temptation, without crying to others to resist that which is no temptation; who can do right simply and naturally, without making a scene, and without calling upon bystanders to come and behold how sublimely they are devoting themselves to the cause of Christ; who can stand erect, without clamoring to be bolstered up by religious nurses, or supported by ecclesiastical standing-stools; who go to church to worship God, and not to be patted on the back by an elder; who walk the narrow path in stout leathern shoes and with their own oaken staff, and do not need to be escorted along on tiptoe by some sturdier servitor.

Different cases require different treatment. There is no law save the universal law of love and wisdom. Doubtless there are times when a gentle and friendly word falls like balm on the wounded spirit. Blessed is the man who pours in oil and wine. Doubtless there are shrinking and sensitive souls that must be won out of their shadowy solitude into the more wholesome sunshine of companionship. There are reckless, rollicking revellers, whom a word may touch, whom a tender solicitude may soften, when sermons and books would glance off, and leave them unmoved. But behind all these remains a class whose stock in trade is innuendoes, insinuations, and accusations against the Church, — men who want to be coaxed and cajoled; who love the little sensation of standing out, and having the Church bemoan itself over its languor and laxity in bringing them in; who reckon themselves a sort of martyr to the neglect of Christians.

To such it seems, sometimes, as if it would be well to preach the gospel after another fashion, — at least, by way of experiment, — and say, "Why, go to the Devil, if you choose. It is nobody's affair but your own. If you prefer dissipation and death to honor and life, who is the loser? You may bring shame to innocence, and grief to gray hairs; but their trouble is short, and to them "joy cometh in the morning." It is your own self, and nobody else, who will bear the sorrow and the scar forever. But you are a free agent. Go your own way. If you prefer to stay outside, on a fancied punctilio, rather than come in to our hospitality and society; if you think it more manly to stand aloof, and criticise the brethren, than to cast in your lot with them, at the risk of being yourself criticised, — do so. "If thou art wise, thou art wise for thyself." But do not think, that, in so doing, you are rebuking the brethren, or approving yourself a martyr. You are but showing yourself a foolish and sentimental young person, who needs, like Mr. Smallweed, a thorough shaking-up. You cannot yourself think your soul is of any great account, if you will maunder on seven years because nobody happened to speak to you about it."

This may seem a harsh gospel, and I admit that it should not be indiscriminately preached; but I am sure there is a mental fibre that needs it.

The ignorant and stupid outcasts of civilization, the unhappy, poverty-stricken waifs who have not so much as heard whether there be any Holy Ghost, any Christ, any loving Father, — these must be minutely and perhaps individually instructed; but why should an intelligent, church-going adult need any one to speak to him about his soul? Especially why should he wish or expect a stranger to do so? It is a delicate matter, when you come to that. There are few more cloistered and sacred possessions than a man's soul. If the principle is once established, that the presence of a person in church is sufficient reason for any member to question him about the most interior concerns of life, the result will be, that persons who have any individuality worth speaking of will stay away from church. Some learned and pious ancient worthy is said to have made a resolution never to talk with any one five minutes, without speaking about the salvation of his soul. Would he think it proper to introduce the topic of a man's income, courtship, or domestic economy after an acquaintance of five minutes? Yet these are concerns far less intimate than religion. They concern only a man's dealings with his fellow-beings: religion concerns his relations with his Maker, — relations which even to himself are but imperfectly comprehended, and by his Maker only are thoroughly understood. Shall the acquaintance of five minutes' standing presume to intermeddle?

But it is said that these relations are of so much more importance than any other as to justify extraordinary measures. Extraordinary caution, but not extraordinary precipitancy. The more momentous and delicate an affair, the more careful should we be in treating it. It is safer to leave the intelligent mind, the enlightened heart, of our age and country, to the influence of the Holy Spirit working through Church and Bible and Divine Providence, than it is to attempt to mould it with irreverent and unskilful hand. When Uriah profaned the ark of God with unseemly touch, he not only lost his life, but he did not advance the ark. The amount of mischief that is done by a coarse handling of the soul's most delicate concerns has never been estimated; but souls are grievously marred. We are told of the persons, here and there, rescued from sin by a rough and ready word; but no account has ever been kept of those who have been repelled, disgusted, and alienated.

I question the kind of conversion that comes of hob-nobbing. Unless a man is convicted of sin, and convinced of truth, strongly enough to come out against the one, and for the other, of his own will and motion, is any thing accomplished? Tea-drinking and caresses and sympathy are pleasant; but they are not principle. It is pleasanter to be taken by the hand to a cheerful home than to go to a boarding-house alone; but it is an appeal to the social, and not to the religious nature. I do not say it is wrong or undesirable: on the contrary, not only Christianity, but humanity, demands, that, on every possible occasion, we should let our light shine, — the light of home and love and human brotherhood no less than that of integrity and uprightness. But that does not dispense with the necessity of discriminating between affection, gratitude, and social magnetism, on one side, and innate rectitude on the other. The result of our ecclesiastical tactics does not indicate so brilliant a success as to forbid all question as to the wisdom of the methods by which it has been obtained. Neither in the quantity nor the quality of our church-membership are we invulnerable. We are not sufficiently rooted and grounded in the faith that conversion is good for any thing only as it affects character. If the only change is, that a man goes regularly to church and Sunday school, while formerly he went to neither, he might as well have staid unconverted. If the only result of the tea-party be, that a young man is now an active member of the church, whereas he was formerly no member at all, the elder who invited him has not got back the money's worth of his tea. A man is not necessarily a particle better for teaching in Sunday schools, or going to prayer-meetings. To draw him into the church by flattering his vanity, by ministering to his self-love, by making him an important and conspicuous partner in a close corporation, is not certainly improving either the man or the church. He ought to come in by his own mind's working and his own heart's leaning. He ought to come in, at once being and becoming a stronger man, more patient, more energetic, more considerate, more temperate or more spirited, more industrious or less worldly, more generous or less prodigal, more severe or more lenient, according to his weakness. It does not signify whether or not he is ready to lead the brethren in prayer; but is he less grasping in his dealings than he was, less vain, less self-centred, less exacting? Do the sinners whom he trades with find him more punctual in keeping his engagements? Is he more careful not to be sharp and selfish at home? Is he more charitable in judgment, more intolerant of rascality, even in respectable garb? It is not those who are the most forward to speak, or to be spoken to, about their souls, who have necessarily the most pure and undefiled and trustworthy religion. There are people who would rather be talked about as backsliders than not be talked about at all. There are people who will boast of the enormity of their sins as if it were a feather in their cap. And I know a woman who never sings more merrily at her washtub than when she has set a whole class-meeting groaning and praying over her "fall from grace."

It only needs a certain degree of self-confidence, self-conceit, and coarseness, to enable anybody to "speak" to anybody. What we need is not encouragement to prey upon our neighbor's privacy, but warning to respect it. Young people need far less aid in laying their personal responsibility upon others, and refusing to be upright, except upon the church's solicitation, than in learning the meaning and dignity of silence, and the profound reverence, which, under all circumstances, and on every occasion, should be paid to the living soul.

THE LAND OF BROKEN PROMISE.

THE LAND OF BROKEN PROMISE.

THE reverend and venerable Dr. Woolsey, late president of Yale College, publicly expresses his dismay at our national plight, and our especial need of hope, "aside from personal considerations, when the affairs of the country are conducted with so little wisdom, and when political corruption seems to be becoming more and more rampant."

Mr. James Russell Lowell is made so uncomfortable by reading American newspapers abroad, that he introduces into a solemn and stately elegiac poem upon Agassiz the teacher, his deep disgust with the country of his birth and of Agassiz's adoption. This song sings he from over the sea:—

> "The festering news we half despise,
>   Yet scramble for, no less,
> And read of public scandal, private fraud;
> Crime flaunting scot-free, while the mob applaud;
> Office made vile to bribe unworthiness;
> And all the unwholesome mess.
> The Land of Broken Promise serves of late
> To teach the Old World how to wait."

And, as all roads lead to Rome, "The Congregationalist," one of the oldest, ablest, and most influential religious newspapers in the country, deduces from the Mill River disaster the rather remarkable moral reflection, that our own community, and our whole nation, should " be admonished by it of a danger in which we are, from the great volume of political corruption reservoired at Washington, which ever and anon gives warning of its dangerous power, and which at any moment may deluge the broad land with distress. Charles Reade's attempted remedy was to ' blow up the waste-weir.' If something could be seasonably blown up at the capital, there might be less danger to the land."

The affairs of this Land of Broken Promise are conducted by — or we may say, "the reservoir of political corruption at Washington" is divided into — three departments, — the executive, the judicial, and the legislative. The President, the head of the Executive Department, is a regularly educated man, a graduate of West Point. The Vice-President is not a graduate, but is a member of an evangelical church in good and regular standing. Of the seven members of the cabinet, the advisory council of the Executive, at least five have a college education. Of the nine judges of the Supreme Court, I assume (what I do not know) that all are graduates of colleges. Of three hundred and forty-eight members of the present Congress, one hundred and seventy are recorded as having received a college-education, most of them being graduates. A very large majority of the remaining one hundred and seventy-eight — so large, that we may say all, with a few exceptions — have received an academic education. The ratio of liberally educated, and even of college educated, men in the National Government, is, therefore, overwhelmingly larger than that outside of government. It is safe to assume (and, if I am wrong, I can easily be proved wrong by exact statistics), that of the eight millions of adult men, who, according to the ordinary rule of ratio, may be reckoned citizens of the United States, not more than fifty thousand are college graduates. Of the Executive Department, then, two-thirds are college graduates. Of the Judicial Departments, all are college graduates. Of the Legislative Department, nearly, if not quite, one-half are college-bred, and nearly all have an academic training; while, outside of Congress, the college-men are only one in one hundred and sixty of the whole male adult population. When we reflect, that, almost universally, the colleges and academies of the country — if not dedicated definitely and formally, like Harvard University, to Christ and the Church — were yet founded in the interests of religion as truly as of science, by devout and learned men, we see that government is not made up of the scum and dregs of our country, nor even of its average " sweetness and light;" but it is the outcome of our churches and colleges, the product of what is considered to be our highest intelligence and virtue. If, then, the average wisdom and honesty of the government be less than those of the outside world, it certainly leads to the supposition, that church and college train to weakness and wickedness, and not to purity and strength. It would seem that the fountains of political corruption are to be found in our nurseries of religion and learning. Nor, I trust, will it be deemed impertinent for me to suggest to college faculties and other clergy, that though standing afar off, and "blowing up something" at Washington, is a favorite and an easy method of political reformation, it may not really be the most thorough, rational, and effective. When our schools and academies, our colleges and churches, have so remodelled their modes of study and their moral influence as to become potent for good rather than for evil; when they can contribute to the government men stronger against temptation, nobler in the adoption of ends, and wiser in the pursuit of means, than are reared outside of college-walls, — then may we look for political regeneration. But so long as the body-politic outside of government — of which the very offscouring of the earth is a large component part, and into which comes liberal education in a severely diminished ratio — is a comparatively virtuous and pure body, and the body called government — though almost entirely free from the low element characterized as the "dangerous classes," and composed largely of the very flower of civilization and Christianity — is so filthy and nauseous as to be a "reservoir of political corruption," from whose defilement the purer outside world should be defended, it must be agreed that our science and our Christianity are both failures, and that the most urgent need of the day is a radical reform in our institutions of learning and religion.

I speak as a fool, "yet as a fool receive me." My acquaintance with colleges is limited; yet such straws as I have seen fluttering harmonize with the above recorded facts in marking the direction of the wind. When a young man of cultivated and honored ancestry, having reached his twentieth year not only without reproach, but with signal honor, becomes a member of that university of which Prof. James Russell Lowell is so distinguished an ornament, to be, in his senior year, expelled with his fair young name tarnished, and his future marred; when, in the same university, a young man attends recitation every day, and is summoned to recite only once in four weeks; when a man whose European reputation is wider even than that of Mr. James Russell Lowell declares that the headquarters of Harvard College are in the Parker House bar-room, and all the Harvard world applauds the " hit ; " when an express-box brought to a student's door suggests " wine " to the first passer-by ; when that member of the cabinet who has been most denounced for incapacity, not to say imbecility, for connivance at fraud, not to say fraud, for insignificance, not to say imperceptibility (I am not now presuming to give an opinion of my own, but am merely stating the case as our journals give it), when this secretary is a graduate with honors from Harvard University, — I cannot help suspecting that no inconsiderable part of the " unwholesome mess " which disturbed the digestion of Prof. James Russell Lowell was cooked at the university with which his name is indissolubly connected. When I hear the president of that college which Dr. Woolsey for many years distinguished by his fame, and nurtured with his counsels, characterizing an assemblage of twenty or thirty of his own students as " a drunken crowd ; " when its attempts at discipline are so clumsy, that a New York newspaper, prominent for courtesy and calm comprehensiveness, and wholly friendly to the college, rebukes it for inflicting " most arbitrary and excessively unjust punishment for questionable offence," — I cannot think that the " little wisdom " of the National Government is the nearest target for Dr. Woolsey's arrows. When the secret society of a college carries its brutal and bacchanal initiation orgies to the cruel death of the student to be initiated; when the servile and stupid custom of hazing has been allowed to take such root in our colleges, that the effort to extirpate it is heard from Michigan to Maine; when resistance to constituted authority goes to the length of a secession of two whole classes; and the relation between teacher and taught, even in our most prominent colleges, is publicly, and without contradiction, characterized as " a system of mere arbitrary and irresponsible power on the one hand, and, of course, of antagonism, and often rebellion, on the other,"— I cannot admit that the National Government is *par excellence* the corporate body which stands in need of more wisdom, and demands the greatest help from hope. It is not unnatural that college officers, with all their traditions and habits of absolute sovereignty, should be impatient at the slow and halting steps of a government hampered by constitutional law and the rights of the individual; but, apart from the fact that our National Government has not the power to compel all men — even in its own employ or its own constituency — to be virtuous, the success of the colleges in compelling their own students to virtue has not been so brilliant as to make any large portion of our countrymen desirous to change, with all its drawbacks, the national for the collegiate form of government.

It cannot be supposed that Mr. James Russell Lowell, writing from a far, foreign country, and loving his own with the idealization which absence and distance always lend, could formally and publicly brand her with a name of dishonor, without an overpowering cause, as well as the bitterest pain.

What was that cause? What does Mr. Lowell mean when he names the United States " The Land of Broken Promise "? What promise has our country made, and what has she failed to keep, that she should be signalized above all nations as *the* land of broken promise? Her Declaration of Independence and her Constitution are the formal statement of her faith and practice, and the standard by which she should be judged. Has she been false to the one or to the other? Has she failed to maintain her independence? Has she faltered in her efforts to secure to her people life, liberty, and the pursuit of happiness, or to derive the power of her government from the consent of the governed? Has she been careless to form a perfect union, to establish justice, to insure domestic tranquillity, to provide for the common defence, to promote the general welfare, to secure the blessings of liberty? Has she been reckless of the Constitution expressly framed for the furtherance of these ends? It is not simply that she fought eight years to maintain her independence, and four years to uphold her Constitution (at what a cost of blood, none knows better than Mr. Lowell): it is that she has been so successful in securing independence, she prizes so highly the freedom she has won, that her pride and exultation have become proverbial, — a theme for the gay banter of her friends, the malignant caricature of her foes. It is that her Constitution is so fixed in the regard of the people, that it forms the ultimate appeal of the bitterest partisan of all parties. The one unpardonable sin of the political world, which is not to be so much as named among us, is violation of the Constitution. What other promise has America made to the world than individual liberty and constitutional government of the people by the people?

Or is it not the government, but the individuals who compose the nation, who give the nation its bad pre-eminence? But when have we even promised to secure universal personal perfection? When and where did this country take out a patent for private individual regeneration? Nowhere but in the brains of theorists. The men who founded, and the men who sustain, this nation, know well that it is not a form of government which moulds character, but character which shapes the form of government. They were never so foolish as to suppose that human depravity would die out in the purest republic: on the contrary, they assume, in the strongest manner, its indefinite existence by making laws to restrain and diminish it. Undoubtedly they believed that what was peculiar in their institutions would not minister to vice; that in the greater happiness, freedom, and prosperity which they wished to secure, there would be less temptation to, less commission of crime. Were they wrong? Is private character less honorable here than in the Old World? Is the standard of truth and honesty lower? Is the word of a gentleman less binding? Is there less payment of debt, more trickery in trade, more cheating of servants, less chastity, less charity, less courtesy to women, less consideration for a neighbor? On the contrary, do not our higher and our lower classes compare favorably with those of any other country? Is an American less trusted in the shops of Europe than a Russian? Is an English gentleman more courteous, is an Italian peasant more comfortable, is a Prussian mechanic more free, is a French tradesman more honest, is a Spanish laborer more intelligent, than his American comrade?

"Crime flaunting scot-free while the mob applauds."

What crime flaunts scot-free? and what mob applauds? Is it murder? is it theft? is it drunkenness? On the contrary, this Land of Broken Promise serves of late nothing more noticeable than a fixed, resolute determination to ferret out and annihilate all malfeasance in office, all breach of trust. No "public scandal" has made part of Mr. Lowell's "festering news," but in connection with, and often in consequence of, an effort to remove it. The great wickedness of Mr. Tweed and the New York Ring was successful only so long as it was secret. It flaunted only to fall. No sooner was it set forth to the world than a universal rage tore down upon it, and scattered its perpetrators to prison and to exile. In a sort of *renaissance* of virtue, our zeal has sometimes outrun our discretion. We have pushed "investigation" sometimes to an absurd and injurious limit, and to the distress and serious detriment of men who were not only innocent, but who would have been considered innocent by a more dispassionate survey. Through mere good-nature, weak, perhaps, and harmful, but not unmanly, offence has been condoned, but never applauded. Criminals have been, through mercy, let off lightly; but their crime has not been flaunted. So strong is the determination to put down fraud, that our censure is often too swift and sweeping. We denounce with too little discrimination. It is because the conscience of the country is so almost morbidly keen and alert, that Mr. Lowell is troubled by "festering news." A single English railway pays regularly every year, without a ripple on the surface of English society, seventy-five thousand pounds sterling to the English parliament for precisely such service as a few congressmen were suspected of having been, for a single session, urged to render in the Credit Mobilier affair, and the mere suspicion of which rocked the whole country with alarm and indignation, and no doubt hastened, if it did not cause, the death of two men most prominently concerned.

Or may it be that our non-resumption of specie payment constitutes us the Land of Broken Promise? But are we alone in resorting to notes of credit in order to sustain the burden of a prolonged and costly war? Is it not the common mode of distributing the expense? What great nation has ever carried on a great war without it? And, if so, may we not have adopted the general course, not from signal and degraded love of cheating, but because there appears to be some inherent wisdom or necessity in the way itself? The United States did in this precisely what England did for twenty-three years during and after the Napoleonic wars, — she had a paper currency not redeemed in gold. England, indeed, went one great step beyond our government, for she made her people take the notes of the Bank of England; whereas our people have been asked only to take their own promises to pay. But, whenever and wherever the United States has agreed to pay gold, gold she has paid. The old debts, maturing when our civil war was flagrant, and gold at an enormous premium, were paid at a fearful cost and sacrifice by our government; but paid they were, in solid coin, to the uttermost farthing. In whose eyes does our Punic faith make us the Land of Broken Promise? Not in those of our own people; for during the sudden and severe panic of 1873, when great houses went down, and no house seemed firm, the nation's notes were in as great demand, and of as sound value, as gold in other panics. Not in the eyes of foreign financiers; for our bonds abroad stand to-day higher than those of any European nation, England alone excepted; and this in the markets of Europe. Our hundreds of millions of Fives sold by the famous syndicate, brought par in coin; while the French Fives, on the market at the same time, were sold at a very considerable discount. It has, moreover, been currently and confidently reported in the treasury circles of Washington, that Secretary Bristow had the most flattering offers for funding the entire amount of United States Sixes as low, possibly, as four and a half, certainly as low as five, — offers, let it be remembered, from the bankers of Europe. How is it that the Land of Broken Promise maintains this high credit by that most sensitive of all tests, the purse? How is it, that, if our promises be lies, the people at home and abroad seem wholly given over to believe the lie? How is it that the bankers of Europe repose the most absolute confidence in our integrity, while an American poet goes abroad to hold his country up to contumely?

I offer no opinion whatever as to the right or the wrong of specie basis, or legal tender, or any monetary measure whatever. It may be that we could have waged our war without paper. It is easy now to say it, and perhaps not easy to disprove it, and perhaps not possible to prove it. At the time, we thought we could not. It may be that we ought to have dispensed with paper credit before this. I leave these matters entirely untouched; but what I do maintain is, that there is nothing to indicate that the nation intends to forswear her plighted faith, or that any large number of men, either at home or abroad, have a lively fear that she will do so. Repudiation did but stir, and she was beaten down. There is a question of ways and means. It may be that a country so wide, with interests so diverse, can arrive at a wise and harmonious conclusion on a question of so vital import, only with infinite debate and delay. It is not enough that a course be right and proper: it must be seen to be right and proper east and west, north and south, by the ignorant and the intelligent, by the freedman and the freeborn. We have never promised the world, or ourselves, to be over-wise in finance; nor do we imagine that wisdom will die with us. We must learn, as other nations learn, truth by experience. They are but dreamers who imagine that any form of government can open a royal road to virtue, fame, or fortune.

Did Agassiz, that Agassiz whose loss Mr. Lowell so tenderly deplores in the same breath in which he stigmatizes the country that welcomed and adopted him, — did Agassiz find it a Land of Broken Promise? From the day on which he came, a stranger, to her shores, till the day on which he lay dead, a well-beloved son, did she fail his hope? Did she refuse him any opportunity, begrudge him any means, deny him any honor?

Charles Dickens, inoculated with what venom I do not know, could write of " that republic but yesterday let loose upon her noble course, and but to-day so maimed and lame, so full of sores and ulcers, foul to the eye, and almost hopeless to the sense, that her best friends turn from the loathsome creature in disgust." But, if she be indeed in such evil case, it would seem more decorous for her own sons not to enshrine her shame in monumental verse, but rather

> "Pay the reverence of old days
>   To that dead fame,
> Walk backward with averted gaze,
>   And hide the shame."

In the midst of the crimination and recrimination, the accusations and investigations, the proved guilt and the uncontradicted slander with which our newspapers abound, it is not strange that uneducated men, whose knowledge of history is derived chiefly from newspapers, whose acquaintance with the experience of other peoples and other ages is but vague and slight, should view the situation with dismay, should feel that we have fallen on evil days, should fear that " political corruption is becoming more and more rampant."

But it is surprising to see educated people doing precisely the same thing. What is culture for, if it be not to enable its possessor to make intelligent comparisons? What is the good of an acquaintance with the past, if it be not to give us a more accurate judgment of the present? The average length of life is said to be about forty years. Looking at this fact alone, and seeing that man is made capable of living comfortably for seventy years, we might despair of the future, and say that his ignorance and recklessness had already reduced his span from seventy to forty years, and set the race on the sure road to annihilation. But, when a survey of the past has informed us that of old time the average length of life was thirty years, we see that our course is really in a different direction; and our jeremiad should be a pæan that science and virtue have already added ten years to the life of man.

Why do not our sages, instead of joining the mob,

and reviling the present for vices and errors which are patent to all, and even for processes which are neither errors nor vices, — why do they not bring out of their treasury things old as well as new, and increase the value of popular criticism by making it intelligent? The mechanic and day-laborer cannot be expected to know; but the professor and the clergyman surely ought to know and teach that society has improved, and not deteriorated, since the early days of the republic. It is less gross, less animal, more pure and elevated; and in this elevation public and political life has shared. What was tolerated then would now consign men to infamy. Charges of corruption were as fierce then as now; but many things which would now be condemned as dishonest were then considered but a part of the " regular routine," and have lost character only as the atmosphere has become clearer, the national and private conscience more sensitive.

The fact, also, that the names which we now hold in highest honor were most sweepingly traduced in their own day, ought, it would seem, to teach our learned men to make allowance for the recklessness of eager and irresponsible persons, whose interest it is to startle. The same shafts of corruption, intrigue, and selfishness that are levelled at the sons were levelled at the fathers. The country was in the same danger then as now of being betrayed and dishonored by the ignorant and unprincipled men who were managing the government. So long ago as March 10, 1779, the disheartened editor declared that "universal despondency seemed to spread itself through every class of men that were led to reflect either upon the weight of domestic calamity or the political derangement of the government."

While Washington was yet alive, there were not wanting those who declared that he had slept away his time in the field till the finances of the country were completely exhausted; that John Adams was always a speller after places and offices, that he never contemplated the origin of government, or comprehended any thing of first principles; that John Jay was always the sycophant of every thing in power; and that the Federalists were but dignified traitors. "The character which Mr. Washington has attempted to act in the world is a sort of non-describable, chameleon-colored thing called 'prudence.' It is, in many respects, a substitute for principle; and it is so nearly allied to hypocrisy that it easily slides into it." The treaty which this imbecile administration made with France had nothing to boast of but the poltroon's right to let another kick him. It was the pusillanimity of the Washington faction that brought upon America the loss of character she suffered in the world. The wanton profligacy of John Adams and his friends made him seem like a debauched libertine, whom a rich and virtuous woman had selected for her husband, spending all she was worth, and getting into debt every day. Parson Read of Massachusetts is accused of getting six dollars a day in Congress, and paying half a dollar to a young sprig of divinity for every sermon preached for the old parson while at Congress. The last day of Washington's administration was hailed with delight as the beginning of an era in which his name should cease to give a currency to political iniquity, and to legalize corruption. Had a fastidious gentleman been living in Paris in 1777 and 1778, his ears would have been as much offended by "festering news" of that mischievous and intriguing commission of which Benjamin Franklin was at the head as they have been by any public scandal or private fraud in this year of grace 1875.

It was Mr. Arthur Lee who found fault, and it was Benjamin Franklin with whom the fault was found, in our negotiations with France. "It is impossible to describe to you," writes this pure, this patriotic, this incorruptible man, "to what a degree this kind of intrigue has disgraced, confounded, and injured our affairs here. The observation of this at headquarters has encouraged and produced throughout the whole a spirit of neglect, abuse, plunder, and intrigue in the public business, which it has been impossible for me to prevent or correct. . . . I see in every department neglect, dissipation, and private schemes." And in almost every distinguished man who was prominent in aiding our cause in France, the pure, sharp, argus eyes of Mr. Arthur Lee saw only a greed of gold, an unscrupulous and dishonest plot to amass wealth for himself.

In 1790 there were not wanting remonstrants against this over-censoriousness. Says one, June 9, 1790, —

> "I wish the Americans were more attentive to their *duty*. Not only numerous complaints are uttered against the measures of Congress, but evil *surmisings* and *predictions*. One predicts they will consume a long session, and disagree at last about the *mode* of doing the business. . . . A third apprehends it is not their *intention* to establish public credit, but to waste one session after another in speculations and intrigues for their private advantage. How irrational is all this! Ask any one of these complainers and surmisers, if *he* would act so unwittingly and inconsistent a part, were he in Congress. He will confidently answer, No! . . . More time having been spent in national arrangements, and forming a system for the establishment of public credit than some expected, *they* are ready to draw the worst conclusions, suppose our representatives will quarrel like children, and part without accomplishing their business. Let us *honor ourselves* too much to believe it possible that we can be so deceived in the men to whom we have committed the honor and happiness of our country."

Would not this gentle rebuke apply equally well to-day? The complaints are the same. The long

sessions of Congress, the failure **to agree, private
greed** instead **of public spirit, prolonged** debate regarding the establishment of national credit: they are
the same sounds with **which our ears are** so familiar.
We have been harping on **my** daughter, and still she
lives. **We have not unsealed an El Dorado, whose**
waters **have power** to quench disease, and **give immortal youth. We have not** established an Utopia,
where all men's good is each **man's rule.** We have
not reconstructed the human **heart, and produced a**
race without sinful tendencies. **We have** not levelled
the partition-wall between rich and poor, or caused that
one star should not differ from another star **in glory.**
But we have secured a greater degree of personal **liberty** and self-government than the world has hitherto
seen in a republic **of** vaster proportions, and with
strength proven by resistance of the severest shocks.
Our working-classes, the rank and file of a nation,
suffer less from the misery of poverty, have an intelligence more widely diffused, and a greater command of
the decencies, the comforts, and the refinements of life,
than those of any other **country.** We are far behind
the optimist's faith; but we are, also, far ahead of the
pessimist's fear. The Old World, which has not largely
dealt **in** an absolutely free criticism of the governor
by the governed, may **be a** little misled by seeing our
secret sins set forth with an almost exaggerated frank-

ness in the columns of the newspapers. But, surely, Americans who have been familiar from their youth up with a freedom of the press which often lapses into license, and which is subject to scarce any other than the natural laws of repression and re-action, they, certainly, ought not to be deceived by any abandonment of self-accusation. One might just as reasonably charge the clergy with crime and corruption, because Henry Martyn and David Brainerd indulged in a fervor of self-abasement. Mr. Martyn and Mr. Brainerd, and a great cloud of newspaper witnesses, use language which strictly belongs only to an estate of great sin and misery; but probably none would be more surprised than themselves to find that this language was not apprehended in a Pickwickian sense. If our literary and learned men would give themselves to teaching us the accurate use of words, the awful force of language, the natural affinities of thought and terms, the wickedness of divorcing an idea from its expression, of filling a word with a meaning that does not belong to it, of transforming a suspicion into a fact, a conjecture into an assertion, an incident into an event, an accident into a trait, gossip into history, — they would do a good service to the cause of truth, of patriotism, and of morality, for which we should all have reason to be grateful.

One of the greatest safeguards of popular government

is popular criticism; and popular criticism is valuable in proportion as it is discriminating, intelligent, and just, not in proportion as it is censorious or laudatory. No easier way of being patriotic offers itself than to decry the methods, motives, and acts of those who are conducting the affairs of the country. There is, and there always will be, sufficient material for censure; but ill-directed censure, general denunciation, indefinite sneers, are of very little use in reforming. If the object of censure be not to exhibit one's own superior standard, but to improve and purify, it should be pointed, accurate, and sure. At the basis of all sound and useful criticism is knowledge. Some knowledge is hard to be got at, and some would seem to be easy of access; yet much resounding censure is apparently founded on an entire absence of both kinds.

With every recurring close of the sessions of Congress, the custodian of public virtue is shocked by the accumulated legislation of the few last weeks of Congress. All the early weeks, he severely declares, are wasted in useless debate; and all the real work is crammed into the closing portion. It is the hot weather, it is the approaching adjournment, which makes members sensible. They dawdle at the beginning, and in the end rush bills through with reckless haste.

But an observer who looks at things themselves,

and not at the mere rumor and surface of things, would see that a great part of the work of legislation is done in committee. Not in the great halls of the house or the senate, but in the small committee-rooms, bills are matured. Each bill is there discussed by a few men selected to represent the opinion of the whole body, — selected by election in the senate, by appointment of the speaker in the house. Yet the speaker is bound in his appointments to represent not his own opinions, but the opinions of the house. These committees have each its own room, where bills are discussed with entire freedom, and often at great length. It naturally happens that the bulk of these bills are ready to be reported at about the same time. When the bills are matured for presentation, Congress can appoint a time for adjournment. That is, the pressure of business does not come because adjournment is fixed; but adjournment can be fixed because business is now all ready to press. During the early weeks of the session, the fifty committees were laboring in their committee-rooms to reconcile opposing opinions and clashing interests, and present measures which should be likely to receive the assent of the whole body. During the later weeks of the session, the same fifty committees are striving to bring forward the various bills, one after another, in as rapid succession as may be. Is it strictly intelligent to say that the processes are useless, the results alone are work? Many bills are of such a character as not to enlist universal interest. Many men trust in these matters to the judgment and honor of the committee that has them in charge, or to the vote of other well-known men; and these bills pass without debate, that is, are "rushed through." Sometimes this confidence is misplaced: a bad bill is passed, and mischievous legislation is the result. But, in a vast majority of cases, confidence is not misplaced. Of this vast majority we hear nothing; but the mischievous bill that slips through makes a great outcry, as is natural and proper: and this is the safeguard. This occasional passage of a bad bill is a reason why people should be vigilant: it is not a reason why they should be despondent, least of all why they should be denunciatory of our institutions. In any case, it is simply impossible that one man should be able to acquaint himself thoroughly, by personal investigation, with the merits of every bill brought forward. The ambition to do it is worse than idle. The man who undertakes to know every thing in Congress is good for nothing, — a failure and a nuisance. The most valuable members are those who have a specialty, and are authority on that point. It is on this principle that business is conducted, and fame acquired, in the English house of commons. More and more, as our country increases, will congressional business be done in committee. That way, danger lies. Danger lies, also, in the direction of too much legislation. It behooves all good citizens to be on the alert. But it behooves them, also, to sight their game before they fire. Random shooting may startle; but it is likely to do quite as much harm as good. Probably there is about as much censurable delay of business from the earlier to the later weeks of the session as there is a censurable delay of sermons from the earlier to the later hours of the week.

Much debate is characterized as useless on questionable grounds. What is a mere truism to the comprehension of the critic may be matter of doubt to the inferior intellect of the congressman, and even of his constituent. It is not enough for the "hard money" man to know that a specie basis is best: he must get the "paper money" man to believe it also. It is not enough for the Granger to know that the cost of transportation is too high: he must put the railroad man under conviction of sin. Whatever is of broad and vital interest is not likely to be passed in the house without prolonged and even heated debate, no matter how closely it may have been discussed in committee. Religious papers may well quarrel with Congress here. They "know a trick worth two" of these national debates. A minister preaches a sermon through, and lets no dog bark. We may think he has left out a fact or two in his argument on the atonement; that there is a flaw in his reasoning on original sin, a cloud in his definition of the doctrine of substitution; but the good minister has put us under such training, that we dare not open our lips, and he has it all his own way. How long would a sermon last, if, every time the Congregational, Evangelical preacher struck a snag, Brother Charles K. Whipple, and Brother Voysey, and Brother Bishop Potter, and Brother Fulton, and Brother Abbott, and Brother Patton should rise and say, "Will the gentleman allow me to ask a single question?" "Will the gentleman permit me to interrupt him a moment?" "Will the gentleman grant me a few minutes of his time to correct a statement of fact?" "Will the gentleman kindly repeat his last assertion?" — if, in short, he were surrounded by eager antagonists ready to claw and clutch at every lapse from logic, and every weak statement or forced inference? Let me not be arraigned for a mover of sedition; but I sometimes think when I hear, as I sometimes do hear, a good man plodding serenely onward in the pulpit, assuming his premises, begging his questions, confounding his terms, mistaking assertions for conclusions, and upsetting his dish generally, that it might not be wholly insalubrious to have a little "useless debate" introduced into the churches. When I read in the Confession of Faith of the Presbyterian Church, that " elect infants, dying in infancy, are regenerated and saved by Christ, . . . others, not elected, . . . never truly come to Christ, and therefore cannot be saved," I think I should like to see that poor little non-elect infant run the gauntlet of the debate in the house of representatives.

The reservoir of political corruption at Washington, built out of the ruins of the Williamsburg flood, is an illustration of the directness and logic of our censure. All investigation points to bad work, ill faith, as the cause of that disaster. The dam was not built according to specifications; and the specifications themselves fell below the safety mark. The foundation-wall should have been laid three feet below the surface, and it was laid on the surface. It was not properly secured at the ends, and was not thick enough anywhere. The moral that sticks up everywhere out of the wreck is a reform in home-manufactures, the necessity of more scientific, conscientious, thorough work. If any political moral be deducible, it is, How can we expect honesty in our representatives, when our own citizens, the solid men of Massachusetts, church-members and property-holders, are so corrupt and reckless, that, to save a few hundreds of dollars to their own pockets, they will wreck millions of their neighbors', destroy scores of human lives, and spread desolation through hundreds of homes?

Instead of which, Massachusetts — the dear old sly-boots — turns her Mill River on to Washington, where its pure water becomes " a great volume of political corruption, which at any moment may deluge the broad land with distress," but which, we must infer, if kept well dammed up, and only let out as it is wanted, is a legitimate source of wealth and power. However, let us not miss any opportunity of " letting drive " at Washington. Where there is a will there is a way; and he who supposes that way is to be blocked up by any thing so trivial as a flimsy Massachusetts dam has little idea of the fervor of our patriotism.

Another moral drawn from the same disaster is the " sure consequences of the American habit of shiftlessness, of running for luck, of trusting that the bridge will stand for this strain." But why American? Is America the only country whose dams give way? In March, 1864, the dam of the reservoir near Sheffield, in England, was broken down; and a body of water covering seventy-six acres of ground rushed down the gorge of the hills, and swept away two hundred and fifty human beings and a vast amount of property. In 1802 a dam gave way in Spain; and six hundred and eight people were drowned.

Remembering Mr. Plimsoll, shall we not believe that ignorance and recklessness and total depravity are traits of human rather than American, or English, or Spanish nature?

"Peccavimus, but rave not thus."

MISSIONARY MUSINGS.

MISSIONARY MUSINGS.

THE idea is somewhat prevalent, that, while our own churches must have ability, a good disposition is the one thing needful in a missionary. We want the first choice ourselves. What is left is good enough for the heathen. But this notion has been supposed to be confined to the unlearned and unthinking. He who has an adequate idea of the magnitude of the work undertaken in christianizing the world must, apparently, admit that the greatest sagacity, as well as the greatest piety, is required in those who are to be its immediate agents.

But it seems otherwise to the gods who preside over some of our missionary boards. The printed commission used by a certain board in appointing missionaries declares that "this appointment is made on condition that the appointee shall agree, without reservation, to the following stipulations ; namely, —

"1. To become a missionary for life."

This seems a little like a blow in the face, to begin with. Are missionaries, then, a separate ecclesiastical order, or do they belong to the same guild as other ministers? Do the ministers of any Protestant denomination take upon themselves vows of perpetual obligation? If a country clergyman, after ten or twenty years of preaching, finds his throat giving out, he retires from the pulpit, and turns stock-broker. If he contracts a distaste for his work, or grows tired in or of it, or thinks he would like something else better, or accomplish more good in other occupations, he enters a newspaper office, or becomes secretary of a charitable society, or commissioner of jails, or a furniture-dealer, or (such things have been known) he buys a snug little house, and lives on the interest of his money. Is there a single Protestant denomination that forbids it? Has the missionary an inferior rank, that he cannot be allowed the same liberty?

Probably the stipulation is made with the praiseworthy purpose of preventing a waste of the money of the churches. The minister pays his own preparatory expenses. The missionary is sent by the Board; and it would not be economical to furnish him with an outfit for a short term. But to make him serve an apprenticeship for life in order to defray the expense of one journey is rating him at a low figure. Our National Government sends the young man through West Point, and demands only an eight-years' service in return. Is not a missionary of more value than many cadets? And what is the attitude of the missionary toward the home churches? Is he the dependent upon or the almoner of their bounty? Is he an office-seeker, clamorous for outfit and salary, to whom the keepers-at-home may say patronizingly, "Yes, we will give you the place you want, on condition that you stay there the rest of your life, and never let us have to provide for you again," or is he a man whom the office seeks, whom the place craves, who earns his salary, who does not barter away his right of self-direction, who is the peer of his appointers, and may be presumed to have sufficient character, ambition, and philanthropy to know when to retire with honor? Gen. Schenck, Mr. Washburne, Mr. Bancroft, are fitted out by government, and can resign and return the moment they touch a foreign port if they choose. Have the ministers of religion less interest in their work, less perception of the fitness of things, less regard for their good name, than the minister of politics? Must they be bound by an oath, lest they run away from their stations? What does it say of missionaries and missionary work, if only a contract can keep them at it? There are many offices to which men are appointed for life; but I know none to which they are forced to adhere for life. This missionary board has so poor an opinion of its appointees, and the work which it assigns them, that it binds them to it by extraordinary and unusual ties, and imposes upon them restraints and engagements to which no class of ministers at home are called upon to submit, and to which, it may be presumed, they would not submit if they were called.

The appointee agrees:—

"3. To go out deeply imbued with the love of Christ and of souls; profoundly impressed with the danger, the folly, and the guilt of men in heathendom; fully sensible of his call from GOD to preach the gospel; a hearty acceptance of the doctrines and discipline of the [apostolic] Church, and well affected toward its authorities; a profound sense of his constant dependence on divine grace to qualify him for the great work to which he devotes himself, and fully determined to labor in harmony with his brethren, to avoid all causes of irritation, to discourage all factions and strifes in the mission, and all attempts to weaken the bonds between it and the Church at home."

If the appointee has any "realizing sense" of Lindley Murray, he must go out deeply imbued with the grammar of the appointing power, and profoundly impressed with the ignorance and the folly, if not the guilt, of men out of heathendom. The heathen, the Deity, and the [apostolic] Church, autocratic bishops, and quarrelsome brethren, are mingled indiscriminately in the draught which is commended to his lips. Nothing human or divine is foreign to his contract. It is not enough that he is called upon to promise, that, at some future time, he will be deeply imbued with certain sentiments, and profoundly impressed with certain facts: he is required to become responsible for the divine Being. The Board is not content to take his view of the case; but it forces him to go up into the heaven of heavens, and tell us the precise part which the Most High took in the arrangement. But can the divine acts be the subjects of human testimony? When a man says he is fully sensible of his call from God to preach the gospel, do we know any more about it than we knew before? It was a great victory in the old witchcraft trials when spectral evidence was ruled out of court as inadmissible; but it was no more intangible than the evidence which modern man can offer of God's plans and purposes. If the [apostolic] Church believes, with the Roman Catholic Church, that the age of miracles is not past, that the blood of St. Januarius still reddens and bubbles before the eyes of the awe-struck people, and the bread of the sacramental table becomes the body of our Lord Jesus Christ; if God still appears to men in dreams and visions to reveal his will, — then it may be that a man becomes fully sensible of his call from God to preach the gospel. But if with the revelation to St. John the divine ceased the special revelation of God to man, a missionary has no other way of being sensible of his call from God to preach the gospel than the dressmaker has of her call from God to make gowns, or the dentist his call from God to fill teeth. We can judge of what God calls us to do only from the human side: the missionary, like the rest of us, must use his own judgment in deciding where to go. Reason tells every one to do the work for which his character, abilities, and circumstances best fit him. One man is born to the purple, and one to be hewer of wood, and drawer of water. If the purple and fine linen are trailed in the dust of defeat and disaster and degradation; if the hewer of wood passes with swinging, steady step from his native forests to the forefront of battle and a nation's highest place, — what is it but the call of God? God calls us through ability. How can a man know his ability till it is tested? Doubtless many a minister, and perhaps many a missionary, has entered conscientiously upon his work, and led a life of disappointment, discontent, and failure, from simple error of choice. I have heard ministers lament, that, under stress of parental influence or temporary excitement, they adopted their profession, exerted but half their powers, and achieved but partial success; while all their tastes led them in another direction, and all their faculties fitted them for another sphere: but, at the time the choice was made, they would have had no hesitation in avowing themselves fully sensible of their call from God. Really the call was from their parents or their emotions: their mature judgment could attribute it to no higher source.

But while the Board exalts its missionaries to the throne of God with one hand, with the other it keeps the balance true by thrusting them down far below those who remain at home. It demands that the missionary shall agree, fourthly, "to observe and keep the rules and regulations both of the Discipline and the Missionary Manual in their present form, or as they may from time to time be changed hereafter; and also to be governed and guided by the general committee and board of managers of the Missionary Society of the [Infallible Apostolic] Church, and by the bishop having charge of the missions, giving due heed to the instructions and suggestions which they from time to time may send in regard to plans and operations."

> "A man I know,
> But shall not discover,"

is wont to terminate all discussion on female suffrage with the terse and intelligible declaration, "Madam, the end of the matter is this: we have got you down, and we mean to keep you down." Very much of this sort seems the attitude of the apostolic Church toward its missionary. They swear him in for life, and they bind him to observe and keep, not only the rules as they now exist, *but as they may from time to time be changed hereafter.* They do not demand from him a declaration of belief in the infallibility of the Board; but they demand a promise which he ought not to give unless the Board be infallible. Of actual rules he can form a judgment, and such he may intelligently agree to obey; but a rule which is not made he cannot agree to keep, except by divesting himself of his manhood, and following a Board as blindly as the most bigoted Roman Catholic follows the Pope. No matter how preposterous a rule some subsequent revolutionary Board may lay down, he has bound himself beforehand to obey it, and has not even the alternative of resignation. No Romanist requirement is more unreasonable than this. He promises:—

"5. To refrain from making known his grievances in communicating with his friends, and especially in writing to newspapers; to avoid calling in question, in any public way, the policy, plans, or spirit of the missionary administration at home, reserving his opinions or complaints for the general committee, the board of managers, or the bishops having jurisdiction severally in the premises, according to the nature of the case."

[*Signed by the bishops.*]

With a single exception, the good bishops have taken every available method of securing order in Warsaw. But they should have made the candidate agree : —

6. Never to put his printed commission into his hat, and especially never to suffer the wind to blow hard enough to blow his hat off, and whirl his commission into the hands of strangers, especially the newspapers, and thus prevent calling in question in any public way the intelligence, policy, or effectiveness of the missionary administration at home.

This wise regulation was not inserted, though it may be one of those future rules which he has constructively agreed to observe. We have, therefore, the opportunity to remark, that the objection which lies against this commission is, that it is founded on the opposite of intelligence. It appeals to ignorant and undiscriminating piety; and in proportion as a man is wise, in proportion as he understands the meaning and use of words, the limits of thought and obligation, the freedom and dignity of the individual, he rejects it, not only with decision, but with scorn. In direct ratio with his fitness to be a missionary is the impossibility of his agreeing to the condition of becoming one.

No man, no committee of intelligence, would make it incumbent on any one to agree to support a contingent discipline. The first requirement of reason is that the mind shall clearly understand the articles to which it subscribes. The Board demands that its servants shall support an unstated proposition, either from a lack of sufficient mental acuteness to see the absurdity of such a thing, or from a dishonorable disposition to take advantage of a similar presumed lack on the part of the candidate. The wise man refuses to be thus blindly bound. It is only the unthinking who are caught.

Again: when a man agrees to "report his acceptance in writing to the missionary secretaries, and place himself under their direction as to the time of sailing, the mode of conveyance, and the preparation for the voyage," he agrees to something definite, intelligible, practicable. But when he agrees "to go out deeply imbued with the love of Christ and of souls, profoundly impressed with the danger, the folly, and the guilt of men in heathendom, fully sensible of his call from God to preach the gospel, and of his constant dependence on divine grace to qualify him for the great work," he agrees to he knows not what. Whose lead and line shall be used in fathoming his love, to tell whether it be deep or shallow? And suppose the party of the second part should at some future time affirm that the party of the first had violated his contract, and was not deeply imbued, or profoundly impressed, or fully sensible, how is the latter to prove or disprove it? He makes a contract regarding possessions which are intangible, immeasurable, incapable of being made the objects of contract. He agrees at a certain future time to be in a certain state of mind. The committee stipulates for emotions. The state of mind may be a very proper one, and the emotions highly becoming to the occasion; but neither the understanding which requires, nor that which subscribes to, these conditions, is of a lofty or discriminating order. The commission is a medley of possibilities and impossibilities, of divine grace and human botch, of sentiment and steamers. The only pleasant feature of the whole form is the painful, scrupulous, ever-vigilant care taken to repress insurrection, and secure obedience. Evidently the venerable bishops have had a hard time of it. Apparently the heathen have not given them half as much trouble as the brethren. These missionaries must be a restive folk. The managers have but a passing word upon the perils of Pagans; but they exhaust the resources of ingenuity in building barricades against the machinations of the men who are conspiring to convert them. One word for the glory of God is followed by ten for that of the board of managers. It is very well for the missionaries and the heathen to depend upon divine grace; but the bishops want it down in black and white. They lift one eye to the hills whence cometh their help; but they keep the other on the valleys, to see that no unruly brother take advantage of their devoutness to indulge in revolt against their dominion. In one breath, the candidate agrees that he will be imbued with the love of Christ; in the next, that he will be well affected toward the church authorities. Not a religious plank is brought forward for the platform, but this belabored Board is sure to be bobbing behind it. Between the secretaries and the manuals, the general committees and board of managers, the bishops and other clergy, the missionary must sometimes be hard pushed to know which king it is to whom he has sworn allegiance.

And the worst of it is, that he cannot have the comfort of writing home to his sweetheart about it. If the Board cannot prevent the formation of steam, it can, at least, shut down the valves, and prevent its escape. The Rev. Mr. Brown may grumble about the stupidity of Secretary Smith in sending him around the Horn, instead of across the Continent; but he shall not permit his grumbling to reverberate in Isabella's epistles. The Board fears its missionaries even writing love-letters. Its model correspondent would be that laconic young man, who, being commissioned to break gently to distant parents the tidings of their son's violent death, fulfilled his mission by writing:—

"MR. A.

"*Dear Sir,*—A coyote has eaten your son's head off."

In short, if we were to judge from this commission, we should say that the missionary force consisted of two parties,— the Board of Managers, which stays at home, and whose work is chiefly and constantly a fierce struggle to maintain and perpetuate its own supreme power; and the missionaries proper, who go abroad, and whose chief industry is to distract the councils, neutralize the action, and destroy the authority, of the Board. He might, also, hazard the conjecture, that, between the upper and the nether millstone, the heathen would be ground exceeding small.

" Another Board appropriates a hundred dollars per child toward their support (the support of 'the children of missionaries, who have been left in this country for education, or who have lost their parents by death'). Mrs. —— and Mrs. —— have been appointed by the American Board to look after the interests of these children. But a further sum is required to meet their expenses; and we write these lines with the hope that some among our readers may be glad to assume the cost of boarding one child for a year or more."

This is beggary. This makes our missionaries mendicants. This is organizing a system with pauperism for one of its foundation-stones.

There may be two opinions about the prudence and wisdom of sending men out to convert the Chinese, the Hindoo, the Zulus, to our faith; there may be two opinions as to the wisdom of sending these men out solitary or in families: but there can be but one opinion about taking care of them and their families after they are sent. We, a great Christian nation, undertake to convert a great Pagan nation. We select men of pure character, of fair, sometimes of eminent abilities, and of expensive education. It is not worth while to talk about the sacrifices they make, partly because that always spoils a sacrifice, and also because they probably make no more than many a man makes in the way of business. Still it is true that their life forbids all hope of wealth, holds out very little prospect of fame, and does, more or less, put them outside the pale of the civilization whereunto they were born. It would seem, then, the least that could be required of us, that we should secure to them a salary sufficient for their support in comfort and respectability. If we are not able to do that, we are not able to found missions. If we are not willing to do that, we need all our missionaries at home.

We raise four or five hundred thousand dollars a year to convert the world to Christianity. It is nothing to boast of. England raises about as much for her royal family. But, perhaps, while it very fairly represents the benevolence of the Church on the one side, it quite as fairly represents the incredulity of the Church on the other. If men really believed that the Brahmins and the Mandarins were in as imminent danger of perishing without their aid, and would be as directly and surely saved by their aid, as the victims of the Chicago fire, they would, no doubt, be as alert and as helpful in the one case as in the other. But though, with only half a million a year, it will take some considerable time thoroughly to christianize the world, it will surely not diminish that time to economize money by degrading missionaries. That is saving at the spigot to lose at the bung. That is bringing Paganism on a level with Christianity by letting Christianity down. We should consider any parish inconceivably mean that should pay its minister so small a salary, that he should be obliged to put his children up at auction, to be bidden off like the town's poor. Ministers in America could not hold their own for a day, if they should go about in the religious newspapers asking people to take their children to board. But missionaries are but ministers, who earn their salaries as really as any ministers. The American Board is but the parish committee that hires them; and the American public, the American Church, is the parish that employs and pays them. If we cannot raise money enough to support ten Christian families, let us support nine, but let us not send out ten, and keep them alive by working the adults, and turning out the children to charity. I think it is better for the heathen to get along with what religion they have, and die in their sins, such as they are, and be judged without law, than it is for freeborn American children to be distrained from their parents, and brought up by charity. If the Chinese go to church in a joss-house, they do no worse than did their fathers before them; but we were reared in a sturdy independence, and, though pulpit and people join hands to make the clergy into a new order of mendicant friars, we cannot succeed in it without serious deterioration. If it is our duty to send missionaries to the heathen at all, it is our duty to furnish them with the means of living comfortably. If it is best to employ missionaries with families, it is imperative to furnish them with means sufficient to support their families without appeals to charity. It is just as disgraceful and demoralizing for the children of a missionary to be hawked about the country in search of homes, as it would be for the children of Boston and Brooklyn ministers. We shall not, perhaps, convert the heathen; but we need not spoil ourselves.

It is not a great while ago that a missionary and his wife (I might as well say a missionary and her husband) were in this country for a visit. They were agreeable and cultivated persons; but the lady was particularly piquant and pleasing. The freshness, simplicity, and grace of youth were combined with the wisdom and mellowness of maturity. They were received with great cordiality, and entertained with much hospitality, by the best people of the country. But I well remember the horror which attended the discovery that the lady in question was wearing a borrowed gown. She was visiting the great cities, constantly associating with silk and satin and velvet and fur. But said the portly and handsome D.D., in spotless linen and faultless broadcloth, "Why, she would better wear a *calico* dress than borrow."

Of course, the horrors of a borrowed gown cannot be exaggerated. But, O *mi fili!* let us see you walking into your own pulpit in a blue farmer's-frock, let us see you presiding over a conference in a flowered cotton wrapper, before fully accepting your dictum in this matter. It is very easy to tell other people to be brave; but conspicuity may be more fearful than cannon-balls. The pity of it is, not that a missionary should borrow a garment, but that we, the home-guard, should suffer her to be reduced to the necessity of borrowing a garment, or going without. We send a woman out to the cannibal islands to lavish her youth and health and life on savages, while we stay at home and enjoy ourselves; and, when she comes home for a few months' rest and refreshment, she has to borrow clothes in order to make a decent appearance among us. It is we who are heathen. We scarcely mend the matter by clubbing together in swift dismay, and providing a silk gown after the discovery is made. That is but a clumsy and unregenerate charity. Our religion ought to have taught us long ago, that a black silk dress should await every missionary wife the moment she sets her foot on the wharf of her country, and that not as a charity, but as the least of her legal rights. Not one of us but would rather take a contract to supply the whole American Board with silk gowns than to settle down in the South Sea ourselves; and, if we can compromise on a handsome outfit and ample support for all goers and comers, we ought to consider ourselves let off very lightly.

Have we any right to be let off at all? I suppose there is no question that the work does drag a little. The debt this year is somewhat alarming. Nor are those years which are free from debt altogether encouraging. The treasurer's report of one such year was received with much gratification, and followed by a hearty prayer of thanksgiving; but it was a little startling to find, later on, that, "the sad reason why the debt has been reduced is, that persons enough could not be found to go abroad, so as to require more money. . . . The most pressing appeals from the secretaries and missionaries — the great burden of the meeting, indeed — were for more men and women to go into the white harvest-fields. It was a piteous cry, almost a wailing."

Of course, there is no inconsistency, and no impropriety, in being glad you are out of debt, even though the reason is that you had no chance to get in. Speaking after the flesh, one would say, that, even had there been people wanting to go, it would have been wiser not to send them, so long as there was no money to do it with. Indeed, may we not reckon it providential that the lack of money was so handsomely met by a lack of men? And, on the other hand, is it so piteous a thing that men do not wish to go? In yet another column of the same paper, I find, " In speaking of the dangers which may burst upon our brethren in China, at any moment, Mr. Goodrich said, 'No man ought to engage in the missionary work who is not willing to be a martyr.' As we looked over the vast assemblage of noble-looking men and women who listened so attentively to his thrilling words, we wondered how it would be, were all of them filled with the martyr's spirit. . . . We felt sure the speaker had faced in sober thought the possibilities of martyrdom."

Now, I must confess, in commonplace honesty, that there was, at least, one of those noble-looking men and women who did not feel filled with the martyr spirit, and who did not see any reason why the rest should. When duty and danger front a man, he is a coward to shirk them; but is it a duty to go around to the other side of the world to court danger? When the Chinese come to our country, we ought to protect them in life, liberty, and the pursuit of happiness, at all costs. There is a clear case for the martyr spirit to have free course, run (forward, not backward), and be glorified. But to sail twelve thousand miles away from our own country, to thrust ourselves into a kingdom that does not want us, and tells us so at the cannon's mouth, seems to me, like swearing,

"Neither brave, polite, nor wise."

"Go ye into all the world, and preach the gospel to every creature," sure enough. But, when Christ was sending out his first missionaries, he bade them expressly, *not* to go to China and Japan and Micronesia, but to New York and Boston and Lowell. "Go *not* into the way of the Gentiles, and into any city of the Samaritans enter ye not. But go, rather, to the lost sheep of the house of Israel." If the heathen did not want the gospel, he did not bid his disciples to force it upon them: he did not bid them stay, and be martyrs, but enjoined upon them to come away. Offer the gospel, but remember that it is for them to take or to leave. A man shall not be forced, even into the kingdom of heaven. "Whosoever shall not receive you, nor hear your words, when ye depart out of that city, shake off the dust of your feet. . . . When they persecute you in this city, *flee* ye into another." Surely, the Bible is not *all* martyrdom. There is room left for the exercise of prudence and reason. Can the fields be considered ripe for the harvest, so long as they bristle with guns? While broad lands are lying opposite our own doors, into which we may enter unopposed, and wherein we may work unmolested, is it necessary to traverse half the globe to dash our life out against the Chinese Wall? The Chinese soul is worth as much to the Creator as the American soul; but the American soul is also worth as much to the Creator as the Chinese soul; and to the American nation it is worth a great deal more; and is, moreover, easier to get at. If we want an alien race to work on, here it is, ready to our hand. The paper from which I have quoted says, "There are thirteen thousand Dakota Indians now under missionary influence. But, besides these, there are, outside and beyond the limits of our own stations, many thousands more, who, as a young missionary said, are ' as wild as any Texan cattle.' " But these wild Texan cattle are our own countrymen. They meet us at every point. It is a matter of life and death. And to this day we know no more what to do with the Indians than did Columbus. We preach to them a little, and we plunder them a little; we feast them, and fight them; and a good many of us have more faith in the fighting than in the feasting. We have been a Christian nation ever since we have had any thing to do with them; but we have not converted them to any great, certainly not to any national, extent; and I presume that the most sanguine expectation we entertain concerning them, is, that they will die out of our way. If we are so powerless for good to an alien race over which we have complete control, and to which we have, of course, free entrance, are we called upon to be martyrs to a race that is an independent power, and exercises its independence by shutting the door in our faces?

The same paper says, that, " in speaking of his late field of labor at Cheyenne, Col. Davis, who now goes as a missionary to Japan, said that town had been termed ' hell on wheels.' And it was a significant fact that women vote and hold office there; an allusion which produced a broad grin and hearty laughter all over the house. In going there, he also remarked that he had in mind the story of the negro who advised his master to go where there was ' the least pay and the most devil.' "

Why, then, does he leave Cheyenne? Why do we leave a "hell on wheels" in the midst of our own country, and sail off to Japan? Has Cheyenne been turned into heaven, or even into a civilized and christianized town on earth? Or have we there as many ministers, and as much machinery, as can be profitably employed?

"The Rev. John T. Gulick will henceforth devote himself to work among the Mongolians. He has found them a cordial, hospitable people, living under a patriarchal government. They are ready to welcome the Christian teacher. Is there any one to go with him to that land?"

Why, indeed, should there be? With what face could we leave a "hell on wheels" driving about here, and set up to reform a nice, hospitable, patriarchal people like these Mongolians? Is it economical or patriotic, is it even right, to send our best men from home, while there is so little pay and so much devil at home? Among those on the platform at the meeting, says a religious paper, "certainly two were young pastors, who, with their wives, gladly go to the heathen, out of the midst of homes and parishes where they have been delightfully settled for two or more years. The Macedonian call moved them. Besides these, . . . we met others on that platform at the same time, agitated and agitating the question, each for himself or herself, 'Am I not called to go?'"

What is the Macedonian call? If it is the wickedness of heathendom that draws them, here is heathendom flourishing like a green bay-tree by our own doorway. If it is the pastoral simplicity and winsome docility of the Asiatics, let us not tamper with them.

For a few years, Japan has been sending young men

to this country and to Europe to be educated. When more than three hundred had been scattered throughout the country, the report of some of our highest religious observers, after four years of trial, was, —

"The Japanese intellect, in the test which has thus been made of it, has proved itself bright, clear, and discriminating. . . .

"From their first coming hither, it has been very manifest, that these boys have been accustomed to the ways of a truly polite and refined society. They are neat in appearance and dress, cleanly in their habits, gentle and winning in their intercourse with each other and with Americans. But more than this has been discovered as time has passed on. There is a moral rectitude among them which is truly surprising. There is almost no tendency to disorder, profligacy, and vice.

"Among the same number of American boys of similar age, picked from any class of society, whether sent abroad or kept at home, no one could hope to find a style of conduct so truly exemplary. Pres. Hopkins might well say, as he did at the late meeting of the American Board at New Haven, that, if all which is said of these Japanese students be true, he could wish that some of them might be kept as models of conduct in our American colleges. As a general fact, they are painstaking and laborious in their habits of study, keeping themselves closely to their books from morning till night; and it is the almost universal testimony in the families where they have lived, that they have shown themselves quiet and agreeable members of the household.

"In conclusion, it may be mentioned as a remarkable fact, that these young men seem to be almost absolutely free from what may be called heathenish superstition, and are ready to receive favorably the impressions which the Bible and our religious institutions are fitted to make upon them. A few have already professed Christianity, and joined Christian churches; and many others seem to be thoughtfully pondering upon this subject."

Is there any thing in this report that seems to make it imperative upon us to listen to the call to martyrdom in Japan?

We were sauntering through the pleasant streets and suburbs of North Adams, on a fine summer morning. Over against one of its little bridges stands the unpretending red brick factory where our modern Sampson has grappled with the problems of labor and capital, of supply and demand, of blood in its unity and diversity, — has wrestled, and seems thus far to have prevailed. We had, like thousands of others, walked through the quiet, busy house, and seen with our own eyes the foreign faces and the untiring, skilful hands. The simple American dress suits ill our ideas of Chinese dignity and luxury; but the long black hair, braided and curled around the head, somewhat after the "Pompadour" style, was any thing but American; and the short, small figures, and soft, beardless faces combined with the braided womanly hair to give an appearance of effeminacy to these celestial immigrants. But that they were in earnest, their unceasing work showed. They scarcely looked up at the approach of visitors; and, if they observed us at all, their countenances maintained a dignified and self-respectful unconsciousness. That they are earnest and aspiring is seen, also, from their schoolroom, where they are mastering the new language and the new modes with a rapidity and persistence quite worthy of the Caucasian race, while maintaining still a most tenacious love of fatherland, a close knowledge of its history, and a fond pride in its traditions.

So, as you stand leaning over the wooden railings of the wooden bridge, listening dreamily to the rush of waters, and looking abstractedly at the commonplace brick factory, you feel that this incursion from the ancient world may dwindle into insignificance, or rise into nationality; but all the same the ancient world is here. The grandeur and the antiquity, the vague, veiled splendor, the secret, sacred learning, are unsealed, and the Celestials are making shoes in a Yankee factory.

We reckon these Chinese as heathen and publicans, to be civilized and christianized. But what do they think of us?

I am sure that those almond eyes are watchful, and theories are forming under those black coronets.

Two women come chattering up the bridge; and we accost each other in friendly country fashion. Among other objects of interest, they point out the Chinese factory. I love information at first-hand; and I ask if our Asiatic friends are welcome.

"No, indeed!" says the portly matron, bridling

with indignation. "They've no business here! Everybody hates 'em but Mr. Sampson; and he worships 'em more than he does his Maker."

It is a new view of the bond between employer and workmen.

"How are they offensive?" I ask. "Do they not behave well?"

"I don't know but they behave well enough. But they have no business here!"

"Are they riotous, quarrelsome, noisy? Do they rob hen-roosts and clothes-lines? Do they mingle in street-fights, and stir up strife?"

"No, they are peaceable enough. They are afraid to do any thing of that kind. They are too afraid themselves. They *dasn't* do any mischief."

"Perhaps they would behave well, even if they were not frightened into it. We might, at least, give them the benefit of the doubt."

"But they've no business here. They don't take any part in the government. They've no wives or families. They don't mean to stay here. They only come to get money, — our money."

"That is an innocent object, if they use innocent means; and we boast that this is a free country, open to all. Perhaps, if we treat them fairly, they will presently bring their families, and become citizens."

"We don't want any more foreigners. There's enough here now."

"But the nation was originally founded by foreigners. And if these people are quiet, honest, and industrious, may they not be a real advantage to us?"

"No: they don't spend any money. They lay it all up, and live on nothin'. If there's a concert or a lecture, Mr. Sampson has 'em all go, and take the best seats. You can't get anywhere, because he's got money, and is just king."

"But they pay for their seats?"

"Oh, yes! they pay for every thing. But I call 'em no better than a mess of hogs."

Evidently this "mess of hogs" is not wholly given over to evil. While I am writing this, I take up a chance volume of Goethe, and find him saying to Eckermann, "Since I saw you, I have read many and various things, among which a Chinese romance has occupied and interested me most of all."

"Chinese romance!" said I. "That is, indeed, something quite out of the way."

"Not so much as you think," said Goethe. "The Chinamen think, act, and feel almost exactly like us; and we should feel perfect congeniality with them, if all they do were not more clear, more pure, and decorous than with us. . . .

"Then you find an infinite number of legends, . . . all turning upon what is moral and proper. 'Tis this severe habit of regulation in every thing which has sustained the Chinese empire for thousands of years past, and will for thousands to come.

"I find a remarkable contrast to this Chinese romance in the 'Chansons de Beranger,' which have, almost every one, some immoral or licentious subject. . . . Is it not remarkable that the subjects of the Chinese poets should be so thoroughly moral, and those of the most distinguished French poet of the present day be exactly the contrary?"

I asked whether the Chinese romance of which he spoke were one of their best.

"By no means!" said Goethe. "The Chinese have thousands of them."

In our own day and country, we see that they are peaceable and docile, eager to learn our language and our ways, and are therefore, of their own accord, putting themselves into very good training for Christianity; while the hostility, the tumult, and the brick-bats are on the American side. Would it not be well to leave the Chinese to themselves for the present, and to see that Massachusetts and California are well stocked with missionaries, whose first duty shall be to preach to American citizens that the Chinese are not a "mess of hogs"? If the Chinese are not human beings, "subject to like passions as we are," we waste money in sending them the gospel: if they are human beings, it must strike them strangely that we thrust ourselves into their homes with the Bible, and receive them in our homes with stones. If we cannot christianize our own communities into a fellow-feeling with the Chinese, what ground have we for expecting to christianize Chinese communities into a fellow-feeling with us? We have long counted Chinese exclusiveness and seclusiveness as a mark of barbarism; but I cannot see that China has expressed her desire to be let alone by America in any more emphatic or barbarous manner than America has expressed her desire to be let alone of China. American missionaries have directly interfered to alter established Chinese institutions; but Chinese immigrants have been only too happy to conform to our laws and customs. They have never attempted to proselyte, or even to modify. They have simply and humbly sought to earn an honest living by supplying labor which we need, at prices which we fix. And they have been met with a ferocity and a brutality which would do credit to the darkest Paganism, and which ought to figure brilliantly in some Chinese "Fox's Book of Martyrs."

The situation is certainly peculiar. We go to great expense in conveying a few ministers to that human hive; but when the bees swarm on our shores, at their own expense, we beat one, and kill another, and stone another, which must seem a little incongruous to the bees. I not long since heard a missionary who had spent many years in China describe her disintegration and demoralization, arising, in part at least, from the opium-war and sundry foreign influences; and when I asked him whether, on the whole, contact with Christian nations had as yet done China more harm or good, he answered promptly and emphatically, "Harm, a hundred times!"

A late writer tells us that one of our early Indian missionaries found a greater obstacle in the lawless and immoral conduct of some of the Dutch than in the Paganism of the Indians. How would it do to turn our half-million of money, and our hundreds of missionaries, into our own land, and keep them there until the nation is so thoroughly christianized, that it becomes by its mere existence a missionary nation; till every ship's crew that leaves its shores on any errand of pleasure or commerce or science shall, by their purity, integrity, unselfishness, preach an irresistible gospel to Jew and Gentiles?

How would it do to let the Chinese worship God their own way in their own land, until we have christianized America up to the point of not plundering and murdering the Chinese when they come to us?

A missionary from China was announced to speak upon the work which had been done in China. It was precisely what I was eager to know; and I took good care to be in attendance. He was very interesting, full of sincerity and simplicity. He drew a contrast between the Chinese and ourselves. Our feet point downward; the Chinese, upward. But that was the paradox of our childhood. We read a book from the beginning to the end; the Chinese, from the end to the beginning. But we learned that before we had left our childhood far behind us. Here, in riding across country, we see church-spires rising all around: there we see no church-spires. But that we could evolve from our moral consciousness. Here we sleep on beds: there they sleep on their ovens. Every one to his taste.

"A bed by night, a chest of drawers by day,"

is not unknown to Christendom. Here our teaming is done by horses and oxen: there you will see a donkey and a woman working together. But we need not leave our own country to see that. In China the ladies pinch their feet to make them small: here they pinch their waists. Does that indicate unquestionable superiority?

All this, and much more, is very interesting; but I can draw from it no opinion at all as to whether we have really put an opening wedge into China, or only driven a tack into the outmost bark. When I learn, that, within the last six or seven years, the missionary has numbered eighty or ninety converts, I begin to see light. That is as many, perhaps, as his American *confreres* have gathered into their home churches in that time, and is an encouraging sign; but I immediately long to know what sort of person a Chinese convert is, how much he differs from a Chinese Pagan, what are his ideas of uprightness and honor, what are his rank and influence in Chinese circles, and what is the rank of a Christian colony or a Christian church in Chinese society. American merchants have told me, that some of their Chinese business acquaintance, unmitigated heathen, have had as high and delicate a standard of integrity and generosity as any Christian community can show. Is this exceptional, or general? My returned missionary says he has no doubt, that, in time, China will be like America. In what time, I wonder; and, outside of the nature of things, what are the grounds of his belief? Besides the conviction, —

> "That somehow good
> Will be the final goal of ill,"

is there actual indication that China will be able to exhibit, for instance, a statesmanship, a financial ability, an unbending integrity, a supreme regard for the rights and welfare of others, approximating those which have illustrated the government of our own commercial metropolis?

We will not give up our Chinese missions, expensive

though they be; for as one little stream, pouring into the fissure of a rock, will finally rend and shatter the whole mass, so our little gospel-rill is going presently to shiver this great Pagan empire, and rear upon its ruins a Christian civilization which shall be a joy to the whole earth.

But, while we are waiting, would it not be prudent and economical to take advantage of other means? We will continue to send out missionaries at great cost; but we will not forget, that, at North Adams and California, the heathen have come to us at their own expense. To be sure, they are not on pleasure or religion bent, but have a frugal mind. Yet if, while they are merely pegging at their boots and shoes, we could quietly convert them into Christians, it would certainly be a great deal cheaper than to fasten them up in China, and convert them there. And, as we have only about half a million a year to spend on the whole world, it must be readily seen that the question of dollars and cents becomes a very important one. We take heart by looking at the Sandwich Islands, which were the seat of a savage society, murderous, idolatrous, licentious. Now they are clothed, and in their right mind. They are governed by a constitution; and they worship 'the true God. So the missionaries preach, and so we believe. But, on the other hand, infidels and unbelievers, and even good Christians, tell us that the natives are dying out. In the good old times, when they worshipped their own gods, and were not hampered by dress, they numbered four hundred thousand. Now they are but sixty-five thousand. The infidels admit, indeed, that this depopulation had begun before the missionaries appeared upon the scene; but their appearance has not checked it. The rate of decrease has even been higher than ever since the mission-work; and they attribute it to the fact that the missionaries have substituted for the natural dress and the natural amusement of the simple islanders the cumbrous dress and the severe manners of their own austere climate.

Have we carried the gospel and the arts of civilization to a nation that was rapidly dying out, and has it been dying all the more rapidly since it accepted us? If so, is it good economy? Is there some offset of which we know nothing? Is there any thing in the position of the Sandwich Islands which makes it incumbent on us to have a Christian people there, even though we slay the natives with the sword of the Spirit, and substitute for them a population transported from our own shores? Is it, at any rate, so important as to compensate us for the pain of seeing, both in the secular and religious newspapers, that our home missionaries are not receiving their usual grants from the Home Missionary Society; that ministers in October, "supporting themselves on a mere pittance any way," have received no payments since the first of August; that five hundred missionaries have waited months for the remittance from New York ("their credit is impaired, their ambition sapped"); that there is untold anxiety in the missionaries' homes, on account of the delay in remitting salaries; that the A. H. M. S. owes forty thousand dollars to missionaries for labor already performed; and that some of them have already sacrificed their furniture and books, and have even sold the horse and cow from their frontier homes, to obtain the necessaries of life?

This, at least, seems indisputable, — that the world is one. He who works at home faithfully is doing as good service as he who sails the wide seas over. Wherever a man's taste, powers, circumstances, call him to go, thither he shall go unblamed; and, if he choose to stay in quiet havens, equally unblamed shall he stay. It is not where he lives, but how he lives, that decides the character of his stewardship. He shall put to the best account his love of novelty, stir, travel, fresh ways and large affairs: but he shall not call it consecration; nor shall he imply that the quiet, home-staying student's life is inspired by indolence or love of ease and self. He is consecrated who does always his best work as unto God, and not as unto man. His consecration may lead him to martyrdom in the deserts of Africa, or by his own fireside, to comfort on the pleasant uplands of India, or to boundless content in the beloved valleys of his fatherland.

THE LAWS OF ANGER.

THE LAWS OF ANGER.

SO far as the Scriptures contain rules, popularly so called, those rules are not for us; and, so far as the Scriptures are for us, they are hardly to be called rules. The rules of the Bible are chiefly to be found in the Old Testament, and were strictly laid down for the Jews. The New Testament widens its scope to embrace the whole world; but it directly and forcibly abrogates rules, and deals only in principles.

It is, in some respects, far easier to be guided by rules than by principles. A rule tells you exactly what to do: a principle leaves you to find out for yourself. A rule demands only obedience: a principle requires judgment. Government by rule attaches responsibility chiefly to the ruler: government by principle fastens it upon the individual actor. Those who are governed can make but one mistake,—disobedience, which is fatal: those who govern themselves may make a thousand mistakes, none of which is fatal, save the mistake of motive. If the divine object were to have an orderly and decorous world, one would say we ought to be governed by rules: if it were to build up a world of intelligent and dignified beings, we should be, as we are, relegated to principles.

Reason teaches us, that if there is any God at all, any God worthy of worship, he is the God of the whole world. He is the Creator and Guardian, not of Jew and Christian alone, but of Gentile and Pagan as well. He did not withhold himself from the human race in its infancy, and come to its help only when it had grown into fulness of days: everywhere, and at all times, he has revealed himself in such ways as seemed to him good. Many ages and many nations have never heard of our Bible; yet in no one of them, says that Bible, confirming the conclusions of our reason, has God left himself without a witness. The Bible may be the clearest lamp unto our feet, and the brightest light unto our path; but it does not profess to be the only light that ever shone upon the world; and the attempt to make it so throws a glamour and uncertainty upon the path. There can be no harmony of the Gospels, no symmetrical plan of salvation, no sufficient theory of life, unless we admit that God is the Father and Friend of the whole human race, that he works efficiently without, as well as within, the Bible, and that not only upon Sinai and Zion may his presence shine, but upon every high hill under the whole heaven.

I think it would not be far wrong to say that the popularly received Christian doctrine of resentment is, that there should be no resentment. "I say unto you, That ye resist not evil: but whosoever shall smite thee on thy right cheek, turn to him the other also. And if any man will sue thee at the law, and take away thy coat, let him have thy cloak also. And whosoever shall compel thee to go a mile, go with him twain. Give to him that asketh thee, and, from him that would borrow of thee, turn not thou away." These and such teachings as these are our warrant for resolving the whole duty of man into a mush of complacency. We have never yet quite succeeded in the effort. We find ourselves ever and anon flaming out into indignation and wrath. If a man smite us on the right cheek, we knock him down. If a man sue us at the law, we stand suit; and if he would borrow of us, we promptly turn away, unless he can give ample security. But we have succeeded so far as to do these things in a shame-faced, apologetic manner. We have succeeded so far as to give those who are outside the church weapons to wield against it which they would not otherwise possess, and which are unlawful to hold. We have succeeded so far as to put an odium upon anger. We do not recognize it as the natural and proper exercise of certain faculties; but we deem it the overflow of evil passions. We by no means obey these precepts of

Christ; but we say they, and they only, ought to be obeyed; and we admit that the reason we do not obey them is hardness of heart.

I admit nothing of the sort. This seems to me a feeble and false presentation of Christianity, as far removed from real Christianity as it is from Paganism. In the first place, it is absolutely unreasonable; and nothing which is unreasonable can be Christian. In the second place, it is impracticable; and nothing which is impracticable can be Christian. But, in the third place, it is utterly antagonistic to the gist of Christ's teachings, and to the whole course of his life. He says explicitly, "Think not that I am come to destroy the law or the prophets: I am not come to destroy, but to fulfil." When he quoted them of old time, who said, "An eye for an eye, and a tooth for a tooth," did he mean to condemn them? He says explicitly not. He introduces a new principle; but he does not withdraw the old. He goes further in the direction which Moses travelled. When they of old time said, "Thou shalt not commit adultery: thou shalt not kill: thou shalt demand eye for eye from thine enemy," they spoke in the interests of truth and purity, of law and order. Recklessness on the one hand, and revenge on the other, were curbed by the law of eye for eye. Whatever communication God may have held with his world outside of the biblical record, we little know.

We do know that there was great need of well-defined laws among the Jews. Moses found his people violent and barbarous; and he repressed them with simple and wholesome laws. When these laws had done their work, Christ came and informed them with spiritual life. Where Moses had forbidden murder, Christ went deeper, and forbade those evil thoughts in the heart, out of which murder springs. Where Moses had forbidden indiscriminate and unlimited revenge, Christ went further, and inculcated forgiveness and friendliness. He did not preach the duty of resentment, because there was no need of it. Anger is one of the earliest and easiest instincts of the human being, and, in the natural course of things, needs to be trained by discretion and discrimination. Forgiveness belongs to a higher and more spiritualized and advanced stage. But that Christ did not mean to extirpate anger, and substitute forgiveness, is proved by the whole tenor of his own life. It is no weak, yielding, namby-pamby figure which the authors of the Gospels draw for us, but a Being of severe and exacting majesty. When the Pharisees shut their eyes to the claims of humanity, and counted a legal phrase more strenuous than human suffering, he looked round about on them with anger. Often his anger burst out in bitter, scorching words: "Woe unto you, scribes and Pharisees, hypocrites! for ye compass sea and land to make one proselyte, and, when he is made, ye make him twofold more the child of hell than yourselves. Hypocrites, fools, blind, whited sepulchres." "Tribunes," "Times," and "Heralds," nay, even "Christian Unions," "Independents," and "Observers" address each other in no more uncomplimentary terms than these. And they are not the words of a well-meaning but short-coming Christian, a man who tried to follow Christ, but found the old Adam too strong for the young Melancthon: they are the words of Jesus Christ himself, the sinless and perfect man, "the only-begotten of the Father, full of grace and truth." Nay, more, his anger was not confined to words. When this man, who was so meek and forbearing, who taught submission to evil, and patience under insult, — when he saw God's temple profaned to profit and pelf, his anger was kindled into an over-mastering fury: he armed himself, and alone drove out the crowd of hucksters and peddlers, scattered their money, upset their tables, ordered out their wares, and made a clean sweep of the whole filthy concern. There was no turning of the other cheek, no giving-up of the cloak also, but a summary and forcible check put upon abuses. If it had been an ordinary church-member, the world looking on, and especially the marketmen who had been turned out of their comfortable stalls, would very likely have said that this reformer and radical had lost his temper, and become as one of us. But he was the Lord Christ in his anger, in his denunciation, in his force, just as truly, just as divinely, and just as exemplarily, as when he cried, "Father, forgive them; for they know not what they do."

The Lamb of God was so meek, that he suffered himself to be slain for us; but there came a time when "the kings of the earth . . . and the mighty men . . . hid themselves in the dens, and in the rocks of the mountains, and said to the mountain and rocks, Fall on us, and hide us from . . . the wrath of the Lamb: for the great day of his wrath is come; and who shall be able to stand?"

God's first revelation to man is man: his second is the law: his third is the gospel. One supplements and complements, but does not contradict, its predecessors. It abrogates only by fulfilment. If the human race guided and controlled itself perfectly, it would need no law: if it perfectly obeyed the law, it would need no gospel. Neither law nor gospel requires the annihilation of any faculty which God has given to man, and which he gave before law or gospel. When the law says, "Thou shalt not kill," it makes no iron-bound prohibition; for this direction is explicitly modified by sundry other directions concerning the modes and circumstances in which thou shalt kill. When the gospel says, "Resist not evil," it furnishes no ground for universal and immoral acquiescence in or toleration of wrong; for the gospel abounds in examples of stern and strenuous resistance of evil. It only means, that along with the right resentment of outrage, of resistance to evil, which the world has always practised, lies another finer right and duty, — namely, that of forbearance and forgiveness. When we are to exercise the one or the other, each man is to judge for himself. There are times when a man does well to be angry; and there are times when he does well to forgive. This is certain: "If thy brother trespass against thee seven times in a day, and seven times in a day turn again to thee, saying, I repent, thou shalt forgive him; nay, until seventy times seven." It must be a little hard when it gets into the four hundreds; but even a transient repentance, a feeble impulse toward right, is to be recognized and encouraged. But stronger than the assertion is the inference, that, if he do not repent, thou shalt not forgive him. The doctrine which I have heard preached as the word of God, the gospel of Christ, — that forgiveness does not depend upon repentance, that we must treat those who have done us a wrong precisely as if they had not done it, — is irrational, unscriptural, and demoralizing. It violates the first instincts of healthy human nature: it puts virtue and vice on the same level, and thus removes a powerful incentive to the one, and preventive of the other:

it makes the man himself the centre of his action, and regards not at all the effect of his course upon his brother, the wrong-doer.

There are certain broad lines of demarcation in Christ's example, which we should do well to trace. We find that his forbearance was exercised towards those who had wronged himself: his wrath blazed towards those who wronged others. His pity and patience were lavished on the poor, the suffering, the ignorant: he spared little to the rich and bigoted, who misled and misruled them. When he saw the multitude, he was moved with compassion on them; but he branded the scribes and Pharisees as blind leaders of the blind, and hypocrites. He forgave, unasked, those who crowned him with thorns, and doomed him to cruel death; but whoso shall but offend one of these little ones . . . it were better for him that a millstone should be hanged about his neck, and that he were drowned in the depth of the sea. When the mob would have cast him down headlong from the brow of the hill, he only slipped out of their hands, and went his way without words; but no denunciation was too strong for those who bind heavy burdens . . . and lay them on men's shoulders, while themselves will not move them with one of their fingers; for those who shut up the kingdom of heaven against men, and will neither go in themselves, nor suffer them that are entering to go in; for those who devour widows' houses, and for a pretence make long prayers; for those who compass sea and land to make one proselyte, and, when he is made, make him twofold more the child of hell than themselves; for those who pay tithe of mint and anise and cumin, and omit judgment, mercy, and faith; for those who make clean the outside of the cup and of the platter, but within are full of extortion and excess; for those who build the tombs of the prophets, yet crucify the successors of the prophets, — for them we hear little of compassion, nothing of forgiveness, but Ye serpents, ye generation of vipers, how can ye escape the damnation of hell?

In all this, Christ spoke the sentiments of honest, uncontaminated human nature. Instinct, reason, experience, and revelation are in perfect accord. It was no nerveless, emasculated, sentimental, and impracticable gospel which he preached, but a gospel of discrimination and emphasis and vitality, — a gospel for the conduct of business and courtesy, as well as of religion, — a gospel masculine, as well as feminine; of strength, as well as of refinement; of self-respect, as well as of self-sacrifice; of force, as well as of feeling.

Let anger, then, resume its place as an original and dignified function of the human organization, and be no more looked upon as the outburst of a rebellious outlaw, or an invincible alien. While we are not to be petty and touchy, easily provoked, self-centred, solicitous of our own dignity, imagining evil, quick to fly into a passion, strict to mark iniquity against ourselves, implacable and revengeful; while we are to be generous and large minded, to ascribe good intent where evil intent is not demonstrable, and not to take offence unless offence is meant, — we are equally under bonds not to level the barriers between courtesy and discourtesy, between justice and injustice, between right and wrong. We owe it to the wrong-doer to throw all the weight of our disapprobation against his wrong-doing. If the wrong be done not to ourselves, but to others, and if, in addition, it be a wrong done to the weak and the helpless, it is difficult to learn from the Bible, or from our own hearts, what expression of indignation would be excessive. So far from the truth is it, that an outburst of wrath must be unchristian, the sudden explosion of surprised but depraved nature, it may rather be that non-explosiveness is but an apathy of the conscience, a dulness of sympathetic perception, an outgrowth of selfishness, a defect of the moral organization. The only man who may be fairly inferred to have lost his temper is the man who never shows that he has any. If he that is angry with his brother without cause is in danger of the judgment, what reason have we to suppose that he who is not angry with his brother when there is cause should go scot-free? When oppression, fraud, malice, are banished from the earth, we can afford to be even-tempered; but, in their present roaring and rampant prosperity, it is more Christian that our hearts should roll up mountain-ranges of disapproval, and occasionally burst into volcanoes of burning indignation. God is angry with the wicked every day, and makes repentance and reformation the conditions of forgiveness. What right have we to look upon the wicked with tranquillity, and take him into our confidence and companionship, as if he had never sinned? To be hasty in spirit, to be angry, is the mark of a petty nature: to be slow to anger is one mark of a large nature: to put a ban upon anger is not the work of the divine nature.

The excesses of anger are to be deprecated. The man who loses control of himself in his wrath is never to be admired. That is a weakness which he should conquer. But he who holds himself well in hand while he hurls his wrath at the evil-doer; he who never loses sight of human weakness, even while the flame of his indignation leaps forth to consume wickedness, — he is not to be apologized for as a halting disciple: he is rather to be rejoiced over as an effective apostle. Blessed are the peace-makers indeed; but blessed, also, is whoever cometh in the name of the Lord, though he come not to send peace, but a sword.

In this, as in every other question, it is well to remember that no one text or precept of the Bible undertakes to set forth in general and in particular the whole duty of man. One phase of the truth is illustrated in one place, and one in another. Every man must decide for himself, on every occasion, as to the bearings of the Bible on his own behavior; as to whether he is right to be angry, or right to forbear; as to whether he demand eye for eye, or resist not evil; as to whether he submit to, or revolt against, the powers that be; as to whether he answer a fool according to his folly, or answer him not. This is an ever-recurring trouble. It gives a man no rest, but keeps him constantly using his observation, his conscience, and his judgment. Nevertheless, it seems to be the divine way, and we cannot help ourselves. We may insist that a part is the whole, that a principle is a precept, that a mariner's compass is a baby-jumper; but such insistence does not alter the facts. The universe with all its laws is around us. The Bible with all its mysteries is before us. Not a hair's-breadth will be changed in the one or the other, because we fail to apprehend them.

THE SIGHING OF THE PRISONER.

THE SIGHING OF THE PRISONER.

WE should be able to reform the world much faster and further than we now do, if we could only have full swing at it; but we are constantly hampered by the necessity of respecting the freedom of the individual. If we could enact and enforce a law, that no man should do what was not good for him, and that all men should do what was for their good, we should save the world at one swoop. We should have no drunkards; for we would forbid the first intoxicating glass. We should have no paupers; for idleness and extravagance should be equally illegal. As it is, the law cannot touch a man so long as he injures only himself, but must wait until he endanger or annoy others; that is, it lays no hand upon him while he is sowing the seed, but only when the evil harvest stands ready to be garnered, which is generally too late to be of much service to the man himself. There seems here to be a great waste: nevertheless, it is the divine way. Man grants to man no more power to hurt himself than is granted him by his Maker.

When we long for absolute dominion, when it seems to us that great good would be done if we could force men to work steadily and thoroughly, to spend their wages economically, and lay up money for future emergencies, to train their children virtuously, and treat their wives justly, and be generally thriving and respectable, we are obliged to remember that evidently God thought not so. Apparently it seems to him better that men should go wrong than that they should go right, under pressure. More is gained by letting them walk alone, even with much stumbling, than by walling them in on both sides, and holding them upright.

Nevertheless, when men have carried so far their liberty to stumble and sin, that they impinge upon the liberty of others, society steps in, and imposes restraints; and there is where we have the opportunity, and where, therefore, our duty lies, to practise our theories of inculcating and enforcing right. So long as a man is outside of prison-walls, he must go his own way, right or wrong. He may abuse his advantages, and ruin his chances, both for usefulness and happiness, and you can only remonstrate and advise; and perhaps not even that will be wise. But once he has forfeited his freedom, once he comes into a state of pupilage, and society can wreak upon him its teaching and preaching, not only with a good heart, but with sound judgment.

There has sometimes been evinced a species of sympathy with prisoners, that is neither politic nor sensible. Feelings are attributed to them which would surprise no one more than themselves. Defects of early education, peculiarities of temper or disposition, are brought forward as palliatives of crime. Doubtless they are palliatives in the eye of the Maker of us all. Doubtless, at the judgment-seat of the heavens, many an earthly decision will be reversed, and many a man whose deserts are unawarded in this world will be ranked below others who on earth forfeited freedom by open and dangerous crimes. Still it remains that we do not have to plead in the courts of heaven, but of earth. Our juries are not called upon to decide moral, but legal guilt. Our judges are not appointed to lay bare the secrets of the divine system, but for the defence of society. It may be that a man has committed burglary, because his father trained him to evil courses; or murder, because his grandfather transmitted to him a diseased thirst for intoxicating drinks. All these things may pass in review before the divine mind; but they do not, and they ought not, to remit or mitigate the penalty imposed by human justice. Legal codes must be founded, so far as may be, on right and wrong. To excuse a man for a wicked act because he has previously done a weak act, is to put a premium on weakness. To pardon a man for criminal violence, because his father never curbed his violent passions when a child, would be to encourage parental indolence ; would be to remove one of the methods whereby society attempts to make up for the defects of home-training.

But when the law has once withdrawn a man from the world, and shut him up in a prison for the good of society, it ought to turn about, and teach and train him for his own good. The freedom of the individual is abolished. Justice has got him under her thumb. It is not enough that the condition of the prisoner is ameliorated, that he is no longer starved and tortured and degraded. The education that he has failed to receive before ought to be furnished him after his incarceration. The habits of industry which he has never formed should be then imposed upon him. In large measure, this is already done ; but there is room for increased effort. When I hear that a man is sentenced to twenty years' imprisonment for midnight burglary, I am moved to no pity for him. If I have pity, it is for the man who has lost, in a night, the labor and love of years : it is for the women and children shocked with sudden terror into illness and death : it is for a neighborhood tortured with long alarm, all that one man, or set of men, may live without regular work, upon the regular work of others. So far from mitigating his penalty, I would, if possible, make his banishment from the world more lasting and more secure.

But let another world be opened to him, which shall not be merely a living grave. He has failed in this: there is for him no second trial. A stigma is affixed to his name, which no tears of repentance can wash out; but in his prison-world let hope beckon, and comfort and motive not be wanting. When I hear that, of the hundreds in a single prison, only half can be employed, because there is not work enough for them, I am moved with pity. To set a hundred wretched minds preying upon themselves is not punishment: it is unintended and unmeaning torment. Punishment should be absolute, but not vindictive. We may admit that it is not remedial, but preventive; but if, while it protects society, it reforms the criminal, is harm done? I would have every prison made, so far as is possible, a reform-school for its inmates. Neither society nor the individual may be wilfully guilty concerning its brother whom it has imprisoned; but, when once it has him in its power, it becomes guilty, if it leave any stone unturned for his benefit. He is often ignorant: he should be taught. He has lived in low ways because he knew of no higher: let him be wisely and warily led into the upper regions. He has had no religious instruction; his spiritual nature is untouched: let the dull and uninteresting preachers prose to what outside ears can be got to listen to them, since outside are many means of grace; but let these imprisoned and dumb lips be touched with live coals. These criminals seldom, if ever, knew how healthful was the process, and how sweet the rewards, of daily tasks well done. Why should it not be taught them, partly by enforcing regular work, partly by investing for them the wages of their work, after deducting the expense of their maintenance? The State does not want its prisons to be pecuniarily profitable for the profit's sake. Suppose a man has spent five years in prison. Suppose his earnings over and above his share of the expenses have been for that time a thousand dollars. It is a very small thing whether that money goes into the State coffers or not; but it is not a small thing if the man have acquired a trade, regular habits, and has a capital of one thousand dollars to begin life with. It may be the difference to him between an honest career and a return to evil courses. It may be the difference to the State between a citizen constantly adding to her wealth, virtue, and strength, and a rogue preying upon all.

Certain cells in a well-ordered State's prison were provided with good kerosene lamps. The keeper said that all prisoners who were condemned for twenty years or more were allowed lamps in their cells that they might read in the evening. This is as it should be. Society often needs that a man should be banished for twenty years; but it never needs that he should not be instructed and improved as far as possible. So far as he is a criminal, he must be punished; but, along with that, so far as he is a victim, let him be helped. If intellectual stimulus be an incentive to virtue, let us minister to his intellect. To the imagination of the classes which furnish the criminals, a prison would be none the less terrible because it was a reform-school as well as a prison; while to those who are actually confined therein, it might prove a savor of life unto life. It is desirable that criminals should feel the power of law; but if they can also feel that law is more benevolent than lawlessness, a double benefit is gained. If there be any thing in geography, history, science, poetry, in Sunday schools and music and Bible, in politics foreign and domestic, in patriotism and helpfulness and humanity, which is calculated to soften the manners, and stimulate the mind, and purify the heart, outside of prison-walls, it is equally so calculated within those walls. And that the men gathered there have been largely destitute of those advantages is the strongest reason why society should attend to them when they are brought under her absolute control. When a man is imprisoned for ever so short a time, let his intellectual and moral, as well as his industrial, education be taken up at precisely the point where it was relinquished outside. If he cannot read, let him begin with the alphabet. If he is a scholar, let his scholarship come into play. If he has robbed, let him restore the amount robbed before his return to freedom. Let him learn the value of daily earnings and accumulated treasures by accumulations and earnings of his own. That is, let not society inflict a purely arbitrary but a natural and logical punishment. He is a wicked man; but half the value of punishment is lost when we remember only the wickedness and forget the manhood. Just as much is gained by treating criminals rationally as by treating children rationally; for criminals are a sort of spoiled children. They have violated State law, but we have no right to violate it towards them. No more should we violate or disregard natural law in dealing with them. Cause and effect, motive and sentiment, have just as full play with them as with outside folk. A violent and desperate fellow entered upon his imprisonment, declaring that nothing should induce him to perform the allotted task-work. When he was brought out with the others, he sat passive. For several days the warden took no notice of him. Then he quietly asked him who he was, why he was there, how long was his sentence, — as if he knew nothing about him, — and then as quietly added that the term of his sentence would be considered to begin from the time when he began to work. The man looked at the warden a moment. A new light broke upon his mind: he went to work at once, and remained, during his imprisonment, one of the most orderly and well-disposed of all the inmates.

I wish I could add that after he came out he led a life of industry, honesty, and sobriety, and died lamented; but that I do not know. I am sure he was more likely to do so than if he had been flogged and "burked" and shower-bathed, and hung up by his thumbs, and kept in solitary confinement in a dark cell.

Let the sighing of the prisoner come before thee, not that he may be released from prison, but that his soul may be loosed from its bonds.

An interesting, and at first sight humane custom has sprung up in the Massachusetts State-prison, and perhaps in the prisons of other States. A sumptuous Thanksgiving dinner is given to all the prisoners,— roast turkey, plum-pudding, and the vegetables, sauces, and other luxuries thereunto pertaining. No one can object to this little festival within those gloomy walls; and, rather than it should fail, private charity would doubtless step forward, and furnish the necessary funds. For these men, "roughs" and "rascallions" as they are, are also, let us always remember, victims,— victims of the ignorance and brutality of their parents and of society,— victims of evil training, and of their own unbridled passions. To whatever gratification can be furnished them without harm to themselves or to the community, they are thrice and four times welcome. Bid them into the circle of human brotherhood; for to that they have a right. Blood-stained it may be, and crime-hardened, still God hath made them of one family with ourselves; and if by any means they can be assured that they are not without the pale of human sympathy, they are removed one step at least toward reformation.

But after the dinner there are certain exercises of a more questionable character. The prisoners are assembled: the warden addresses them, and announces to a certain number unconditional and immediate pardon, granted by the governor and council. The character of the crime, the duration of the sentence, seem not to enter into the case. The last newspaper announcement I have seen is simply this, omitting the names:—

"After dinner, Warden C. made an address, and announced the pardons granted by the governor and council. The convicts liberated were A. B., sentenced to the institution from Boston, July, 1863, for life, for committing the crime of rape, and who is now fifty years old; C. D., sentenced June, 1868, for life, for committing murder in Worcester, now fifty-two years old; E. F., sentenced June, 1866, for twelve years, for robbery by force and violence in Boston, now thirty-seven years old; G. H., sentenced October, 1865, for fifteen years, for manslaughter committed in Boston, and now sixty-two years old."

This is all. There is no explanation of the act, no presentation of the grounds for pardon. No one intimates that a single prisoner was unfairly tried or unjustly convicted. There is no hint of any new evidence changing the complexion of their act. There is simply a Thanksgiving dinner, followed by "exercises;" and four men, every one of them guilty of the worst crimes against society, every one of them guilty of force and violence, of the infliction of unspeakable horror, of death, and worse than death, are let loose upon the community, in spite of the law which was brought to bear upon them and the justice which was supposed to be meted out to them. A. B., sentenced for life, for rape, was pardoned after being in prison eleven years, and has still nineteen years of life before him. C. D., sentenced for life, for murder, is pardoned out at the expiration of six years, and has eighteen vigorous years to brandish knife and pistol among his fellows. E. F., for robbery by force and violence, was sentenced for twelve years, and at the robust age of thirty-seven is discharged, after eight years of confinement. G. H. killed his man, and his fifteen years are reduced to nine, leaving him, at that, only eight years to try his hand, according to the allotted age of man. What is the use of all our expensive paraphernalia of law, if its decisions and its sentences are to be thus set aside? Why should men be brought from their farms and their counting-rooms to serve on jury-seats? Why should lawyers be clothed with dignity, and judges with power, if the result of their efforts is to be brought to nought by an outside authority? Do the governor and council know more about the case than lawyers, judge, and jury? Then why be at the expense of lawyers, judge, and jury? If the court is not so well informed as the council, let the court be abolished. If the men whose business it is to examine the case thoroughly, if the men who are liberally paid for that, and for nothing else, do not comprehend it so well as men to whom it is only a side issue, one incident among many duties, why be at the expense of maintaining the unprofitable servants? Either let our courts of law be abolished, or let their decisions stand.

There is annually published in Massachusetts a Blue Book, in which the governor records for the legislature the number of the pardons he has granted and the reasons for which he has granted them. I have never seen a copy of this volume, and I fancy it has no very general circulation; but, from such extracts as I have seen, we could hardly gather arguments in favor of the practice of pardoning.

The Blue Book for 1875 records eighty-seven pardons during the year 1874. In more than a dozen cases, pardon was granted because the sentence was considered too severe; in one, because the sentence was illegal; in one, because the prisoner was evidently insane when his crime was committed; in one, because the council felt there was reason to believe the witnesses against the prisoner were perjured; in twelve cases, because the prisoner was intoxicated at the time of committing his offence; two, because a comrade in crime had been pardoned; one, because his twin-brother, from whom he had never been separated, was to leave prison at an earlier day, and the pardon was necessary to prevent their separation. In no one case do these extracts show that new evidence had been discovered. Even in those cases where the reasons, had they existed, would have been sufficient, there is but the smallest proof that they existed. Insanity of the prisoner, perjury of witnesses, belong, one would say, to lawyers, judge, and jury, the regularly appointed ministers of justice, who make its administration the business of their life; not to an outside body, with whom it is a mere incidental duty. Many of the reasons alleged are purely frivolous; and some are immoral and disastrous, calculated to foster, rather than repress, crime.

Side by side with these festive and fraternal pardonings, we read such paragraphs as these: —

"K. L., the notorious horse-thief, sentenced to the M. State-prison for six years, and pardoned about a year ago, was again arrested at O., charged with the same crime.

"P. R., the burglar who was captured in the unoccupied house on B Street, Wednesday, is an old thief, and has a history. He was first arrested Aug. 6, 1865, for breaking and entering a dwelling-house. He had, about that time, broken into several dwelling-houses, and carried on his burglarious operations with the aid of two accomplices. The two latter were arrested after a desperate fight. When the case was tried, P. R. and one accomplice received a sentence of twenty years each; the other, five. P. R. was pardoned out November, 1872, after seven years' imprisonment."

Is six years too long a time for a notorious horse-thief to be confined? Before he was pardoned out, had he made restitution to all the men whose property he had stolen? Did P. R. make any amends to the owners of the houses he had broken into? Had he atoned for the fright, the anxiety, the apprehensions, which his violence, his fightings, and his burglaries had caused among women and children? What extravagance and folly, what mockery of law, what satire upon justice, is it that rises up in the glow of roast turkey and plum-pudding, and without any pretext of new evidence, or any allegation of undue severity in the judge, coolly throws open the prison-door, and lets the notorious horse-thief, the brain-rapping burglar, the murderer, and the devil incarnate go forth again up and down the earth, seeking whom they may destroy!

The least we can demand is, that the way out of prison shall be as well barred as the way in. If lawyers, judge, and jury are necessary to protect a murderer against a community, they are certainly just as essential to protect a community against the murderer. To try the burglar in open court, with lawyers to defend him, and then to let him out of the prison to which they have sentenced him, without giving the community so much as a warning, or any opportunity to protest, is to bring law into discredit. The power to pardon should be taken out of the hands of the governor and council, or should be hedged round by as many safeguards against abuse as is the power to convict and punish.

Is this a strange theme to introduce into ordinary discussion? Is it a matter which pertains to professional men, and not to untrained citizens, idiots, and women? Did the children murdered in Boston by that young fiend who was pardoned out of the Reform School belong any less to women than to men? It is only a few months ago that the murder of a woman shocked the whole country. A little New England family was living its quiet, happy, affectionate family life, as so many New England families do. Three women, domestic, industrious, independent, cultivated, and refined, doing their own work, enjoying society, music, literature, passed their gentle, harmless, helpful days in the midst of a community that loved and respected them. Up to this tranquil hearthstone tramped a hardened, a dehumanized sot, who had been twice imprisoned for " felonious assault " and " assault with intent to kill," and once pardoned out from a twelve-years' sentence, after four and a half years' detention, clutched the helpless woman, defaced her delicate and beautiful features, bruised and crushed her tender body, tore out her life with such reckless and brutal violence, that even the cold report of a municipal inquest affirms that the lovely face bore the expression of a person " dying in extreme agony," leaving to the unspeakable sorrow of her friends no consolation but that it is all over; that her woe was past before theirs had begun; that whatever heaven awaits the pure in heart was hers long before they knew she had gone from earth; that, out of the horror of great darkness, she escaped swiftly into the ineffable and all-atoning light.

The young monster who has infested Boston and vicinity for the last few years made it his amusement to lure little children into by-places, and there torture and mutilate them. He was presently caught, and sent to the Reform School, where, as the supply of small children failed him, he seems to have behaved himself. Thereupon some mischief-maker, wiser in his own conceit than seven men that left the law alone, had the young monster pardoned out, and turned loose among the little children again. Naturally enough, he improved his opportunities. With his appetite, of course, increased by long-enforced abstinence from his game, he gratified it to a greater extent, and tortured his little victims to death. Two innocent children, a boy and a girl, are supposed to have lost life at his cruel hands; and he now stands in custody, awaiting the execution of his sentence, planning meanwhile, and partially executing, new crimes; and social science is baffled to know what to do with him.

Meanwhile other developments of a similar character cry aloud to social science. There is said to be a boy in the Reform School at Westborough, who, at eleven years of age, drowned, without provocation, a schoolmate five years of age, simply, as he said, "to see the little devil kick in the water." He had diverted himself before with stealing, with throwing stones on the railroad-track, and such pleasant sport, and never could be brought to express regret, or any thing but indifference, to the act for which he was arrested, convicted of murder, and — sent to the Reform School.

Then we hear of another case; and this time it concerns the gentler sex. A young girl, Henrietta Waibel, fifteen years old, takes to burning houses, clothes, and particularly little children. She has no other motive or excuse than that she has a mania for it; and she serenely informs her employer that she has often tried to burn places and children before.

The metaphysical and perhaps the moral nature of these deeds belong to science; but the protection of the little children who remain alive belongs to society, — to you, and to me, and to every person. It is not necessary to decide whether a boy inherits his propensity from a butcher-father and a butchery-witnessing mother; it is not necessary to describe the exact measure of guilt attributed to him by divine Justice: but it is necessary to prevent him from sticking his jackknife into any more little girls and boys. Many demand that he be hung. Others denounce such a demand as brutal. In this they are wrong. The demand may not be wise, but it is not brutal: it is the cry of terror over the danger of little children; it does not spring from brutality, but from fear.

We may admit, for the time, that Jesse Pomeroy is not morally guilty; that he has inherited a thirst for blood, and has not inherited a will strong enough to overcome it. He is not, let us say, a fit object for moral indignation, and is only to be restrained from evil deeds. But how? We restrained him once. We sent him to a reform school; and some interloper forthwith stepped in, snapped his fingers at the law, and Jesse Pomeroy was pardoned out. If we send him to the State-prison for life, he is as sure as statistics to be pardoned out at the end of six years, by which time he will be a man; and if a youngster kills two, and tortures twenty, before he is sixteen, who can tell what feats of homicide he may perform at twenty-one? If he is put into a lunatic asylum, the chances are that he will be sane enough to escape, or to lull his keepers into a belief in his sanity.

The creature has a defective organization, and probably has no idea of the real nature of the torture he inflicts. He has no sympathy to tell him the frenzy of agony and terror which he enforces upon his victims. If this intellectual deficiency could be helped out by a little experimental knowledge, it would probably sharpen somewhat his moral perceptions. If, for instance, a strong man should stand over him as long as he stood over each little boy, and give him as many cuts with a jack-knife as he dealt out to his victim, — not by way of revenge, but simply to let light into his darkened mind, and show him how a jack-knife feels, and what pain and dread and terror and helplessness are, — it might be a good thing for him. The old Jewish law, An eye for an eye, and a tooth for a tooth, seems the very perfection of penal law, the most accurate transcript of natural, which is divine, law. But society seems to have agreed not to carry it out, even where it was practicable. It is useless to say that we abolish it on account of the Saviour's condemnation; for we do not in the least accept his alternative, which was non-resistance: so that we have now neither the law of the old nor of the new dispensation, but a substitution of our own. Since, then, the *lex talionis* is not in force, it only remains to do the best we can under such laws as we have. The law does permit restraint, which has been tried, and found not only useless, but fruitful of fresh crime and greater grief. The law also permits and prescribes the penalty of death.

When Nature turns into the world children so unfortunately constituted as these stabbing, burning, drowning wretches, one feels for them a pity so profound that one would never subject them to the vicissitudes of this world, — a world which has very vague ideas on the subject of inherited traits and emotional insanity, and contemplates their possessors with horror and hate, — but would send them out of it as speedily and as mercifully as possible. To whatever world they may go, they cannot find one that has less use for them, or is less adapted to their peculiarities, than this. It is done, not to punish the children, but on the ground that Nature has put out a bad piece of work, and we send it back on her hands. Does this seem to be trifling with the sacredness of human life? But the Author of Nature does not, apparently, consider human life too sacred or inviolate. What God seems to be resolved on is to have his own way, to carry out his own plans; and he does have his own way, and he does carry out his own plans, though thousands fall at our side, and ten thousand at our right hand. Gases will explode, and waterspouts must burst, and gravitation hold good, though families are overwhelmed, and cities perish. I do not quarrel with this. I admit that God's way and God's plans are the best. I only say that always and everywhere he makes individual life subordinate to general law. More than this, he does not consider human life too sacred to be put into human hands. Man gives, and, to a very large extent, man takes away. If poor little Kitty Curran's life was not too sacred for Jesse Pomeroy to take, surely Jesse Pomeroy's life is not too sacred for society to take, in preservation of all the little Kittys who are not yet buried under his ash-heap. Human life, the human soul, is sacred, — too sacred to be profaned by such travesties as Jesse Pomeroy and Henrietta Waibel and the Westborough reform scholar. If some imperfect, distorted, or mischievous coin comes from the mint, we send it back to be recoined, without misgiving. It is not that we undervalue, but that we rightly value, the worth of money. Through somebody's violation of the law, which is holy and just and good, these unhappy children are in the world, defective, distorted, monstrous, fatal. They can never have any fair showing here. They are weighted with incapacity and with crime. The law has provided a way by which we may make it possible for the divine Being to give them a better start; and they certainly cannot have a worse one. Divested of the burden of weakness, or vice, or brain-disease which disabled them here, they may be born again in some other world as pure and perfect as the happy infants of this. This, of course, is the merest possible conjecture; but they should certainly have the chance.

But the main object is to keep down the crop of little monsters that seem to be springing up in the wake of Jesse Pomeroy. Henrietta Waibel may not have been to blame for her mania; and we may none of us understand, or make proper allowance, for the powerful nature of that mania; but if, while we are striving to make it out, it is thoroughly understood that society has a mania for hanging all little girls and boys who have a mania for murdering other little girls and boys, we shall be likely to keep the mania under till such time as we shall be able to repress it altogether. I have never been able to persuade myself that the Salem witchcraft was wholly an intentional fraud; but I do believe, that if the young people whose antics brought it to a head had been soundly punished, without reason, or argument, or mercy, every time they showed the first symptom of floundering into fits, instead of being coddled and cosseted, they would have been speedily brought to their senses. Whatever devil was at the bottom of it would have been succinctly driven out; and good old Rebecca Nourse would have died in her bed, full of years and honors. In like manner, while we are, as is proper, investigating the moral status of these young monsters, defining the cause and end of their being, divesting them, so far as may be, of their guilt, and relegating them to the divine compassion, I would at the same time have it deeply impressed upon the public mind that moral guilt and legal guilt are wholly different things; that children who murder their playmates for fun shall be just as surely hung as if they did it for greed, anger, or revenge; that, the younger they are when they deliberately and consciously kill, the more hopeless is it to try to make them over, and the more imperative is it to take the first step to their reform by sending them out of a world where such temptations assail them.

The right or the wrong, the wisdom or the unwisdom, of capital punishment, does not, however, enter into this question, except by courtesy. It is a question of the might and majesty of law. It is whether the law, or the opinion of a few persons concerning the law, is the stronger, the more powerful, the more worthy of respect. The time may come when we shall consider capital punishment a relic of barbarism; but it is not yet so considered. We are to act, not according to a standard of civilization which may be set up a hundred years from to-day, but according to the standard of to-day. To-day capital punishment, imprisonment for life, imprisonment for longer or shorter terms, are the penalties appointed by our highest legal authorities for certain crimes. There are equally authoritative modes for administering these punishments. Are these laws to be executed, or are they to be set aside on purely sentimental or positively immoral pretexts? The severity of the laws is not in question : if it were, we might say that one assault with intent to kill is enough to condemn a man to restraint for the rest of his life ; that unconditional liberty after a second similar assault is an outrage upon the honest and peaceable ; that it is only, if at all, less than murder in the first degree to send a man who has twice attempted the life of his fellows forth upon the world, after four and a half years of confinement, to beat down to agony and defilement and death a helpless and unoffending woman.

It is simply this : if the law has any dignity, let it be executed. If it has none, let it be repealed, but let it not be tampered with. Capital punishment may or may not be wise ; but so long as it is the punishment prescribed by the law, for murder, let it be enforced. Imprisonment may or may not be wise ; but, so long as it is the law of the land, let it be inflicted in exactly such measure as the law imposes, and not be curtailed or meddled with by irresponsible agents. Theorists may think, that, because a man is orderly under confinement, he will be orderly when set at liberty; but they should be refrained from trying the experiment on their own account. There is no clamor for blood; there is no frenzy for revenge: but there is the cry of weakness for protection, of suffering for justice, of assailed innocence for the law inviolable and inviolate.

FAIR PLAY.

FAIR PLAY.

O extol the weakness of the strong as strength is as injurious as to make a mock at sin. To overlay Nature with religious phraseology is not to regenerate or to consecrate Nature.

In a little book published by the Tract Society, called "Lady Huntingdon and her Friends," there is a remarkable commingling and confusion of the fruits of the Spirit and the fruits of the flesh.

For instance, an extract is made from a letter of the "unhappy Lady Marlborough."

"Your concern for my religious improvement is very obliging. God knows we all need mending, and none more than myself. . . . I have no comfort in my own family; and, when alone, my reflections almost kill me, so that I am forced to fly to the society of those whom I detest and abhor. Now, there is Lady Frances Sanderson's great rout to-morrow night. . . . I do hate that woman as much as I hate a physician; but I must go, if for no other purpose but to mortify and spite her. This is very wicked, I know."

"This, then," moralizes the biographer, "tears away the trappings of wealth and station, and startles us by a sight of the bad passions which lie cankering beneath. Let it be contrasted with the freshness and beauty of the believer's life."

"What blessed effects does the love of God produce in the hearts of those who abide in him!" writes Lady Huntingdon to Charles Wesley. "How solid is the peace, and how divine the joy!" &c.

But, as we go on in the book, we find that these very hearts display qualities more akin to those of the unhappy Lady Marlborough than this solid peace and joy. The Dissenting churches received the new preachers with indifference and bitterness. Doddridge was severely censured by his brethren. Angry and threatening letters were sent to him from various quarters. Then the new preachers themselves began to quarrel. "The breach widened between Wesley and Whitefield," says the biographer; "for on both sides there were friends and followers who fanned the flame. . . . Their counsels divided, and their ranks broken, there seemed to be a weak betrayal of their Master's cause." "A bitter household squabble," the contest is called. When the churches in connection with Mr. Wesley held their twenty-seventh annual conference in London, it "gave birth to a controversy, perhaps one of the hottest, and most barren of spoils, in the annals of Protestant theology. It was a kindling of the old flames that so nearly consumed the friendship of Wesley and Whitefield more than twenty years before." Lady Huntingdon took sides " with an honest though hasty warmth." " However powerful may have been the arguments wielded on either side, tools, also, of a sharper point were freely used. Acrimonious and intemperate expressions were hurled back and forth. Both parties, instead of convincing or retreating, were driven to the extremes of their own principles, and made unguarded assertions of themselves and their opponents, the effect of which was to alienate the hearts of Christian brethren, . . . and widen the breach between those who really loved the Lord."

Nor were Lady Huntingdon's differences with her friends limited to theological matters. When Rowland Hill started in his career, she " received the ardent and self-forgetting young man with an open heart, and gave him a cordial welcome beneath her roof. Subsequently a coolness seems to have sprung up between them. Though mutually respecting each other, and mutually wishing each other God-speed in *separate* paths of usefulness, they do not appear to have wrought harmoniously together." In short, not to put too fine a point on it, Lady Huntingdon absolutely refused to let him preach in her chapel.

Now, I submit that it is entirely unfair to set over against Lady Marlborough's frank and witty badinage the cheap, pious reflections of Lady Huntingdon. I say cheap, because they are worth absolutely nothing but the paper and ink they are written with. The proper comparison is not between the bad passions of the world and the freshness and beauty of the believer's life, but between the bad passions of the world and the bad passions of the believer. To take the world at its bad, and the Church at its best, will never give us just views. Yet, so far as we see from this book, it is the only way to give the Church the desired superiority. I cannot see that tearing away the trappings of wealth and station reveals the cankering of worse passions than a tearing-away of the trappings of ecclesiasticism and theology. Lady Marlborough's simple hatred of Lady Frances Sanderson seems no deeper or more bitter than the twenty-years' quarrel of the churches over divine sovereignty and electing grace. Lady Marlborough calls a spade a spade; while the religious biographer calls it " an acrimonious and intemperate expression." I confess I like the spade best. Can wealth and station do any worse thing than make " unguarded assertions of themselves and their opponents " ? They would probably call it by the ugly names of lying and slander; but it would be very much the same thing at bottom. Lady Marlborough hated Lady Frances, but went to her rout, and, no doubt, spake her peaceably. Whitefield and Wesley " loved each other; " but their "friendship" was "clouded;" and Whitefield wrote in a "recriminating tone," and Wesley took possession of Whitefield's Kingswood School, and drove his "spiritual children" into "a temporary shed" for shelter. One said, I will not, but afterwards he repented and went; and the other said, I go, sir, and went not. The world's hatred cankers no more than the Church's love. If you are reckless, implacable, slanderous, what difference does it make whether you are quarrelling over divine sovereignty, or ball-room precedence?

On one occasion, Lady Huntingdon sent for a distinguished revival preacher to spend a few weeks in her "fields." His reply is any thing but complimentary to his flock, any thing but indicative of blessed effects in their hearts.

"I am determined," he says, " not to quit my charge again in a hurry. Never do I leave my bees (though for a short space, only), but, on my return, I find them either casting, or colting, or fighting, and robbing each other; not gathering honey from every flower of God's garden, but filling the air with their buzzings, and darting out the venom of their little hearts in their fiery stings. Nay, so inflamed they often are, and a mighty little thing disturbs them, that three months' tinkling afterward with a warming-pan will scarce hive them at last, and make them settle to work again."

Certainly the Duchess of Marlborough does not show off badly against the freshness and beauty of these believers' life.

No one disputes that Lady Huntingdon and her friends were sincere Christians, and served God, and wrought righteousness, in their day and generation; and if their biographers would be content with pointing out the good they attained and executed, we would not complain, even though their defects were hidden. But when their imperfections are softened with sacred phrase, and the imperfections of the world set forth in glaring colors, the instinctive sense of justice rises in revolt. Not by such help is the kingdom of God to be advanced.

Lady Huntingdon and her chaplains, says her biographer, often journeyed during the summer, making their presence a means of religious revival wherever they went. "There is something grand and beautiful in the laborious and unselfish ministrations of the band of preachers who thus went out into the highways and hedges of England, publishing the gospel message as if fresh from Christ and Calvary." One of these journeys, "though undertaken for the countess's health, seems really to have been a home-missionary tour. Returning again to society, Lady Huntingdon may be seen journeying through Wales. . . . Is it a jaunt of pleasure, a tour of aimless excitement, a seeing of new things for the sake of killing time? We now find her travelling in different countries, following up with her presence the labors of her missionaries, inspecting her chapels, investigating the doings of trustees and committees, regulating salaries, directing funds, counselling, controlling, and encouraging, with an unspent force of mind which was marvellous to behold."

What we wish to get at, in all history, personal and national, is things as they are. That Lady Huntingdon was a woman of remarkable energy, ability, and excellence; born for command, and not for subordination; of a masculine force of character, not to be suppressed even by English conventionality; of an executive ability, guided by Christian principle, and seldom surpassed either in man or woman, — this book indicates, and these journeys illustrate. But that there was any thing noticeably unselfish in the ministrations of this band of preachers, that there was any self-denial in these home-missionary tours, that they were, in any respect, *not* jaunts of pleasure, it is difficult to see. They were something besides pleasure-tours; but surely they were pleasure-tours. The biographer, unconsciously no doubt, uses the common "question fallacy" in the form of interrogation, as if a pleasure-tour and a tour for killing time were one and the same thing. But let us look at Lady Huntingdon's journeys.

"The party is large, composed of her two daughters,

her sisters (Anne and Frances Hastings), several clergymen, and other religious friends." One of these clergymen was Griffith Jones, a popular preacher, whose "very presence was like the ringing of the sabbath-bells for the people to come and hear." Another was Howell Harris, so popular that he had to form his followers into societies. Another of her clique was Whitefield, who could hardly make his way along the crowded aisles to the reading-desk, and who had to leave Bristol secretly, in the middle of the night, to avoid the ceremony of being escorted by horsemen and coaches, and whom crowds went to hear so early in the morning that the streets were filled with people carrying lanterns, — a man of remarkable grace, fair complexion, dark-blue eyes, and uncommon sweetness both of voice and countenance. Would a journey with such a party make a special draught upon disinterestedness? On their preaching-tours, these men, and such as these, addressed immense crowds from all the country round about. So far from requiring unselfishness, this jaunting was exactly what Lady Huntingdon liked. She had her family, her friends, her ministers; and she ruled the whole caravan. She was the mother-superior. She was to them "good Lady Huntingdon." They stole her hymns and sang them. They drank her health. They sounded and resounded her praises. They preached in her parlors. They took orders from her and reported progress to her. A jaunt of pleasure, indeed! Imagine a handsome, high-spirited, well-born American widow, of ample means and fine mind, making up a party to the Yellowstone. She invites, first, her pretty and agreeable daughters; then her sisters, who have been belles and beauties in their day and are still held in high consideration; then, let us say, Prof. Barbour, unhappily now of Bangor, to the long lament of Massachusetts; and Mr. George Field, snatched also from Boston to the benighted realms of Maine; and Dr. Swing, and Mr. Beecher; and as many other friends as she likes; and she keeps them all well in hand: and we talk of unselfishness. They may preach seven times a week, or seventy times seven, and call it a missionary tour, if it so pleases them; but their rose by any other name is just as sweet. Lady Huntingdon loved large affairs. She loved to organize and superintend and direct. She loved company and excitement and respect and deference. She could not content herself with the quiet, humdrum domestic and social life which occupies most women, and with which many women are forced to be content. Like the resolute, capable, and virtuous, nay, splendid woman that she was, she moulded life to her likings as well as her uses: she found a sphere for her powers: she ordered men about in a way that it is refreshing to read of. She fulfilled her mission; but she fulfilled it exactly as Charlotte Brontë fulfilled hers when she wrote "Jane Eyre," and as Mrs. Siddons fulfilled hers on the stage, and Christine Nillsson hers with her voice, and another woman hers in the forever unveiled seclusion of her kitchen and nursery. I see no more reason for attributing unselfishness and denying pleasure to Lady Huntingdon than to Jenny Lind. To go off on a journey with her family and friends, and half a dozen popular preachers, all training in her company, is a cross which the most selfish woman would gladly take up. We have only to look upon Lady Huntingdon and her people as human beings, who were hungry and thirsty, and gay and gallant, as well as pious; who were perfectly familiar with the advantages of good birth and breeding, as well as of gospel privileges,—and all things become simple and natural. They were no anchorites; for at Mr. Nimmo's they drank her health every day; and that means wines and meats and desserts and luxurious living. No doubt the Ladies Hastings "hungered for the living manna," and the preacher's "words fell upon good ground," and Lady Margaret "embraced the truth as it is in Jesus;" but, all the same, it remains that the preacher's marriage with the earl's daughter was a very brilliant match for him; and there is no doubt that the Rev. Benjamin Ingham saw it just as plainly, and enjoyed his courtship just as young-manfully, as if he had not been "leading her to the Saviour" while leading her to himself.

The laborious and unselfish ministrations of these peripatetic preachers do not seem to me one-half so striking, so laborious, or so unselfish, as the ministrations of those preachers who stay at home. Novelty, excitement, irresponsibility, adulation, even opposition, stimulate them. But to stay in one place, among people who are perfectly used to you, and hammer away at the same old sins, with the same old truths, and yet strike fire, — that is work.

Let us call things by their right names. We do what we like, and it is not self-denying because it happens to be beneficial. The choice we make is not unselfish because it pleases others, any more than it is selfish because it pleases ourselves.

"Lady Huntingdon," says her biographer, "had been exemplary as a wife and mother, and free from the corruptions of fashionable society," even before she became technically a Christian.

We must not corrupt society, even for the sake of making a foil to Lady Huntingdon's purity. At the age of twenty-one she was married to the Earl of Huntingdon, who is mentioned as "a man of high and exemplary character." "He was sincere, just, and upright: he was courteous, considerate, and charitable. . . . In the stately household, no earthly good was withholden, nor were earthly blessings abused by riot or excess. Dignity, sobriety, and refinement presided over the homes and halls of the earl. Lord Huntingdon had several sisters, whose thoughtful cast of mind made them particularly welcome to his house. In them Lady Huntingdon had found kindred spirits. The earl was a man of unblemished character; and, though not a believer in the distinctive theology of his wife, he courteously entertained her religious friends."

Here then was a whole family (and the only family to whom we are fairly introduced) in the first and most fashionable circles, maintaining as good a reputation as it is possible to find in the most devout of religious circles. Whatever we may say about frames of mind, states of heart, words of the lips, no one can be any thing better than sincere, just, upright, courteous, considerate, charitable, exemplary. As we meet incidentally other members of this same fashionable society, we are not altogether unfavorably impressed. They thronged her house to hear Whitefield preach, and, having heard him once, desired to come again. Lord Bolingbroke was moved, and asked Whitefield to come and see him the next morning; and "Whitefield used the current compliments of address common to that period,— more fulsome then than now." Lord Bolingbroke "heartily despised the gospel, yet affected to reverence it;" which was certainly good-humored and civil. He also "desires his compliments and thanks to Dr. Doddridge, and hopes he shall continue to deserve his good opinion."

So it seems he had deserved it. Lord Huntingdon, the son, had a dislike to religion; but he was "most tender, respectful, and kind to his mother," as well as "interesting, elegant, and accomplished" in corrupt society. Lord Chesterfield used a "polished sarcasm" toward the faith; but he offered his chapel to Lady Huntingdon's chaplain during their summer tours; and, "at Lady Huntingdon's solicitations, he often contributed to the cause of Christ," though it would seem as if delicacy could not have asked him to contribute to a cause in which he did not believe. Surely here the worldly gentleman shows to better advantage than the Christian lady. "He had been the early friend and companion of Earl Huntingdon, after whose death he seems always to have remained on a friendly footing with the countess. Toward the young earl we find him acting as toward an adopted son, — a circumstance which Lady Huntingdon is presumed not to have been able to control, and which must have occasioned her no little sorrow."

Not quite so fast, if you please, worthy biographer. Your facts and your presumptions, and your forced inferences, are commingled too precipitately. It was, surely, not a bad trait, even in a "corrupt" man, to act the part of father to his dead friend's son. Nor was Lady Huntingdon, with all her devotion, in the least insensible to the advantages of birth and position. She and Mr. Whitefield were quite aware when the "great ones" heard them patiently. She got her daughter a place at court; and her subsequent marriage to the Earl of Moira "seems to have given much satisfaction." Another daughter's honor, in being appointed one of six to help Princess Augusta bear the train of Queen Charlotte on her coronation day, was sufficiently appreciated to pass into history. Her marriage with Col. George Hastings was much approved by her mother; and at Paris the eldest son, just become of age, "is warmly greeted by the most distinguished English residents, particularly, introduced, as he is, by Lord Chesterfield." With Lord Chesterfield remaining on friendly terms with Lady Huntingdon all his life, and paying her compliments, and at her solicitation, and in most polite phrase, contributing to her cause, in which he had no faith, I see not a particle of evidence that his friendship to her son was to the mother a source of sorrow, or a thing which she had any wish to hinder.

Other most exemplary friends of Lady Huntingdon in this corrupt, fashionable society seem to have been **Lord and Lady Glenarchy**, "just returned from the gayeties and excitement of a Continental tour," and Lord and Lady Sutherland, of whom Lady Huntingdon says, "Never have I seen a more lovely couple. Although they have not yet been led to 'the fountain of living waters,' they may, indeed, with justice, be called the flower of Scotland."

In short, while we declaim, in general terms, on the frivolity and vanity of fashionable society, a close acquaintance with it reveals about the same proportion of excellence that is found in any society. As we meet its members in these pages, they by no means bear out the charge of corruption so lightly and easily made.

Let us glance at the society of Lady Huntingdon's liking. "Her princely mansions were open with a tireless hospitality to every one who loved her Lord." But is that the true principle of hospitality? "If ye love them which love you, what reward have ye?" This is not a strict statement of fact; but it is as pertinent as if it were. Lady Huntingdon did open her house to those who did not love her Lord; but her biographer seems not to think that counts for any thing in the general summing-up. "During the lifetime of the earl, Lady Huntingdon's time was necessarily engrossed by many cares, which withheld her from the friends and the interests which lay nearest her heart." But what right had she, the wife of a man of unblemished character and chivalrous courtesy, to any friends nearer her heart than her husband, to any interests more close than his? A pretty religion that, in whose path a high-minded husband is a hinderance! "As mistress of his princely mansion, she had duties to general society which could not be slighted. Respect and affection for him controlled her private preferences; and, without making her disloyal to her religious convictions, blended her interests with his own. The tie is now broken; . . . and henceforth we find unfolding that lofty energy of character which has identified her name with the revived Christianity of her day." A revival, it is significant to remember, in which her husband and her son did not share.

And how did Lady Huntingdon reconstruct society when her husband was no longer alive to restrain the indulgence of her private preferences? Chiefly on a basis of preaching, one would say. Certainly the amount she underwent was appalling. Not content with her tours and her chapels, she was constantly having sermons in her own house. "Ashby Place," one of her homes, writes Whitefield, "is like a bethel. We have the sacrament every morning, heavenly conversation all day, and preaching all night." There is no disputing about tastes; but certainly this seems too much of a good thing for a steady, well-balanced life. Surely any conversation carried on all day, and day after day, would cease to be heavenly. With "five clergymen beneath her hospitable roof," and an indefinite number of dear Lady Fannys and Annes and Bettys, they appear all to have been in a state of unmitigated happiness. Women are good by nature, and clergymen are good by grace; but it seems as if their religion would have been more nervous, sinewy, and commanding, more effective, perhaps, upon the husband and son, if a few brawny sinners had been let in upon them, speaking the language of the world, the flesh, and the devil, and permitting, not to say compelling, religion and infidelity to put off their fine array, and meet in a real hand-to-hand combat. But the church sang songs over the harpsichord, and talked heavenly talk all day in the drawing-rooms; and the world indulged in "polished sarcasm" and "severe denunciation" outside; and both interchanged fulsome personal compliment; and "Lord Huntingdon died as he had lived;" and around the dying moments of Lord Chesterfield "the blackness of darkness, accompanied by every gloomy horror, thickened most awfully;" and Horace Walpole scoffed to the bitter end.

With a resolute endeavor to have the sheep distinctly arranged on one side, and the goats on the other, even in this world, Lady Huntingdon's biographer tells us, that, in 1773, she "lost two friends with whom she had been long and differently associated, — that indefatigable servant of God, Howell Harris," and, as Wesley would call him, that servant of the Devil, Lord Chesterfield. The biographer is not content to compare the lives of these two men, but dutifully and formally follows the footsteps of Lady Huntingdon, and contrasts their deaths as an argument regarding their creeds. Let us, therefore, look at it a little more closely.

"That indefatigable servant of God," writes Lady Huntingdon to Romaine, "Howell Harris, fell asleep in Jesus last week. When he was confined to his bed, and could no longer preach or exhort, he said, 'Blessed be God, my work is done, and I know that I am going to my God and Father, for he hath my heart, yea, my whole heart. Glory be to God! death hath no sting: all is well.' And thus this good man went home to his rest.

"In contrast with the death of Howell Harris stands that of Lord Chesterfield. 'Death' he declared to be ' a leap in the dark;' and dark and dreadful did he find the leap to be. As the pains of dissolving nature increased upon him, and human help was vain, his cold and mocking scepticism could offer neither present alleviations nor future hope. 'The blackness of darkness, accompanied by every gloomy horror, thickened most awfully around his dying moments,' says Lady Huntingdon."

But what is the biographer's authority for her statements? and what is Lady Huntingdon's idea of horror? I distrust both as witnesses. Both seem to judge by shibboleth. I find no account of Lord Chesterfield's death-bed shrouded in gloomy horror, except in Lady Huntingdon's letter. Lord Mahon says he "retained his presence of mind to his latest breath.... His dissolution had not been thought so close at hand; and his intimate friend, Mr. Dayrolles, had called to see him only half an hour before it happened; when the earl from his bed gasped out, in a faint voice, to his *valet-de-chambre,* '*Give Dayrolles a chair.*' His physician, Dr. Warren, who was present afterward, expressed himself as much struck at these the last words he was heard to speak. 'His good breeding,' said Dr. Warren, 'only quits him with his life.'"

It seems to me that Lady Huntingdon unconsciously transferred to Lord Chesterfield her own feeling about him, and attributes to him the sensations she imagines she should herself feel, were she, with her convictions, in his situation; which is not unnatural, but is certainly not biographical. Apart from the fact that he could not frame to pronounce her shibboleth, the polite lord's death-bed does not contrast unfavorably with the Christian minister's. The latter is chiefly concerned with himself: the former cares for the comfort of his friend. But kindly service is as likely to contain the essence of Christian religion as the most fluent self-gratulation. It may be said that Mr. Harris had more cause for self-gratulation than had Lord Chesterfield. Mr. Harris was a preacher, and, if we may believe his admirers, was a faithful and effective preacher. Of his private life we know little or nothing, nor of his public life any thing not told by his admirers. Lord Chesterfield is held up to view by friend and foe; yet, in spite of all his faults, we find him in his will, finished on the February preceding his death in June, writing, "I most humbly recommend my soul to the extensive mercy of that Eternal, Supreme, Intelligent Being who gave it me, most earnestly, at the same time, deprecating his justice." I do not find Lord Chesterfield's humility less impressive than Howell Harris's confidence.

For his life-work we are told, that in the outset, in his first embassy to Holland, he displayed great skill, and attained universal reputation; that his second embassy confirmed and renewed the praises he had acquired by the first; that Sir Watkin Wynn, though neither his partisan nor personal friend, said that he " had a head to contrive, a tongue to persuade, and a hand to execute, any worthy action;" that his career deserves the praise of humane, liberal, and far-sighted policy. After the rebellion, while all his colleagues thought only of measures of repression, the dungeon, or the scaffold, disarming-acts and abolition-acts, Chesterfield was for schools and villages to civilize the Highlands. His course as Lord-lieutenant of Ireland was brilliantly useful. He was the first since the revolution who made that office a post of active exertion. He left nothing undone, nothing for others to do. He was the first to introduce at Dublin the principle of impartial justice. He proscribed no one, and was governed by none. His measures were so able, he so clearly impressed upon the public mind that his moderation was not weakness, nor his clemency cowardice, he so well knew how to scare the timid, and conciliate the generous, that he soothed even the turbulence of Ireland into a greater tranquillity than her settled and orderly periods often show. His administration was so wise and just, that his authority was appealed to, even by those who departed most widely from his maxims; and his name lives in the honored remembrance of the Irish people, as, perhaps, next to Ormond, the best and worthiest in their long vice-regal line.

These are the statements of a biographer who has a clear eye for Lord Chesterfield's defects, — so clear, indeed, that he impugns his motives, and neutralizes the virtue of his acts by ascribing them all to selfishness. Nevertheless, it remains that his public career, with which alone we are concerned, was as honorable as that of Howell Harris, and I think it is not too much to say more difficult and distinguished. So far as his life-work is concerned, he would have been as much justified as Howell Harris in looking back with exultation, and forward with confidence. Nor is it at all certain that Mr. Harris was more free from the errors of his profession and position than was Lord Chesterfield from his. Had Mr. Harris been as frank or as penetrating as Lord Chesterfield; had he been as keen, as analytic, and as fearless; did we know as much about the private life of the one as of the other, — we should be far better able to pronounce judgment than we now are. Mr. Harris is not to be absolved by reason of his freedom from Lord Chesterfield's sins, but by his power of resistance to his own temptations, of which we know nothing.

But whatever may have been the life of these men, their death does not prove, on the one side, the truth of the Christian religion, nor, on the other, the fragility of scepticism. We may admit that they died as they lived; and it only remains that the minister talked exultantly of himself, of what he had done, and what he was to receive; and the nobleman was to the last courteous and considerate, — not flippantly and jestingly so, like Charles the Second, but with that instinct of politeness which is scarcely to be distinguished from the Golden Rule of Christ. Lord Chesterfield lived in a society which does not think it good manners to talk much about yourself, or to display your feelings. Howell Harris lived in a society which cultivates egotism as a Christian duty. Each, in truth, died as he had lived. Mr. Harris may have been the happier man. Self-contemplation may be a more satisfactory thing than consideration for others. Rapturous anticipation of the glories of the next world is a thrilling and impressive experience, compared to which a quiet performance of the little duties of this is but commonplace. To feel that you are deservedly a favorite of the Almighty, and have a reserved seat in heaven, must give a far more jubilant sensation than humbly to cast yourself upon the divine mercy with a sense of ill-desert. So much we can allow. Beyond this we may not go. A conjecture cannot be permitted to do duty as a fact. Edifying as it would be to paint Lord Chesterfield's departure from the world in the most horrid tints, much as the cause of Christ will lose if he be allowed to depart in peace, we must not gloss over the truth, but measure the gloom and horror of his death-bed from the testimony of eye-witnesses, and not from Lady Huntingdon's imagination.

The ladies of Lady Huntingdon's clique, we are told, had hard work to hold their own against the strong temptations presented by a frivolous court, a witty peerage, and a learned bench in favor of a formal religion. "Nothing but the 'joy of the Lord' could have sustained them in such a sphere. Happiness in religion was the best security for their holiness. They could not be laughed out of a good hope through grace. . . . Neither the severe denunciations of Warburton or the polished sarcasm of Chesterfield could touch the *consciousness* of peace in believing, or of enjoyment in secret prayer, in the hearts of those peeresses who had found at the cross and the mercy-seat the happiness they had sought in vain from the world."

As martyrdom, this makes but a poor showing, although it is the nearest the peeresses can get to martyrdom. Polished sarcasms can very well be borne when they are accompanied by hundred-dollar notes for the chapel satirized: at least, Lady Huntingdon's long friendliness with the satirist proves that she thought so. Let us see whether "the severe denunciations of Warburton" were wholly in the nature of persecution, or even of opposition to the gospel, and the enjoyment of secret prayer.

Mr. Romaine was one of those travelling chaplains whose laborious and unselfish ministrations contained something grand and beautiful. Beautiful they undoubtedly were to himself; for not only was he of Lady Huntingdon's party, but Lady Margaret Hastings "felt a cordial sympathy for Romaine in his London trials and reverses, and — and generously eked out his small income from her own purse."

This unselfish, grand, and beautiful Mr. Romaine, travelling with Lady Huntingdon at Lady Margaret's expense, had been guilty of what the world called a shabby little trick toward Mr. Warburton. Mr. Warburton had published his "Divine Legation." Mr. Romaine preached against it a sermon, afterward published by Beltenham. About the time the sermon was preached, Mr. Romaine wrote to Mr. Warburton, and, professing to be his admirer and defender, obtained certain advantages, which, when his sermon was published, excited Mr. Warburton's great chagrin and displeasure. In his indignation, he published Mr. Romaine's letter, with his own comments; whereupon Mr. Romaine rushed into print to declare that Mr. Warburton might have made a better use of his capacity and learning than to think "he deserved, or that I meant *in earnest*, those compliments in the letter." But he, an entire stranger to Mr. Warburton, had spoken to him of "your last excellent book. I had read it more than once with a great deal of pleasure, and had ever admired your elegant style, great learning, and strength of argument, and had been used to hear the same praises from others." What is here to indicate that he was not in earnest? or that, either in writing the compliments, or in denying their earnestness, he was not what Warburton calls him, — an "execrable scoundrel"? Even Beltenham, who published the sermon, so much disliked Romaine's retort on Warburton, that, when Romaine took it to be printed, Beltenham replied, that "it was a knavish business, and he would have nothing to do with it." Think of that, and a publisher!

Of course, these little doublings and turnings did not prevent Mr. Romaine from being "a warm and intrepid champion of the cross," or Lady Margaret from contributing her own purse to make him comfortable, or the other peeresses from their peace in believing; but it ought to make us a little charitable toward poor, rough-tongued Warburton, even if his denunciations were a little severe. And severe, indeed, it must have seemed to these high-bred ladies to hear their "dear Mr. Romaine" called "a blunderbuss" and "a poor devil!"

It, no doubt, seemed to them severe to be classed with "idle fanatics;" but had not the indignant bishop some reason for his characterization? What were the effects produced by the preaching of the men whom Lady Huntingdon countenanced and encouraged? Mr. Berridge, her especial friend and correspondent, held forth to his congregation till they responded with shrieking and roaring and gasping, like people half strangled. Some fell down as dead. An able-bodied, fresh, healthy countryman dropped down with great violence, shaking the adjoining pews with his fall, and lay kicking and stamping, ready to break the boards. Among the children was a boy eight years old, who roared above his fellows, with a face as red as scarlet, as well it may have been. A stranger, well dressed, fell backward to the wall, then forward on his knees, roaring like a bull. One Thomas Skinner came forward, his large wig and hair coal-black, his face distorted beyond all description. He roared incessantly, throwing and clapping his hands together with his whole force. Several were terrified, and hastened out of his way. And no wonder. Presently he fell on his back, and lay roaring for hours. "Almost all," says the reporter naively, — " almost all on whom God laid his hand turned either very red, or almost black."

These things did not disturb the peeresses; but they did irritate the bishop, who, though not serene, was sensible. I do not find that he anywhere denounced secret prayer. What he did denounce was public roaring. He was willing to grant peace, but not tumult, in believing. Mr. Wesley condemned prudence as the mystery of iniquity and the offspring of hell, when the question was of preaching against the body of clergy to which he belonged. Is it strange or persecuting, that Mr. Warburton should have pounced upon him for counselling Whitefield that it was imprudent to publish the letter against himself, or for proposing to meet another minister halfway, and offering never to preach publicly against Mr. G., if Mr. G. would promise never to preach against him?

Mr. Wesley thought and taught, that true religion did not consist in living harmless, using the means of grace, and doing much good, but in God's dwelling and reigning in the soul. But, if God's dwelling in the soul turns men black in the face, must not the bishop be pardoned, if he preferred the Gospel according to St. James to the Gospel according to St. John Wesley? The account of Lady Huntingdon and her friends is published by the American Tract Society; but nine out of ten of the supporters of that society would utter just as severe denunciations of the proceedings in question as did Bishop Warburton — if they knew how. It was not the frivolous court, the witty peerage, the learned bench, that made the strongest temptation to a formal religion: it was the ignorance, the vulgarity, the boundless license of fanaticism, into which religion lapsed, when, rejecting forms, it rejected also decorum and decency. By his own confession, it tickled Whitefield's vanity to be mobbed; but the man, who, in making proposals of marriage, could bless God that he was free from the foolish passion which the world calls love, *deserved* to have dead cats thrown at him. It is not necessary to suppose that these men were hypocrites; but, in certain respects, they lacked a perception of the relations of things; and it was this lack, as well as the purity of their doctrines, which provoked opposition. Indeed, Wesley himself, in his mellow old age, considering the wrong-headedness of his earlier years, marvelled that the people had not stoned him. Formalism, ministering at the altar in priestly robes, is not religion; but neither is fanaticism, kicking its heels against the pews, and roaring like bulls of Bashan: and, if peeresses do not see it, let us be thankful that Chesterfields are raised up to level at it their polished spears of sarcasm, and Warburtons to bring down upon it their huge cleavers of indignation. To call these men hostile to religion because they saw and repelled the vagaries and extravagances of some of the preachers of religion, to condemn them without noticing the weakness and wickedness which elicited their disapproval, is to falsify history, to misuse opportunity, and make the word of God of none effect by our traditions. Lady Huntingdon and her peeresses were good women; but they would have been none the less good if they could have been touched by severe and deserved denunciation, by polished and rightly pointed sarcasm. A keener sense of the ridiculous, a stronger power of discrimination, would have made them no less singlehearted, and, one would say, more really efficient and influential. It was no credit to their penetration, that they flocked after their preachers through thick and thin, bleating as trustfully among the morasses of superstition and sensation and tergiversation as in the green pastures, and beside the still waters, of righteousness.

Mr. Venn, an amiable and excellent clergyman, lost an admirable wife, to whom he was much attached. But even in the midst of his tears for his unspeakable loss, so inalienable is the egotism of a certain type of piety, he had the composure to look through his fingers, as it were, and mark how his grief affected the beholders. "For his own cause, I cannot but conclude the Lord does it, since, immediately upon my unspeakable loss, the opposers cried out, 'Oh! now you will see what will become of his vauntings of the power of faith and the name of Jesus.' They knew our great happiness; and they said, 'You will see your vicar just like any one of us in the same situation.' But my God heard and answered."

That is, the wife died, that the Christian faith might be illustrated by her husband's resignation. Of course, no one can disprove this; though the overwhelming probabilities are, that Mrs. Venn died in the simplest earthly manner, — of inherited or legitimately acquired disease; but, surely, this habit of posing and living with a view to what other people think of you indicates and develops an unwholesome and unnatural character. In course of time Mr. Venn again became engaged, and thus wrote to the lady, "Long was I very backward to think of entering again into the marriage-state, though so blessed in my first connection; but the gracious God, whom I serve, and whose I am, has provided for me one of his own elect."

Did Mr. Venn suppose that God took any more interest in his love-affairs than in another man's, or that he brought about his marriage in any other way than he brings about all things,— by the use of the requisite means? Is it piety that speaks of the Most High as a match-maker, and man a mere puppet in his hands, not using his own eyes to find his wife, but taking the one provided for him? How did Mr. Venn know that God had selected this woman to be his wife? When Whitefield wanted to marry, he wrote to the lady's father, "I write only because I believe it is the will of God that I should alter my state; but your denial will fully convince me that your daughter is not the person appointed by God for me." Very sensible in Mr. Whitefield. A flat refusal from a resolute father is certainly a strong indication of the Lord's will. Whitefield evidently had less faith in heavenly than in earthly revelations. He might be mistaken in interpreting the one; but there was no doubt about the other. But this time the divine will was conveyed, not through the lips of the father, but of the daughter, which was even more decisive. If the trumpet of the

Lord ever gives a certain sound, it is from the mouth of a determined woman saying 'No' to her suitor. After strong crying and tears at the throne of grace for direction, Whitefield married the Widow James of Abergavenny, "a despised follower of the Lamb." Before his child was born, he prophesied that it would be a boy, and become a preacher of the gospel. It proved a boy, but died in four months; whereupon he philosophized that "Satan had been permitted to give him some wrong impressions, whereby he had misapplied several texts of Scripture." Moreover, his marriage turned out not to be a happy one: so it seems that those who depend upon the Lord for wives are no better off than those who fall in love on their own account. And, on the whole, what reason is there for supposing that God supervised Mr. Whitefield's and Mr. Venn's courtship any more closely than Mr. Smith's or Mr. Brown's?

Mr. Wesley seems to have been a more manly man than Whitefield, more human, more natural, less vain, worthy, indeed, of a happy domestic life; yet he fared ill, fared especially and grievously ill, in his fortune with women. The nineteenth century has thus far developed nothing more farcical, more scandalous, more preposterous, than the loves of John Wesley. In his friendship for "Miss Sophy," his heart was deeply enlisted. She was young, pretty, and intelligent. He was thirty-five, handsome, well bred, and of genial manners. He was passionately fond of her; and she liked him, and, doubtless, more than liked him. She dressed in white because it pleased him; and, when he fell sick, she nursed him. It was the nicest little love-affair that could be dreamed of, with nothing in earth or heaven to hinder. But there is a third estate, which always finds some mischief still for idle hands to do; and, in an evil moment, Mr. Wesley, instead of acting out of his own manly, loving heart, propounded the matter to the bishop, and then to the elders of the church, through all of whom God commanded him, he says, to pull out his right eye, meaning to give up Miss Sophy; but, hesitating, Miss Sophy pulled it out herself by marrying another man. What pique of pride, what wounds of disappointed love, the young girl suffered, we can only divine; but poor Wesley was sorely driven of the wind, and tossed. After he had incurred Miss Sophy's displeasure by listening to the Moravian adversaries, he could not bear the thought of separation from her, and begged her to break her rash engagement with the other man, and marry himself. After her hasty marriage, he could only comfort himself by the reflection, that he should have been so happy with her that he should have given up preaching. Poor dear! One pities him, in spite of all these hundred and fifty years. Doubtless, also, it was some comfort, though a trifle spiteful, for him to write that her husband was "a person not remarkable for handsomeness, neither for greatness, neither for wit or knowledge or sense, and, least of all, for religion;" and "presently God showed him yet more of the greatness of his deliverance by opening to him a new and unexpected scene of Miss Sophy's dissimulation." I do not feel so sure of that. Perhaps Miss Sophia would not have dissembled, if mischievous Moravian outsiders had not taken from her the handsome, great, and wise man whom she loved, and piqued her to fling herself hastily into the arms of a man whom she can hardly be supposed to have loved. At any rate, Mr. Wesley was so hampered by the bonds of his church and his love, that he could neither marry her, nor let her alone; and he was presently defendant in a scandal suit brought by Miss Sophia's husband, from which, after three months of waiting for trial, he escaped by hiring four renegade debtors to row him away in a boat by night. Whether God commanded him to plan this little escapade does not appear.

Several years afterwards, the movings of the Spirit led him to Grace Murray, who also had nursed him when he was sick; and again the Most High spoke through his brother Charles and Whitefield, for the excellent reason that she was already engaged to John

Bennett, one of his lay-preachers, whom she had nursed before **Wesley fell ill**. His brother and **friends** counselled her to keep to her engagement. Naughty John Wesley, **did** God command you **to make love to another** man's betrothed? He is excused, on the **plea of not** knowing **that she was** engaged to Bennett; **but** after Bennett and Grace wrote him a joint letter, asking his consent to their marriage, he must have suspected that all **was not** going smoothly with his suit. Still, as **Mrs.** Murray seems **to have** changed her mind with each change of lovers, perhaps Mr. Wesley is not much to be blamed for holding **on**. Doubtless, he thought he had as much right to win, and was as likely to win, as the other man. In the morning she told John Wesley she loved him a thou**sand times better than she ever** loved John Bennett: **in the evening** she promised John Bennett to marry **him. A** week after she told Mr. Wesley she was determined to live and die with him, and wanted to be married at once. If **Mr.** Wesley could only have come up to the mark then, **all** might yet have been **well;** but, madly enough, **he wished some** delay. Grace said she would not wait more than a **year**; and she was as good as her word, for in three weeks she was married to Bennett. Then the **defeated** one in **this game** of see-saw thus **bemoans** himself, "Since I was six years old, I never met with such a severe trial." He had forgotten that little operation of pulling out his right eye. "I thought I had made all sure, beyond a danger of disappointment. But we were, soon after, torn asunder as by a whirlwind. I fasted and prayed." But what was the good of fasting and praying after it was all over? How much better to have stepped up and married her when she was ready to his hand, and then have had a day of thanksgiving! for, as she made an excellent wife to Bennett, she would, doubtless, have made an excellent one to Wesley.

Mr. Bennett seems to have been a perfectly proper match for the lady, being a man of classical education, and superior native talents. It is just possible that he may not have been particularly pleased with this little episode; and that his subsequent defection from the Wesleyan ranks, and his opposition to Wesley, may have been somewhat influenced by this bit of personal history. It is to be noticed, that, though Mr. Wesley submitted to the will of God and John Bennett, he was much offended with his brother Charles, who enforced it, and interfered against the match as soon as he found it out.

Not only without were fightings, but within were fears. When Wesley had no inclination to marry, he had published a treatise in favor of "remaining single for the kingdom of heaven's sake." Now that his heart was fully set on marrying, it was necessary for him to explain, that he only meant "to remain single for the kingdom of heaven's sake, unless when a particular case might be an exception to the general rule." Admirable distinction! And his was the particular case.

He then gathered his friends together, and consulted them, and was clearly convinced that he ought to marry; which shows the remarkable reasoning power of his friends. He fully believed he " might be more useful in a married state, into which, upon this clear conviction, and by the advice of my friends, *I entered a few days after.*"

> "But fixed before, and well resolved was he,
> As men who ask advice are wont to be."

All this was accomplished in about a year after the whirlwind had torn him from Grace Murray. But I do not mind Grace Murray. She was a widow, and thirty-four, and abundantly able to take care of herself. It was pretty Sophy Hopkey in her white dress that he ought to have married, and kept from breaking her heart and his own in a fit of girlish pique. Such a bright, happy life she would have led him!

But there was the slippery bridge, and the sprained ankle, and the Widow Vazeille lying in wait to nurse him; and it was all over with John Wesley. Surely, never had man more need, or less heed, of the warning of Mr. Weller, senior, to his son Sammy. In eight days from the sprained ankle, she and her four children were married to him. She robbed him; she wounded him; she betrayed him; she secretly spied upon him; she searched his pockets; she dragged him about by the hair, and pulled it out by the roots; she published every thing which would bear a construction unfavorable to him, and accused him of deadly sin with the wife of his brother Charles. Verily, it was not so much of a deliverance, after all, — out of the hands of Miss Sophy into the hands of Mrs. Molly. Was this what the divine Being was aiming at? Verily, Miss Sophy had as much to console her in John Wesley's wife as John had in the contemplation of Miss Sophy's husband. All this did not prevent the wife's tombstone from eulogizing her as a woman of exemplary piety, a tender parent, and a sincere friend. But let us not be too harsh upon the dead lady, to whom her husband used to write, —

"Be content to be a private, insignificant person, known and loved by God and me."

"Leave me to be governed by God and my own conscience; then shall I govern you with gentle sway."

"Of what importance is your character to mankind? If you was buried just now, or if you had never lived, what loss would it be to the cause of God?"

"Are you more humble, more gentle, more patient, more placable, than you was? I fear, quite the reverse. I fear your natural tempers are rather increased than diminished."

One wonders he had a hair left in his head!

Suppose, now, after reading such a letter as this to herself, one of the letters she found while searching Mr. Wesley's pockets happened to be this to Mrs. Sarah Ryan: —

"The conversing with you, either by speaking or writing, is an unspeakable blessing to me. I cannot think of you without thinking of God. Others often lead me to him; but it is, as it were, going roundabout: you bring me straight into his presence. . . . I not only excuse, but love, your simplicity. . . . Upon what a pinnacle do you stand! Perhaps few persons in England have been in so dangerous a situation as you are now. I know not whether any other was ever so regarded, both by my brother and me, at the same time."

Being an unreasonable and jealous woman, the wonder is she left him his head!

And this Sarah Ryan, whose simplicity was so sweet to him, whose words were an unspeakable blessing, whose presence was the pathway to God, had been, like his wife, a servant. She left service to marry a mechanic who already had one wife. He ran away from Sarah; and then she became engaged to an Italian sailor. Before the marriage she happened to nurse an Irish sailor named Ryan, with what appears to have been the usual result: she married him. He went to sea; and she married the Italian until he came back; and then she returned to Ryan, and lived with him till he went to sea again. He wrote to her from America, wishing her to come over to him; but she refused. And, with three husbands living, Wesley appointed her housekeeper, or matron, in his theological school at Kingswood, and made her his intimate friend, and the confidante of his domestic troubles. And when they were all sitting comfortably at dinner, Wesley with his ministers, and Sarah at the head of the table, in burst the irate Mrs. Wesley upon them, hurling the coarsest insults at Mrs. Ryan, and narrating bits of her personal history to the astonished company.

A hundred years and more have passed away; and it may scarcely be said that stain or speck mars the white fame of Wesley. The vast majority who revere his memory know nothing of his whims or weakness, but only his energy, his zeal, his wonderful effectiveness, his marvellous power. This is as it should be. In this world our treasure must be put into earthen vessels. We are often indignant and disappointed to find it so. A man arises with some gift of song or speech, so brilliant, so magnetic, that it lifts him above his fellows; and we would fain believe it is the voice of a god, and not of a man. But, in the common affairs of life, we find him sharing the common lot, falling into the same folly, the same mistakes, which have entrapped ourselves; and we are enraged. We feel ourselves deceived. True; but it was ourselves deceived ourselves. The greatest eloquence, the most irresistible power over masses of men, will not prevent a man from crying out, when he is drowning, "Help me, Cassius, or I sink!" Our mortal god will shake when the fever-fit is on him, and beg, "Give me some drink, Titinius," as a sick girl; and, in the fever-fit of love, is not likely to be half so sensible as a sick girl. Our gods are not really any more foolish than ourselves; but our own follies are acted, not scanned, and no one knows them. John Wesley makes a poor figure in love; and John Smith is very angry with him on that account. But if all that John Smith said and did when he was in love had been published in a memoir, word for word, doubt for doubt, pang for pang, thrill for thrill, would it read any better? In the case of most of us, the reason we are not covered with blushes for our silly sentimentalisms, or our sillier rejections of them, is, that our obscurity has kept them from being of the slightest interest to the world. If we had made as fine a figure as John Wesley we should have made as poor a one. Being nobodies, we enacted our follies without so much as suspecting they were follies; and when a man comes towering so far above us, that even his weaknesses are learned and conned by rote, we rage as if some strange thing had happened unto him, and not that which is common unto man. But even that is better than to hold up these weaknesses as virtues and graces to be extolled and imitated. Did all this self-examination, this consultation with the elders, this dependence upon divine direction, amount to any thing? These people certainly made no better marriages than those who fall in love the natural way, and say nothing about it. Nor do I believe that they got any more happiness or holiness out of their strong crying and tears than an honest lover gets in making love to a nice girl. If the human mind is capable of comprehending the divine will, courting, and not crying, is the Heaven-appointed pathway to marriage. When Whitefield was spreading his letters before the Lord, and blessing him that he was not in love, he was despising the means of grace, and setting up unmanly methods of his own; and he ought to have had a poor wife, or have been made miserable by a good one. All this backing and filling seems childish. All this talk about the divine direction is worse than childish. Wesley thought the heavens and the earth should come together to decide whether he should, or should not, marry. What does that remind one of but the most inflated and exasperating self-conceit? It is not impossible that a man may marry because he thinks it is the divine will that he should; but, the less he says about it, the better. The world will be sure to think scornfully of him; and the world is very likely to be right. It is impossible to give credence to a man who brings in the Deity as an excuse for doing what he wants to do. All the saints on earth would not make us believe that God was any thing more than an accessory after the fact. He who falls in love, and marries a woman with simple, straightforward sincerity, *because* he loves her, is just as much in the path of duty as if he had all the elders of the church to pray over him. Why should a man make a great merit of going around by Robin Hood's barn, when all the world reaches the same place by taking a straight cut across the fields?

The Rev. Mr. Venn, writing to the lady who was about to become his second wife, says, "I begin to feel more concerned than I at first did, lest my children should give you trouble; for, just in proportion as I love and value you, I must feel any thing that in any degree may affect you. And I say to myself, 'How should I be able to bear seeing my dear wife in tears, or void of her sweet cheerfulness and vivacity of spirit, by any of my children, to whom she has so kindly shown herself a friend in need?'"

Which was certainly amiable in Mr. Venn. But how about the children? The grown woman was much better able to take care of herself than were the five children under thirteen years of age to take care of themselves. They were helpless, and had no voice in the matter. She knew what she was about. She went into battle with her eyes open. They could give her trouble; but she could mar their life. He was to them under the strongest bonds that one human being can be to another. She was to take, or to leave; and, after all, the decision was in her own hands. Sound sense, accustomed to look at things on all sides, would have had a little anxiety to bestow on the children, and would not have lavished it all, however sweetly, on the mature and independent woman.

Dr. Doddridge seems to have been a most courteous and agreeable person. Even the bristling Warburton roared him gently. But what is that peculiar mental organization which makes it edifying for a man to spend his time in writing out in set phrase, "As a husband, may I particularly avoid every thing which has the appearance of pettishness. . . . May it be my daily care to keep up the spirit of religion in conversation with my wife, to recommend her to the divine blessing, and to manifest an obliging and tender disposition towards her"? What sort of tenderness is that which a man resolves upon? How shall he go to work to take care to keep up any thing in talking with his wife? What elaborate and cumbersome machinery where there should be spontaneity! And if a good man must needs grind out his emotions in this laborious fashion, and his biographer cannot conscientiously hush it up, why should he not soften it down by referring it to the pompous custom of the age, and not blindly blazon it as something admirable, and worthy of imitation? No one would divorce religion from the marketing and the house-rent; but no one wants the marriage-ceremony performed every morning. Self-survey and attitudinizing do not neutralize the excellence of a good man; but simplicity and self-forgetfulness are better.

When Lord Dartmouth was rebuked for his tardiness in waiting upon the king at a morning ride, he replied, " I have learned to wait upon the King of kings before I wait on my earthly sovereign." Could any thing be more ill bred, indecorous, priggish? Yet the biographer finds heart to say, " May the lofty and uncompromising tone of his religious character ever distinguish the institution which bears his name!"

Let not the graduates of Dartmouth College flatter themselves that any president would long retain in his cabinet an attorney-general or a war secretary who could not rise early enough to keep his appointments.

The probability is, that he would presently find his religious character to be not the only uncompromising thing in the world, and would speedily and deservedly be relegated to that private station where he could take his own time to his devotions.

Nor does his inflexibility as a devotee seem to have been carried into his duties as a statesman, since the profane historian tells us, that though, in the administration of his own department, he at first assumed some degree of independence, "he soon betrayed a want of consistency and firmness, which, although he was inclined to good measures, led him to join in sustaining the worst." We are told that there are odds in deacons; but we would much rather know that Secretary Fish could be depended upon for maintaining the honor of the country intact than that he kept President Grant waiting while he said his prayers.

Lady Huntingdon wished to build a chapel.

"Wherein could she curtail? There lay her jewels, long since put aside for a pearl of infinitely greater price; and these she determined to offer to her Lord. They were sold for six hundred and ninety-eight pounds; and with this she erected a neat house of worship.

"During her last years, Lady Huntingdon's style of living befitted less an English peer than an heir of glory. Her equipage and furniture were extremely simple; and, although her income was much increased at her son's death, so ample were her benefactions, that she allowed herself but one dress a year, — a degree of economy that might well shame many a Christian woman whose adorning consists far more in the 'putting-on of apparel' than 'the hidden man of the heart in that which is not corruptible.'

"She maintained the college at her own expense; she erected chapels in most parts of the kingdom; and she supported preachers, who were sent to preach in various parts of the world. This was, indeed, consecration to God. 'Go thou . . . and do likewise.'"

The real lesson of Lady Huntingdon's energy and beneficence are likely to be lost in this headlong omnivorousness. Such utter confusion of thought would be amusing, as well as amazing, if it were not mischievous. Lady Huntingdon laid aside her jewels for the pearl of greater price. Are the two incompatible? From the day when Abraham's pious servant adorned Rebekah with jewels of silver, and jewels of gold, ear-rings upon her face, and bracelets upon her hands, until the day when the holy city, the New Jerusalem, came down from God out of heaven, wholly made up of gold and precious stones, these gems have been held in honor, the type and emblem of all pure and priceless things. Does the Tract Society mean to teach, or does it believe that St. Peter meant to teach, that the young schoolgirl, wearing a gold locket on her velvet ribbon, and a silk bow on her braided hair, cannot be a Christian? Does the oyster secrete a substance that is fatal to piety?

Lady Huntingdon offered her jewels to her Lord, and got six hundred pounds for them. We must not suppose, however, what the language indicates, that the Lord was the purchaser. They probably went no farther than the show-case of a London jeweller. But, if jewels are incompatible with religion, what right had Lady Huntingdon to sell hers? She ought to have destroyed them. That she wanted to build chapels with the proceeds is nothing to the purpose. Shall we ruin some souls to save others?

Was it right that her style of living befitted less an English peer than an heir of glory? At the most, she was only an heir-expectant of glory; but the peerage was a present fact. It was her duty to live in a manner befitting her actual earthly rank as much as her supposed heavenly rank. The very best way to prepare for the next world is to discharge the duties of this.

Does the Tract Society mean that the rich ladies of Boston, New York, and Washington,— the wives of the merchant-princes, the great lawyers, the cabinet ministers, — should have no jewels, should ride always in horse-cars, should carpet their floors with straw-matting, buy only one gown a year, and devote their money to building meeting-houses, and supporting ministers? If this is not meant, what is meant? "This was, indeed, consecration to God." Where in the Bible, where in the whole realm of reason, can such a doctrine be found? It is the creed of monasticism, not of religion. The teaching of the Bible is, that, if a man be just, and do that which is lawful and right, if he have not oppressed any, if he have executed true judgment between man and man, he is just, he shall surely live, saith the Lord God. If a man sell his jewels, and support preachers, and build meeting-houses, he shall be holy to God, saith the Tract Society. If Lady Huntingdon must shame her Christian sisters because she had but one gown a year, how much more those holy mendicant friars, who have but one sackcloth shirt in seven years!

I do not believe that Lady Huntingdon was half so objectionable a woman as her biographer makes her out to be. Her independence, her strength, her zeal, her grasp and control of circumstances, were altogether admirable. She was not always, but she was often, clear-sighted. Her activity, her vitality, were marvellous. But when we are taken to her shrine, and bidden to bow down and worship, we instinctively straighten up so rigidly, that we are in danger of bending backward. We are called upon to admire weakness as strength, to revere tastes as virtues. It may have been wise in Lady Huntingdon to spend her substance in building chapels; but to point the moral, "Go and do thou likewise," is an impertinence. It was no more an offering to the Lord for her to sell her jewels than it is for another woman to wear them. An heir of glory may enclose as much sin in one gown a year as in six or sixteen. The woman who never erected a meeting-house in her life, nor ever gave a ten-cent scrip to the Tract Society, the woman who rides in her satin coach, and is draped in velvet, and hung with diamonds, may be as truly consecrated to God as was Lady Huntingdon. What has God done that gold and silver and purple and scarlet and fine-twined linen should not be his now, as in the olden time? Of the temple is left not one stone upon another; but know ye not that your body is the temple of the Holy Ghost? Therefore, glorify God in your body.

Real biography would be the most interesting reading in the world; but that we can seldom, perhaps never, command. Nor is it prohibited to friends and admirers to veil defects. But it is not lawful to sum up character without reference to defects. Still less is it lawful to depict them as beauties. The cause of right living is not to be promoted by such aid. What we want is to see things as they are, not to point a moral, or to support a theory. And any religious society, or any religious person, who wilfully distorts the truth, or who ignorantly mingles good and evil, wisdom and folly, in a weak moral mush, and then deals it out as the bread of life, is likely to do more harm by nauseating the healthy than service in feeding the hungry.

THE END.

www.ingramcontent.com/pod-product-compliance
Lightning Source LLC
Chambersburg PA
CBHW030545300426
44111CB00009B/863